T0281852

TWILIGHT OF THE SHADOW GOVERNMENT

TWILIGHT
OF THE SHADOW
GOVERNMENT

HOW TRANSPARENCY WILL
KILL THE DEEP STATE

KEVIN SHIPP AND

KENT HECKENLIVELY, JD

Skyhorse Publishing

Skyhorse Publishing books may be purchased in bulk at special discounts for
sales promotion, corporate gifts, fund-raising, or educational purposes. Special
editions can also be created to specifications. For details, contact the Special Sales
Department, Skyhorse Publishing, 307 West 36th Street, 11th Floor, New York,
NY 10018 or info@skyhorsepublishing.com.

Skyhorse® and Skyhorse Publishing® are registered trademarks of
Skyhorse Publishing, Inc.®, a Delaware corporation.

Visit our website at www.skyhorsepublishing.com.
Please follow our publisher Tony Lyons on Instagram @tonylyonsisuncertain

10 9 8 7 6 5 4 3 2 1

Library of Congress Cataloging-in-Publication Data is available on file.

Hardcover ISBN: 978-1-5107-8206-8
eBook ISBN: 978-1-5107-8207-5

Cover design by Brian Peterson

Printed in the United States of America

All statements of fact, opinion, or analysis expressed are those of the authors and
do not necessarily reflect the position or views of the Central Intelligence Agency
or any other US Government agency. Nothing in the contents should be construed
as asserting or implying US Government authentication of information or Agency
endorsement of the authors' views. This material has been reviewed by the CIA to
prevent the disclosure of classified information.

For some time, I have been disturbed by the way the CIA has been diverted from its original assignment. It has become an operational and at times, policy-making arm of the government.

President Harry S. Truman, "Limit CIA Role to Intelligence," op-ed in *Washington Post*, December 22, 1963

Dedicated to those who love freedom.

CONTENTS

INTRODUCTION

THE EMPIRE OF LIES

On the day my coauthor and I signed the contract for this book, March 19, 2024, the *New York Times* published an op-ed with the title, "It Turns Out the 'Deep State' Is Actually Kind of Awesome" by Adam Westbrook and Lindsey Crouse.[1]

As a seventeen-year employee of the Central Intelligence Agency, who has worked in all four directorates of the Agency (and three years in the State Department, which we referred to as "CIA-lite"), I couldn't believe the absolute idiocy of this clumsy persuasion play by the former practitioners of my profession. Let me catalogue a few of the mistakes.

The concept of the "Deep State," a cabal of intelligence actors lying to the American public to generate a string of low-grade military conflicts for the benefit of the defense contractors, as well as keep supposedly liberal democrats in power, has for years been portrayed in the media as a right-wing, paranoid fantasy.

The *New York Times*, and their idiot Project Mockingbird handlers in the intelligence agencies, had just shown their hand.

Instead of continuing with their former approach of deception behind smoke and mirrors, they came up with a new one in this painfully obvious piece.

The Deep State is not only real, it's "kind of awesome," like working at a cool, new tech startup such as Google, Facebook, or Instagram. (Which in all likelihood are intelligence agency schemes to gather your data.) It's one thing to try to control the United States, it's quite another to do such a pitifully bad job of it.

It's not good propaganda if you can spot it a mile away.

Let's imagine you're a liberal voter with just the slightest knowledge of what your conservative brethren in the country believe. You may not agree that the "Deep State" exists, but at least you know what the Right believes it to be.

If the *New York Times*, your "paper of record" and trusted news source, is going to tell you that the Deep State is "kind of awesome," you'll have a moment of confusion.

"I thought the Deep State didn't exist," you'll say to yourself.

Then the cognitive dissonance will set in, and you'll say, "Of course there's a Deep State. Everybody has *always* known that." You pick yourself up, realize you've always suspected there was a Deep State, but you believe they're the "good guys" hiding in the shadows. You expect you'll meet some intelligence agents, maybe a few undercover operatives (as I once was), and they'll share with you the dangers of the profession, as well as the good they're doing for America.

But you won't get anything like that.

The six-and-a-half-minute video clip which formed the basis of the op-ed, opened predictably with former President Donald Trump denouncing the Deep State and vowing to break it up. Got the propaganda 101 setup? Trump is the liar, and now we, the *New York Times* (and our intelligence agency friends), are going to tell you the truth.

In the video, our narrator tells us he's jumped in the car to travel across America to find the real Deep State. (The piece was so bad it would have been embarrassing even if it had played on *Entertainment Tonight* in the 1970s.)

Narrator: But who are these bureaucrats, and what makes them so dangerous? We needed answers. So we took a trip across America in search of the people behind this threatening entity. First stop, Huntsville, Alabama. Sure looks like some nefarious government activity happens around here.
(We see footage of a non-descript-looking office building.)
Narrator: Meet Scott Bellamy.
("Scott" is a pudgy-looking guy with a beard and thinning hair who looks like he'd be winded by a flight of stairs, much less chasing bad guys down an alley in the Middle East. Imagine a younger version of the cartoon character, Homer Simpson.)

Scott Bellamy: I'm a Mission Manager in the Planetary Missions Program Office.
Narrator: He drives a Nissan Titan 4 x 4. He's loved *Star Trek* since he was a kid.
Scott Bellamy: Of course I have a favorite character. It's either Captain Kirk or Mr. Spock.[2]

Can you see the bad persuasion play at work here? He's not just a nerd, (because he likes classic *Star Trek*), but he's also the kind of guy who drives a 4 x 4 truck. But the Project Mockingbird intelligence folks are so out of touch with current science fiction, they stick to the 1960s characters. What about going for some of the newer *Star Trek* characters like Captain Jean Luc Picard or Commander Data from *Star Trek: The Next Generation*, the female captain, Kathryn Janeway from *Star Trek: Voyager*, or the African American, Benjamin Sisco of *Star Trek: Deep Space Nine*?

I guess those Diversity, Equity, and Inclusion goals go right out the window when you're engaged in propaganda. But just like in those *Star Trek* movies, nothing less than the survival of the Earth itself is at stake.

Narrator: And he may have quite literally saved the planet from annihilation.
Scott Bellamy: Potentially.
Narrator: You see, Scott managed a mission called—
Scott Bellamy: The Double Asteroid Redirection Test.
Narrator: And back in 2022, his team used your tax dollars to pull off something kind of incredible.
Scott Bellamy: You have an asteroid and you have a spacecraft. And you fly the spacecraft into the asteroid and try to change the directory of that asteroid. It's like playing pool in space. Everybody was holding their breath. This is the moment of truth. Did we hit it?[3]

I'll spoil the surprise by telling you they did hit it, and it did successfully redirect the asteroid. But the *New York Times* wants you to believe this is the kind of guy Trump is talking about when he brings up the Deep State.

Trump wants the Earth to get hit by an asteroid.

That's what they want you to believe.

Just like they want you to believe Trump's in favor of lead in drinking water. The next location the narrator goes is to Washington, DC.

> Narrator: This is Radhika Fox.
> Radhika Fox: I'm the assistant administrator for Water at the Environmental Protection Agency.
> Narrator: She loves Pilates, making salads, and watching the Taylor Swift Eras tour on TV with her family.
> Radhika Fox: I think we're all pretty 1989.
> Narrator: Oh, and she led an operation to make our drinking water lead-free in ten years.
> Radhika Fox: That's the dream.[4]

How the Environmental Protection Agency and lead-free drinking water has anything to do with the Deep State, is never explained. But I guess we simply have to assume that was one of the secret missions undertaken by James Bond or Jack Ryan, which unfortunately never got turned into a big screen movie or an Amazon series.

The final stop on the *New York Times* magical mystery tour investigating the Deep State was Chicago, Illinois, to interview Nancy Alcantara.

> Nancy Alcantra: I am the acting director for the Wage and Hour Division for the Midwest Regional Office for the US Department of Labor. I had to take a breath, yes.
> Narrator: She still eats Lucky Charms for breakfast, trains for marathons, and loves Latin dancing.
> Nancy Alcantra: Cumbia [Colombian dance], Bachata [Dominican Republic dance], cha-cha-cha, you name it, I did it.
> Narrator: And she uses your tax dollars to get kids out of working in dangerous slaughterhouses.
> Nancy Alcantra: Thirteen, fourteen, fifteen-year-olds working on the kill floor, cleaning body parts, animal carcasses. They're working with machinery such as skull-splitters, bone splitters.[5]

This is the fevered, paranoid world the *New York Times* wants you to believe about Trump, the Republicans, and pretty much everybody who calls themselves conservative, or even middle-of-the-road.

They want an asteroid to smash into Earth and destroy all life.

They want your children to drink water polluted with lead and lower their IQs.

They don't care if teenagers work in slaughterhouses and get their limbs amputated or die.

How can the media blatantly promulgate such lies about their fellow Americans? Have they no decency?

Let's look at some other lies they've been caught telling.

***

In June 2022, the Information Technology and Innovation Foundation published an article listing ten stories it believed showed a consistent pattern of misinformation from the mainstream media. It began with:

1. In Ferguson, Missouri, according to contemporaneous press reports that became enshrined in popular culture, Michael Brown had his hands up, while saying, "Don't shoot!" Subsequent investigations by the U.S. Justice Department revealed that while the Ferguson Police Department "engages in a pattern of unconstitutional stops and arrests in violation of the Fourth Amendment," as many protestors contended, that was not the story in this case: The evidence shows Brown fought, tried to take the gun, and was moving back toward the officer who shot him.

2. The Steele dossier, with its allegations of Donald Trump's salacious misconduct and cooperation with Russia, was widely reported to have come from "highly credible" former British intelligence sources. But the document was opposition research that turned out to consist of thin and unsubstantiated information.[6]

As an intelligence analyst, the truth is what you're struggling to uncover. Often, that means you're presenting shades of grey, not just a simple black and white tableau of villains and heroes.

The specific Michael Brown incident should not have been the controversy, but the use of many municipalities to target poor areas with excessive fines as a way to raise funds for the local governments. (Strange, how that never became a topic of discussion, right?)

What do I think was the issue people DIDN'T talk about in regard to the Steele Dossier case? How about the fact Steele was a former British intelligence agent, and he was paid by the Hillary Clinton campaign? Isn't that foreign interference in our elections, in collusion with a presidential campaign? The list continued:

3.   Initial social media videos appeared to show Nicholas Sandman and a group of fellow students from Covington High School on a field trip to the National Mall taunting a native American elder while chanting "Build the wall!" Most mainstream media outlets ran with and amplified this story, making it into a huge national issue. But subsequent reporting revealed that the students did no such thing.

4.   The Black Lives Matter protests during 2020 were widely described as "mostly peaceful." But while analyses have found that 94 percent of the protests were peaceful, the media downplayed the remaining 6 percent which were the most violent protests across the United States since the 1960s, in which 2,037 police officers were injured, with 2,385 cases of looting, 625 cases of arson, hundreds of police vehicles burned or seriously damaged, and an estimated $2 billion in property damage in 140 U.S. cities.[7]

A commonality I would notice between these two stories is how much they push the population toward violence, which as you'll read later, is a common CIA tactic when they're attempting to overthrow a government. Divide and conquer, was the operating principle of the British Empire as it sought to exert its influence around the globe. It should come as little surprise that it's also a tactic the CIA uses.

The list continued with five being the claim that Russia was placing bounties on U.S. soldiers in Afghanistan, while six was the assertion that the theory that COVID-19 had leaked from a virus lab in Wuhan, China was a "racist conspiracy theory."[8]

If you want to be a discerning reader, I suggest you withhold judgment on any international story which immediately makes you want to inflict pain and destruction on some country or leader.

Take a breath and ask yourself if the claim makes rational sense.

Why would Russia want bounties on American soldiers when the Taliban was already ready to kill our soldiers anyway? It's similar to the story about Syria using poison gas on its citizens, just as President Assad was on the verge of winning that country's civil war. Why would he do the very thing which might cause the international community to rise against him?

COVID-19 was a special case, because the facts today seem to suggest that what the intelligence agencies wanted to conceal is the Wuhan lab was doing biological weapons research on their behalf. A hallmark of a lie from the intelligence agencies is that it doesn't make logical sense. In the case of COVID-19, how is it racist to say the virus escaped from a sophisticated Chinese laboratory, yet not racist to say the virus came from a Chinese seafood market where people were eating bat soup?

The list continued, with seven being the claim that the Hunter Biden laptop was "Russian disinformation," while eight was the falsely reported story in the *New York Times* that Capitol police officer Brian Sitnick died as a result of injuries sustained when January 6th protestors struck him with a fire extinguisher.[9]

These two stories are quite important, as they both suggest to me that our own intelligence agencies are intervening in domestic politics, which forms the basis of much of the main thesis of this book. Corruption is not merely a democratic problem, as this book will argue, but permeates our entire governmental system.

I urge you to take a closer look at those individuals the media wants you to dismiss as "dangerous" or a "conspiracy theorist." You're more than likely to find an individual with a well-sourced and well-reasoned critique of our political and governmental system.

The final two stories from the article on misinformation were the campaign against ivermectin as a treatment against COVID-19, and the story of Illinois teenager, Kyle Rittenhouse, who was claimed to be a white supremacist after shooting three men who attacked him during the course of a riot.[10]

Many Republican politicians and commentators supported the campaign against ivermectin or stayed silent in light of the Big Pharma media attack on it, as did a monolithic left wing.

But this is about all of us.

There is no left-wing or right-wing COVID death, just as there is no left- or right-wing cancer death.

If you followed the Kyle Rittenhouse case, you understood that a seventeen-year-old young man answered the call of an Indian American businessman to protect his car dealership from rioters, who had already destroyed part of his business. The police had abandoned efforts to protect property in that area of Kenosha.

What Kyle Rittenhouse did, whether you believe it was rational or not, is exactly what we ask firefighters, soldiers, and police to do every day, to willingly step into dangerous situations.

Why was Kyle painted as a "white supremacist?"

Because somebody somewhere, felt that served an agenda.

This book investigates who that might be, their possible agenda, and how we might combat it.

If you are a moderately fair person and followed many of these stories, you will already understand there are things you are not being told. What are the agendas and biases of those involved?

When there are so many lies, it can be difficult to catch up.

And this doesn't even consider all the various Russian hoaxes, such as the claim Putin blew up his own natural gas pipeline to Europe, or that Russia is behind the anti-vaccine movement, as alleged by Dr. Peter Hotez.[11]

But while the media has been telling these lies, my years as an intelligence agent have convinced me that these fabrications are not coming from the media.

Instead, I believe they're coming from the people I used to work for, the CIA, particularly the Operations Directorate, who learned long ago how to overthrow other countries, and whom I believe are now fixated on doing the same in this country.

They do not want you to be informed. They want you misinformed, emotional, filled with fear of your fellow countrymen. Because when you are afraid, you will let the government take away their "enemies" in the middle of the night, make them the subject of ridicule and disdain, or destroy their source of income.

These ploys have sadly become all too common, and we must not let them continue.

We must drag the intelligence agencies into the light and expose their misdeeds.

It is the only way to save our country.

The years ahead must belong to the patriots, not those who hide in the shadows.

CHAPTER ONE

THE LIES OF
BOB WOODWARD

**The Director of the CIA lay dying, and it was my job to
protect the peace of his final hours.**

The year was 1987, the director of the CIA was the legendary William
Casey, the country was in the throes of learning about the Iran-
Contra scandal, and I was assigned to the protective detail keeping a
twenty-four-hour watch over the director in his room at Georgetown
University Hospital.

My father was brought to Washington, DC, from Utah to work for
the CIA, a fact that my five siblings and I did not know in our child-
hood. In fact, I was only informed of this fact in 1985, after I had joined
the Agency.

Although I'd applied to the Agency in the winter of 1984, at the height
of the Cold War, I did not expect the be accepted. Many years earlier, in
college in the 1970s, I'd been a wild man, known for relentless partying
with the whole package of drugs, alcohol, and women. Because of my
unsavory past, I never imagined I could make it through the CIA's stringent security clearance process. I had an undergraduate degree in biol-
ogy and was working in a lab testing blood pressure medications for Big
Pharma. At first it had seemed exciting to work in a lab, but I eventually
grew bored of it.

I was twenty-nine, and felt my life was going nowhere.

However, a close friend (whom I would later learn was with the Agency) talked me into making an application. "Just tell the truth, Kevin," he said to me. "The CIA isn't like Hoover's FBI of the 1950s. They know people are human and can change. You're not that person anymore and haven't been for several years."

Was my father, or one of his buddies, helping my application along as well?

A few months later I got a call asking if I was interested in my application going forward.

I said yes, and three months later, I got a call asking if I wanted to be interviewed at CIA headquarters in Langley, Virginia.

On the day of the interview, I walked into the spacious lobby of headquarters and was immediately confronted as everybody is by the marble wall with more than fifty engraved stars (today there are one hundred and forty), CIA officers killed in the line of duty. Many had no names listed because the agents died while undercover, and that anonymity remains, even after their death.

To the left, in huge letters on the marble wall was a verse from John 8:32, "And ye shall know the truth and the truth shall make you free." In all that I have done, I have striven to live by that motto. The National Security Act creating the CIA was signed into law in 1947 by President Harry Truman to avoid any American president ever being surprised by another Pearl Harbor style attack.

The great failure of the Act was that it combined intelligence-gathering AND covert actions into a single agency, an arrangement unique in the world's intelligence services. It's been said by many that "design is destiny" and if you have a flawed system, you will get flawed results, regardless of the people. The problem, as I would come to realize over the years, is that instead of giving the president information, and waiting for his decision, the CIA massages the intelligence to maneuver the president into acting the way they want him to act.

But I didn't see any of this on that day in 1985 when I walked into CIA headquarters. Instead, I was just a nervous young man, hoping to be of service to his country. I was escorted down a back hallway, given a visitor badge, and sat down in the waiting area. A woman dressed in business attire eventually came through a door and asked me to follow her.

I was led to an office where a silver-haired man was sitting behind his desk, casually smoking a cigarette. The room was thick with cigarette smoke as he invited me in and asked me to take a seat. I heard the door close behind me, took a quick look back, then gave my attention to the older man. He quickly got down to business.

"Kevin," he said, "have you ever broken the law?"

"Yes, sir. I have."

"Why don't you tell me about it?"

I laid it out for him chapter and verse. I know that to many the CIA is the place where secrets are kept. But at the time, I fervently believed those secrets were kept for the benefit of our policymakers and country. We might lie to others, but we told the unvarnished truth to our leaders. We were Americans, it was a dangerous world, and we had to do difficult things to keep our country safe. That was the agency I thought I was joining. And while I believed my past would disqualify me from that patriotic mission, in what I expected to be my single encounter, I would show them that I believed in that ideal.

I figured that was it, he thanked me for my candor, and I left the office.

A few months later, I got another call from CIA, asking for me to come in and take a polygraph exam.

Before the exam, the polygraph examiner asked if I had anything I wanted to discuss.

Just as I'd done in my previous interview, I told him about my wild, college past, wanting to be completely honest with him. He nodded, as if he'd heard similar stories over the years, and told me to answer as honestly as I could.

I was connected to the wires, sat in a chair, and was asked a very specific set of questions.

They say you can tell a lot about a person by the questions they ask, and I think the same is true for the Agency. As I sat for the exam, listening to, and answering their set of very specific questions, I felt I was getting a better feel for what they considered important. They weren't looking for any ideal psychological profile or background. Mostly, it seemed they were concerned whether I was an honest person. After the emotional build-up, the actual test went smoothly, flying by in about two hours, which I later understood is a good sign.

Apparently, telling the truth takes a lot less time than telling a lie.

After the interview I got calls from people I knew, saying that some guy in a dark suit "from the FBI" had visited them and asked questions about my background. I was a little surprised that people bought the story the agent told and never suspected I had an application in with the CIA.

A month later, I got another call from the CIA, stating my background investigation was still in process, but they wanted to "provisionally" hire me. The Agency had a new program, identifying valuable potential employees who hadn't completed their security investigation, but that they wanted to prevent from applying somewhere else. I felt I was now halfway inside the CIA, identified as a promising recruit, allowed into the building, but not yet in the club.

It may sound crazy in retrospect, but I was processed into the Agency, then placed in a room behind a combination locked door for eight hours a day with the other applicants of promise who had yet to complete their security clearances. We were encouraged to bring books or magazines to read to pass the time, and there was a good assortment of non-classified reading materials they provided.

This lasted seven weeks.

During that time, many of those in the room got the news they'd failed the background check, and that was the last we saw of them.

Finally, I got word of the results of my security background check.

I had passed and was now a junior member of the club.

The excitement was even greater because those of us who had passed were now shepherded to an auditorium deep within the bowels of headquarters, where we were given a three-day presentation, called an Enter on Duty (EOD) briefing, on what really goes on inside the CIA.

I had officially passed into the world of shadows.

I did not know it as I sat in that auditorium, but among the many jobs I would have over my seventeen years at the Agency, I would eventually become the senior EOD briefer, telling these new recruits what the CIA actually did, the good, the bad, and the ugly.

As much as I can, I like to believe I'm continuing in that mission to inform, but you, the general public, are now my audience.

***

After I joined the CIA, I underwent testing for the Security Officer Recruiting and Training (SORT) program. I passed and was admitted into the CIA Office of Security, staff security officer generalist program, where I underwent the intensive security officer training program.

It was in this capacity I would be assigned to protect CIA Director William Casey. There was a command center at his house, one outside his office on the seventh floor of CIA headquarters in Langley, Virginia, where he'd often meet with Senators, Congressman, and others, and later, when he became sick, at George Washington Hospital. I would work at all three of his command centers.

To most agents, Casey was an intimidating figure, a legendary intelligence operative from World War II who placed agents in occupied France. He was Reagan's 1980 campaign manager, a man who didn't suffer fools gladly. He could have a short temper and was also something of a mumbler, making it difficult for the agents to understand what he wanted.

But I always seemed to get along with him.

I don't get intimidated by people, so one day when he walked into the command center and asked for a special phone line to be set up, I asked if he was still having trouble with his next-door neighbor. He stopped, stared at me for a moment, and I held my breath for a moment, wondering if he was going to chew me out.

Instead, he acknowledged that he was (he often used that phone line to handle the neighbor problem) and talked for a few moments about it. I noticed that agents often got stiff when Casey came around, and thought I'd try a different approach.

In future interactions, I asked how his wife, Sophia, was doing with her charitable projects, and his face would lighten up as he talked about what she was doing. I'd just always try to make that human connection with him, making small talk about non-serious things, and it seemed to work.

In the CIA, generalist security officers are responsible for a wide variety of tasks. They include internal and external security, applicant background screening and clearances, staff periodic reinvestigations, the protection of defectors handled by the CIA, the protection of CIA station chiefs while they are overseas, the deputy director of the CIA, as well as the director of the CIA. Security officers are also responsible for operational security during Directorate of Operations (DO) missions. In other words, when CIA agents are operating in a foreign country, guys like me are responsible for making sure they get back safely.

My training as a security officer began at what's affectionately known as "The Farm," a beautiful tract of land in Virginia, equipped with all the latest agency training props, toys, and role players. Most nights it's quiet at the Farm, and you feel a remarkable sense of calm, the silence only broken by the occasional burst of automatic weapons fire. The program at the Farm consisted of how to perform internal CIA investigations, interviewing, interrogation, as well as surveillance detection and counter-surveillance. Our final training involved intensive, scenario-driven training on operational VIP protection, including how to use several advanced weapons systems.

It was humbling to realize that as a security officer, I could very well be killed on assignment, and end up as the newest engraved star on the marble wall in the CIA lobby.

***

If one has read much of the news at any time over the past fifty years, you will be familiar with the name of reporter Bob Woodward.

I don't think it's an understatement that for much of his career he has been regarded as our country's most respected journalist, starting with the work he and Carl Bernstein did for the *Washington Post*, investigating the Watergate scandal which brought down President Richard Nixon in 1974.

However, there's considerable evidence to suggest that Woodward is not to be trusted. And what's more concerning is evidence he may have been acting as an intelligence agent throughout the entirety of his career.

My analysis convinces me that Woodward is likely to have been the most successful disinformation agent on behalf of our intelligence agencies in American history.

But before we examine those charges, let's proceed directly to Woodward's own website so that we may see him as he describes himself to us.

College and the Navy–Woodward was born to Jane and Alfred Woodward in Geneva, Illinois on March 26, 1943. He enrolled in Yale University in 1961 with an NROTC scholarship and studied history and English literature. He received his B.A. degree in 1965 and began a five-year tour of duty in the U.S. Navy.

The Washington Post–After being discharged as a lieutenant in August, 1970, Woodward considered attending law school but applied for a job as a reporter for *The Washington Post*. Harry M. Rosenfeld, the Post's metropolitan editor, gave him a two-week trial, which he failed. After a year at the *Montgomery Sentinel*, a weekly in the Washington DC suburbs, Woodward was hired as a *Post* reporter in September, 1971.

Watergate & All the President's Men–In 1972, the reporting of Woodward and Bernstein in the *Post* was regularly denounced by the Nixon re-election campaign, Republican leaders, and the White House. For example, on Oct. 16, 1972, White House Press Secretary Ron Ziegler denounced the reporting as "hearsay, innuendo, guilt by association."[12]

Remember, this is Woodward's own account of his rise to success. He enrolls at Yale University (a prime recruiting ground for the intelligence agencies), studies history and English literature (the better to understand people and their motivations), on an ROTC scholarship (patriotic type who wants to serve his country), then goes into the Navy, where he spends five years, before being discharged as a lieutenant.

What he fails to mention is how high he made it into the Navy, becoming a briefer for General Alexander Haig, who would become chief of staff in the Nixon White House, just as the Watergate scandal began to swirl. (Haig would also serve in the Reagan White House as secretary of state, memorable to most Americans at the time for taking the podium after

Reagan had been shot in March 1981, declaring, "I'm in charge here at the White House." This was widely derided and mocked in the press at the time for not only being wrong under the Constitution but giving the image of a power hungry general. Haig's relationship with Reagan was rocky, and he resigned in June of 1982.)

A 2019 book about Haig by Ray Locker, twice nominated for a Pulitzer Prize as well as being an editor at *USA Today*, detailed the Woodward/ Haig relationship.

> He [Woodward] gave no indication in his column that he had known Haig since his days as a young navy lieutenant delivering messages to Haig at the NSC [National Security Council] for his boss, Adm. Thomas Moorer, the chief of naval operations and then the chairman of the Joint Chiefs of Staff. Woodward also mentioned nothing about his coverup for another former commander, Welander. Seven years earlier, Woodward's articles for the Post about the spy ring also failed to include that he had worked for both Moorer and Welander.[13]

Why would Woodward be interested in concealing that as a Navy service member he'd worked on behalf of the National Security Council, the future chairman of the Joint Chiefs of Staff, and the future White House chief of staff. Isn't that something you'd be shouting from the rooftops as a young man in your twenties trying to get people to pay attention to you? That seems like unparalleled access to the most powerful men in the country. Or could it be that to reveal such information to his bosses at the *Washington Post*, they might have questioned his objectivity?

Doesn't it seem that if Haig and Woodward were being honest, they might have mentioned their relationship to the White House press secretary? Are we genuinely supposed to believe that the chief of staff of a White House under siege by a very specific reporter, wouldn't think to mention that the reporter in question once reported to him?

In what world does hiding this relationship comport with the rules of objective journalism?

In the concluding section of his book, Locker makes the following claims about Woodward, and Haig.

Despite what Haig's associates at State and elsewhere noted as a close relationship with Woodward, neither Haig nor Woodward could get their stories straight about when they first met. They both denied what others such as Melvin Laird and Moorer confirmed—that Woodward and Haig knew each other while Woodward served in the Navy. Haig said he did not meet Woodward until he and Bernstein showed up at Haig's home in September 1974, while Woodward put the date sometime in early 1973. Given Woodward's long service on Haig's behalf as a journalist—covering up the spy ring, hiding Woodward's relationship with the top military officers, masking Haig's identity as a source in *All the President's Men*, and writing a helpful column to push Haig over the hump in the Foreign Relations Committee—their protestations ring hollow. The close relationship between Haig and Woodward that Clark noted at State was no accident and no recent occurrence.[14]

If the 1970s were supposed to be the golden age of journalism because of the efforts of people like Bob Woodward, maybe we should reappraise our understanding of those times, as well as those which followed.

We return to Bob Woodward's own site to learn of his remarkable accomplishments. In light of the revelations of Woodward's close connections to the intelligence communities, perhaps his "blockbuster revelations" should be viewed through a different lens.

Six months later, on May 1, 1973, Ziegler reversed himself and said, "I would apologize to the *Post*, and I would apologize to Mr. Woodward and Bernstein . . . they have vigorously pursued this story and deserve the credit and are receiving the credit."

Subsequently, the investigations of the Senate Watergate Committee, the House Judiciary Committee and the Watergate Special prosecutor showed that the Woodward-Bernstein reporting had been accurate and perhaps understated the scope and depth of the criminality and abuse of power.

Over 40 people went to jail because of Watergate investigations, including Nixon's top White House aides H.R. Haldeman and John Ehrlichman, and Nixon's main attorney's, former attorney General

John N. Mitchell, White House Counsel John W. Dean and Herbert Kalmbach, Nixon's personal attorney. The Senate report follows and supports much of the reporting of Bernstein and Woodward on the Watergate break-in, coverup, Nixon White House and 1972 re-election campaign espionage, sabotage, and fundraising.[15]

The question which later researchers would ask is whether the Watergate scandal was an "inside job" designed to bring down the Nixon presidency, which had won the greatest landslide reelection victory in American history in 1972, as Nixon was successfully winding down the Vietnam War, had integrated schools, and even founded the Environmental Protection Agency. Key pieces of evidence in support of this belief show that four of the five Watergate burglars were former CIA agents, and that Woodward's famous anonymous "Deep Throat" source was later revealed in 2005 to be the number two man at the Federal Bureau of Investigations, Mark Felt, who had been passed over to lead the agency by Nixon. From the *Encyclopedia Brittanica* account of the Watergate break-in and scandal:

> Early on June 17, 1972, police apprehended five burglars at the office of the DNC in the Watergate complex. [It was later claimed they were looking for evidence of a Democratic ring of call girls who were being supplied to politicians.] Four of them formerly had been active in Central Intelligence Agency (CIA) activities against Fidel Castro in Cuba. (Though often referred to in the press as "Cubans," only three of the four were of Cuban heritage.) The fifth, James W. McCord, Jr., was the security chief of the Committee to Re-Elect the President (later popularly known as CREEP), which was presided over by John Mitchell, Nixon's former attorney general.
>
> The arrest was reported in the next morning's *Washington Post* in an article written by Alfred E. Lewis, Carl Bernstein, and Bob Woodward, the latter two a pair of relatively undistinguished young reporters relegated to unglamorous beats—Bernstein to roving coverage of Virginia politics, and Woodward, still new to the *Post*, to covering minor criminal activities.[16]

In 1972, at the time these events took place, there was not as much suspicion among the general public about the workings of our intelligence community. It would only be after the hearings led by Senator Frank Church in 1975, that most Americans would get a glimpse into the covert actions of the CIA, including the manipulation of foreign elections, the corruption of American journalists, and the assassination of political figures. Much attention has been focused over the past decades on getting to the bottom of the possible CIA involvement of the John F. Kennedy assassination in 1963.

But perhaps similar attention should be focused on whether a nonviolent coup (utilizing Nixon's own penchant for secrecy and paranoia) was used to end the Nixon presidency in 1974. It may also be shocking to realize that after Nixon's resignation, this cleared the way for his vice president, Gerald Ford, to become president. As a congressman, Ford had served on the Warren Commission investigation into the Kennedy assassination, concluding the president was killed, not as a result of any conspiracy, but by a lone, deranged gunman, Lee Harvey Oswald.

When one genuinely looks at the facts of this period of American history, one comes to realize it was a relatively small group of powerful men, who were circulating in and out of these top governmental positions.

Now let's look at perhaps the central figure of the Watergate scandal, the anonymous Bob Woodward source who was only known to the public for decades as "Deep Throat."

I was a young man, living in the Washington, DC, area at the time, and trying to determine the identity of "Deep Throat" was a national guessing game, a secret that was successfully kept for many years. From the History Channel website article with the title, "How 'Deep Throat' Took Down Nixon from Inside the FBI":

Former FBI Deputy Director William Mark Felt, Sr., age 91, broke his 30 year silence and confirmed in June 2005 that he was "Deep Throat," the anonymous government source who had leaked crucial information to *Washington Post* reporters Carl Bernstein and Bob Woodward, which helped take down Richard M. Nixon during the Watergate scandal . . .

Throughout the 1972 election campaign and beyond, Deep Throat fed Woodward and Bernstein a steady flow of information which exposed Nixon's knowledge of the scandal.

The idea to break into the Democratic National Committee's office and tap their phones was the brainchild of G. Gordon Liddy, [former CIA agent] Finance Counsel for the Committee for the Reelection of the President (CRP). He took his plan to White House Counsel John Dean and Attorney General John Mitchell, who approved a smaller-scale version of the idea.[17]

One might question how a relatively junior reporter like Bob Woodward, not even a year on the *Washington Post*, could so quickly cultivate sources like the White House chief of staff and the number two man at the Federal Bureau of Investigation.

It doesn't sound like Woodward was your typical journalist at the start of his career. His journalism career seemed to be curiously "supercharged."

And perhaps it's worth getting a little more information about Mark Felt, the number two man at the FBI, passed over by Nixon for the top job, and whether he upheld his responsibilities as a lawman. The same History Channel article notes that, "In 1978, Felt was indicted for ordering FBI agents to search the homes of Weather Underground members and other leftist groups without a warrant. He was found guilty in 1980 and pardoned by President Ronald Reagan in 1981."[18]

It seems that Felt wasn't above breaking the law when it suited him, either. He seemed to be at home in J. Edgar Hoover's culture of corruption, surveillance, and blackmail that marked some of the darkest days of the FBI.

How much was the FBI running interference for the CIA?

We can't know for sure, but there are some things that are part of the public record, which suggest that perhaps they should be seen as part of the same agency.

In February 1973, Nixon appointed Gray [L. Patrick Gray] permanent FBI director. His tenure was short, however, when he was forced to resign after it came to light he had destroyed a file on CIA Officer E. Howard Hunt, one of Liddy's Watergate co-conspirators. Gray then recommended Felt for the job, but Nixon and his Chief of Staff Alexander Haig were concerned Felt was leaking information to the press and chose William Ruckelshaus instead.

Felt and Ruckelshaus had a strained relationship. In June, Ruckelshaus directly accused Felt of leaking information to *The New York Times*. On June 22, Felt resigned and ended his 31-year career with the FBI.[19]

Mark Felt was prosecuted and convicted of violating the civil rights of Americans. And yet, for those who know of his role as "Deep Throat," they likely don't know about that part of his career. Felt was suspected of breaking the law by his coworkers, and yet never copped to the crime. Is that what we expect of top justice officials?

No, we expect their behavior to be above reproach.

And what does it say about the top management of the FBI, that during his brief tenure as FBI director, L. Boyden Gray destroyed a CIA file on one of the Watergate burglars, E. Howard Hunt, probably one of the most notorious figures in CIA history, active not only in the failed Bay of Pigs invasion, but the CIA-assisted murder of Cuban revolutionary, Che Guevara, in Bolivia, and long-suspected of playing a key role in the assassination of President John F. Kennedy?

Did Bob Woodward ever investigate those allegations?

He did not.

Let's return to Bob Woodward's own description of his heroic life from his personal website.

Woodward's first book with Bernstein, *All the President's Men*, became a #1 national bestseller in the spring and summer before Nixon resigned in 1974. The 1976 movie version of *All the President's Men* became a classic, with Robert Redford as Woodward and Dustin Hoffman as Bernstein.

David Halberstam, in his book, *The Powers that Be*, reported how Seymour Hersh of *The New York Times* did important reporting on Watergate, especially on the payments of hush money to the

Watergate burglars. But Halberstam wrote of Hersh, "Woodward and Bernstein were always ahead; he was amazed at how good they were and how hard they worked, he who had always outworked everyone else, he was in awe of their energy and drive. His recurrent nightmare was of arriving at some lawyer's office and seeing Woodward leaving it. Often that nightmare turned out to be true . . . It was an unusual feeling for Seymour Hersh, the feeling that someone was always just a little ahead of him."[20]

At the time, Seymour Hersh was arguably the most important journalist in America, having won the Pulitzer Prize in 1970 for his reporting on the My Lai massacre in Vietnam, in which twenty-five US Army officers and enlisted men killed more than five hundred unarmed Vietnamese civilians.

How is it that Woodward, a junior reporter at the *Washington Post*, was able to scoop Hersh, a Pulitzer Prize winning journalist?

Probably by having the White House chief of staff (Haig), the number two man at the FBI (Felt), and likely a host of other still undisclosed members of the intelligence community feeding him information and shaping the narrative, Woodward appears to have been able to pull off something unprecedented in American history, the resignation of a sitting president.

But this begs the question of whether the reporting was journalism, or an intelligence operation directed against a popular commander in chief?

***

All of this leads to my own experience with Bob Woodward.

As I've mentioned, in 1987 I was assigned to CIA Director William Casey's staff as a protective agent, as he lay terminally ill of cancer in a secure room at George Washington Hospital. I spent many hours in what we called the "hot seat," right outside of Casey's hospital room. There was no higher priority than protecting Casey, as I detailed in my 2012 book, *From the Company of Shadows*:

As Casey lay dying in the hospital, death threats from radicals and bizarre individuals, convinced he was controlling the globe, continued to come into the CIA. As agents assigned to assess the threat against the Director, we continually received, analyzed, and if warranted, followed up on these threats. During his tenure as Director of Central Intelligence (DCI), his time terminally ill in the hospital, and even after his death—death threats continued to arrive by mail and via the telephone (to Agency operators). Several letters claimed Casey should die for his involvement in the Iran Contra scandal, and others came from unstable or mentally ill people who thought either they were super-intelligent and ruled the universe, or the CIA was controlling their brain. Most disturbing was the fact that Ayatollah Khomeini had placed a significant price on Casey's head.[21]

The other important fact to note is that Casey's tumor attacked the language centers of his brain, and although his cognition was intact, he had lost the ability to speak. Bob Woodward would claim in his book, *Veil: The Secret Wars of the CIA, 1981–1987*, that he was able to penetrate the CIA's security cordon at George Washington Hospital and interview the ailing director and obtain a few, final, devastating admissions from him.

I believe this is a bold-faced lie.

Woodward was never able to get through our team.

The problem with Woodward's work, noted by many commentators, is that like many first-rate liars, he does an excellent job of telling you nine true things, then when you've been lulled into believing him, the tenth thing he tells you is a lie. There is also no doubting that when he wants to be, Woodward, can be a thorough, competent writer. This is what he writes early in *Veil*.

In the couple of years before he joined the Reagan campaign, Casey had started another book, his best, he believed. Tentatively entitled "The Clandestine War Against Hitler," the six-hundred-page book recounted OSS [Office of Strategic Services, the forerunner to the CIA] spying in World War II and had two main characters. The first was Casey. The second was Casey's mentor and surrogate father, General William "Wild Bill" Donovan. Casey drew a loving portrait of the OSS founder, a roly-poly man with soft blue eyes and an unrelenting curiosity and drive. Donovan had been twice the age of the thirty-year-old Lieutenant (junior grade) Casey when they met in Washington in 1943, but he had closed the multiple gaps of generation, military rank, education, and social background. Donovan wanted to know what someone could do. Results counted. "The perfect is the enemy of the good," Donovan often said. Casey would have walked through fire for him.[22]

As far as I know, everything in that paragraph is accurate. Casey was a genuine intelligence hero of the Second World War, working with the predecessor agency to the CIA. Woodward's book, more than five hundred pages long in the paperback version, is filled with great detail about CIA operations.

When Woodward lied about getting into Casey's room, my perspective was that Woodward was simply doing it to sell more books.

However, with the passage of time, I've come to a different perspective. Casey allowed Woodward great access to him, more than any other journalist. This struck me as odd. If Woodward's reputation was to be believed, he was a president-killer.

He was the guy who always got the story.

If that was true, why did Casey give him such extraordinary access? Unless he wanted a "certain" story to come out, suggesting it had somehow been weaseled out of him,

One thing I need the reader to understand is that even in the intelligence community, there are secrets. In fact, most of the intelligence community is walled-off from information in a way little different than the general public. We are trying to do our job in an honorable way, but we don't know what the guys in the next cubicle, the next office, or on the floors above or below us are doing.

Thus, as an agent on the protective detail for Casey, I would wonder why he seemed to be so close to Bob Woodward.

I could not come up with a reason.

As I have grown older an explanation has emerged for me. But like much in the clandestine world I cannot tell you it is true.

However, it does explain all the known facts.

I believe Bob Woodward is the authorized disinformation agent of the most secret parts of our intelligence agencies. For some reason, these agencies wanted Nixon gone, and Woodward was their witting agent.

If that's true, it explains why the Agency let Woodward talk so much with CIA Director Casey, who at the time was the focal point of the Iran-Contra scandal which threatened to bring down the Reagan administration. I think Bob Woodward's book, even his fake account of that final deathbed meeting with William Casey, was an attempt by the Deep State to rehabilitate Casey's reputation in the face of democratic attacks in Congress.

Consider if you believe this to be an indictment of the CIA director, or a celebration? In my estimation, Woodward is telling the public that no matter what they hear about the CIA, they should still trust its inherent goodness.

> The previous year Casey had told me that he had read a review I had written of John le Carre's *A Perfect Spy*. Casey said he agreed with my interpretation of the le Carre's view of espionage, that the better the spying, the better the deception. I had quoted him one of my favorite lines from the book: *"In every operation there is an above the line and a below the line. Above the line is what you do by the book. Below the line is how you do the job."* Casey just took it in, an intense, almost gloomy, look on his face. He could be so distant. What did he think? I had asked. No response. Did he agree? Nothing.
>
> Casey had been an attractive figure to me because he was useful and because he never avoided the confrontation. He might shout and challenge, even threaten, but he never broke off the dialogue or relationship. Back in 1985 when we had exposed the covert preemptive teams to strike against terrorists, he had said to me, "You'll probably have blood on your hands before it's over."[23]

Let's think about how Woodward wants this to come across to the general public. The CIA director is telling the intrepid journalist that he agrees with the reporter's interpretation of the intelligence community's methods. But our patriotic CIA director won't go any further than that, leaving it unclear how much they might break the law in attempting to fulfill their mission of protecting the public.

In your secret heart, don't you hope our intelligence agencies will do just about anything to stop terrorists? We don't admit it in public.

But in private we hope those shadow warriors are on the wall, protecting us.

And we're happy to know that at least in Woodward's telling of it, they are also honorable men.

While we're at it, let's also consider the "expose" of secret terrorist execution squads, that supposedly so upset the CIA director.

What strategy is best for deterring potential terrorists?

Finding them in their secret hiding places and killing them before they strike?

Or might it be even better to release stories in the "free press" that intelligence operatives are lurking in the shadows, possibly observing your terrorist group right now, ready at a moment's notice to end your lives? Personally, I think it's better if you convince your enemies that any attempt to attack you will meet with immediate failure.

Maybe Woodward's pose as a check on government power is the greatest lie he's told over the course of his career.

Instead, I think Woodward's purpose in writing *Veil* was to wash the stain of sin off the CIA, for their many violations of law and human rights. Consider how he ends the book:

> Several days later I returned to Casey's room. The door was open. Scars from the craniotomy were still healing. I asked Casey how he was getting along.
>
> Hope and realism flashed in his eyes. "Okay . . . better . . . no."
>
> I took his hand to shake it in a greeting. He grabbed my hand and squeezed, peace and sunlight in the room for a moment.
>
> "You finished yet?" he asked, referring to the book.
>
> I said I'd never finish, never get it all, there were so many questions. I'd never find out everything he'd done.
>
> The left side of his mouth hooked up in a smile, and he grunted.[24]

How's that for a picture of a brave, public servant of the secretive intelligence agencies, engaging in good-hearted battle with a member of the independent press? The picture Woodward paints is of two men on opposite sides of a debate, and yet still interacting with great respect. The account continues, building to an emotional climax worthy of an Academy Award-winning film.

> You knew, didn't you, I said. The Contra diversion had to be the first question: you knew all along.
>   His head jerked up hard. He stared, and finally nodded yes.
>   "Why?" I asked.
>   "I believed."
>   "What?"
>   "I believed."
>   Then he was asleep, and I didn't get to ask another question.[25]

Woodward's account is a complete and total fantasy.

A few days later, Casey was taken home by his wife, Sofia, and allowed to die in his own bed. Woodward's account of his meeting with Casey a few days before his death is absolute garbage. The CIA protective detail would have prevented him from getting into the room, and Casey couldn't talk.

I know, because I protected the CIA director in those final days. I was often in the room with Casey, his wife, Sophia, and Casey's daughter, Bernadette, and Bob Woodward was not.

Reaction to what Woodward had written was swift and strong. First out of the gate was Casey's widow, Sophia, as reported in a September 28, 1987, article in the *Los Angeles Times*:

> Sophia Casey said that when Woodward, the Washington Post's assistant managing editor for investigations, attempted to visit her husband in the hospital, guards stopped him before he could enter Casey's room. She also said that Casey was unable to speak during his hospitalization because the right side of his neck and tongue were partially paralyzed. "My husband could not converse," she said.[26]

I agree with this claim, as Sophia and Casey's daughter were always at his bedside. I'd come to know Sophia well, often manning the command post at their hours before Casey became ill, and she was as kind and gracious as her husband could be gruff and intimidating. I have to mention I've often observed this pattern among powerful, intimidating men. Their wives are usually the epitome of friendly and approachable, almost as if they function as two sides of the same human being.

Another person who spoke up at the time was Charles Colson, who'd been a member of the Nixon team, imprisoned for his role in Watergate, but later became a popular Christian minister who eschewed politics. Politics were no longer part of Colson's makeup, only being faithful to God. Colson wrote in an opinion piece in the *Washington Post* on October 1, 1987:

> Coincidentally, I underwent major surgery and was a patient at the Georgetown Hospital during the entire month of January. I occupied the room immediately below Bill Casey's. Without wishing to impugn anyone's veracity I feel compelled because of my personal experience in the hospital to comment in The Post article.
>
> One evening, a hospital official visited my room. He mentioned in passing that Bob Woodward, under false pretenses, had attempted to enter Mr. Casey's room but that he had been turned away by security personnel. These personnel, by the way, had maintained a 24-hour vigil in front of Mr. Casey's door since his operation. Hospital officials were less than pleased with Mr. Woodward's attempt to invade the privacy of a man who was gravely ill.
>
> In the latter part of January–it was either the 26th or 27th–I was invited by Mrs. Casey to visit Bill since we had been associates in the Nixon administration. I did so: it was for me a very moving experience to be able to offer spiritual counsel and pray with an old friend. He was unable, however, to communicate other than by squeezing my hand and making grunting sounds that were unintelligible.[27]

In 2010, I published a book, *In From the Cold: CIA Secrecy and Operations*, and in addition to taking direct aim at Woodward's claim, included what we noticed about Casey in the aftermath of the Colson meeting.

After Colson's visit, Bill Casey became a changed man. Formerly a gruff man who did not suffer fools lightly and regularly reprimanded the agents, or anyone else for that matter, for even small mistakes, he became a kind, gentle man. During his last days in the hospital, although he could not speak, he went out of his way to communicate to the agents and nurses how much he appreciated them and what they were doing. Some of the agents were shocked at the change. An agent, and close friend of mine, who accompanied him as he was transported back to his home in New York relayed to me Casey spent his last days requesting by gestures his nurse come into his room and read the Gospels to him as he lay in bed. On May 6, 1987, Willian Joseph Casey passed away in peace, leaving the legacy of a true American patriot.[28]

I'm sure there are those who will claim I'm giving too much credit to Casey, that even when I was a new agent the CIA was involved in nefarious activities, and I acknowledge that some of that criticism is likely to be warranted.

However, in fairness, I believe it must be balanced against our fears of Soviet communism at the time, which had held Eastern Europe in its iron grip for more than four decades. Just as in our current situation, only a few are properly awake to the fear of Chinese influence with its fascist combination of governmental power combined with corporate interests, there are many reasonable perspectives of the situation.

The CIA I entered seemed focused mostly on our country's external threats.

What I worry about today is that the CIA's powerful influence has been turned against our own citizens, something which we must resist with all our power.

To some extent, this potential threat may have always existed with the structure of the CIA, because of its dual responsibilities for intelligence collection and direct action, but for decades this poisonous plant lay mostly dormant.

And Bob Woodward may have lay at the center of this threat.

Let's continue to follow this thread and consider the question of whether Bob Woodward is a witting or unwitting spreader of lies and misinformation.

In 2012, *Politico* published a long article on six instances in which Bob Woodward's honesty has been called into question by other journalists, beginning with a claim "that legendary *Washington Post* editor Ben Bradlee once expressed 'fear in my soul' that Bob Woodward had embellished elements of his reporting in the Watergate scandal . . . "[29]

The six instances of alleged deception involved the claim that his Watergate source, Deep Throat, had signaled him with the placement of a potted plant on a balcony which was visible from Woodward's apartment. However, many claimed that Woodward's window faced an inner courtyard, with no other balconies visible.

Casey's deathbed confession scene was the second claim, followed by an alleged quote from then CIA Director George Tenet, that the evidence for weapons of mass destruction in Iraq was a "slam-dunk."[30] A claim in Woodward's book on the Supreme Court, that one Supreme Court justice had changed his vote on a crucial case to avoid offending another justice, also came in for sharp criticism.[31]

The fifth controversy also came from Bob Woodward's book, *Veil*. But this time it concerned President Reagan being in the hospital, after his March 1981 assassination attempt. (Which if it had been successful, would have allowed his vice president, the former head of the CIA, George H. W. Bush, to become president.)

In "Veil," Woodward also describes Ronald Reagan's recovery from the 1981 attempt on his life as quite poor. He reports on a scene in which Reagan collapses into a chair. Woodward further writes that in the days after his release from the hospital, Reagan could "concentrate for only a few minutes at a time" and in the following days would only be able to "remain attentive only an hour or so a day."

Reagan's physician, Dr. Daniel Ruge, disputed this portrayal, telling the AP that "his recovery was superb . . . I never saw anything like that [description in the book] . . . it's certainly news to me and I was there all the time."[32]

The question is not just what was true, but whether Woodward was choosing a more dramatic story, Reagan asserting his strength before the public, but behind the scenes being much weaker. Were these just rare mistakes on Woodward's behalf, or were they symptomatic of something much deeper, which might show itself even outside of a political context?

The comedian John Belushi certainly wasn't political, but his friends and family didn't recognize the portrait which emerged from Woodward's book, *Wired*.

> Close confidants of Belushi expressed outrage at the way the comedian was portrayed in Woodward's biography, "Wired," alleging that some scenes were fabricated.
>
> "There were certain things that he just got patently wrong. He painted a portrait of John that was really inaccurate–certain stories in there just weren't true and never happened," said Dan Aykroyd, a fellow Blues Brother and close friend, in the book, "Live from New York: An Uncensored History of Saturday Night Live."[33]

It must be some kind of record for a reporter to have people as diverse as the legendary Ben Bradlee of the *Washington Post*, presidents Nixon and Reagan, the CIA, and the wife of the deceased director of the CIA question your reputation for honesty.

Others, like Joan Didion, saw something a little different than the picture of Woodward as a fabricator. She saw him as an empty vessel, waiting to be used uncritically by those he chose to profile, as detailed in an article from 2013 in *The New Yorker*.

> In a 1996 essay for the *New York Review of Books*, Joan Didion wrote that "measurable cerebral activity is virtually absent" from Woodward's post-Watergate books, which are notable mainly for "a scrupulous passivity, an agreement to cover the story not as it is occurring, but as it is presented, which is to say, as it is manufactured."
>
> Woodward's 2000 book on Alan Greenspan, "Maestro," which was clearly based on extensive access to the Fed chairman, is a good example of what Didion was talking about. As an inside account of what Greenspan said and did, it included some arresting, if largely irrelevant, narrative details, such as one in which the great man, disturbed by his wife, Andrea Mitchell's, desire for a canine companion,

asks one of his colleagues, the chairman of the Philadelphia Fed, "Well, how do you tell your wife you don't want a dog?"[34]

The author continued her critique of *Maestro*, noting it didn't reveal the impact of Greenspan's policies on the country, how he came to rise to godlike status in the financial world, or predict the stock market bubble caused by Greenspan's policies, which would result in the dot-com bust of the stock market in 2001.

The criticisms of Woodward, from his apparent fabrications of critical dramatic moments in several of his books, to his passivity in regard to his subjects, while well-founded, misses what I believe is the best explanation for the mystery of Bob Woodward.

And the answer would come from none other than his famed partner in breaking the Watergate story, Carl Bernstein.

***

On October 20, 1977, Carl Bernstein published a 25,000-word article in *Rolling Stone* magazine, with the title, "The CIA and the Media."

It would reveal a massive influence operation by the intelligence agency to deceive the public during the Cold War, shortly after the formation of the CIA. This is how the article opened:

> In 1953, Joseph Alsop, then one of America's leading syndicated columnists, went to the Philippines to cover an election. He did not go because he was asked by his syndicate. He did not go because he was asked to do so by the newspapers that printed his column. He went at the request of the CIA.[35]

When this information was first released to the public in 1975 as a result of an investigation by US Senator Frank Church, it shocked America. The public thought they understood the basic compact between the government and the press. The press was often referred to as the "fourth estate" or the "fourth branch" of government, as independent from Congress, the presidency, and the courts, as those three branches were to each other.

But the CIA had rigged the game from its inception.

The public thought they were getting independent information, gathered by unbiased journalists with a code of ethics that would prevent them from even having a meal with a public official, for fear of it compromising their objectivity. America was learning that at least for the important issues of the day, the intelligence community was shaping the information they were receiving. Like mushrooms in a basement, the public was being kept in the dark and fed crap.

> Alsop is one of more than 400 American journalists who in the past twenty-five years have secretly carried out assignments for the Central Intelligence Agency, according to documents on file at CIA headquarters. Some of the journalists' relationships with the Agency were tacit; some were explicit. There was cooperation, accommodation, and overlap. Journalists provided a full range of clandestine services–from simple intelligence gathering to serve as go-betweens with spies in Communist countries. Reporters shared their notebooks with the CIA. Editors shared their staff. Some of the journalists were Pulitzer Prize winners.[36]

The CIA broke the sacred compact of American journalism during the Cold War, and it was decades before the public found out. I want you to reflect on that when somebody tells you secrets can't be kept. (Maybe the next time you hear about a foreign country "detaining" an American journalist on charges of being a spy, you'll pause just a minute before rolling your eyes.)

This CIA operation was named Project Mockingbird. (The mockingbird is a bird which mimics the sounds of other bird species, as well as the sounds of insects and amphibians. Scientists are uncertain why the birds engage in this activity. It is believed the female of the species may prefer males who can mimic a wide variety of sounds. Think of mockingbirds as the cover band of the animal kingdom.) Bernstein continued his account of the investigation into Project Mockingbird:

> During the 1976 investigation of the CIA by the Senate Intelligence Committee, chaired by Senator Frank Church, the dimensions of the Agency's involvement became apparent to several members of

the panel, as well as two or three investigators on the staff. But top officials of the CIA, including former directors William Colby and George [H.W.] Bush [Reagan's two-term vice-president, US President from 1989 to 1993, and father of US President George W. Bush, 2000 to 2008] persuaded the committee to restrict its inquiry into the matter and to deliberately misrepresent the scope of the activities in its final report.[37]

When one is trying to wrestle with the question of who really runs our country, consider how George H. W. Bush was able to lie to the Church Committee in 1976, become Reagan's vice president in 1980, serve as president from 1989 to1992, and maneuver his son, George W. Bush, into the presidency from 2000 to 2008.

When one considers the possibility that perhaps important parts of the supposedly independent media are actually secret propagandists for government interests, a different picture of the past, as well as our present situation, begins to emerge.

I also think it's important to realize that spooks and journalists share a number of the same qualities as well as background, and worldview, as Bernstein's article noted:

> Within the CIA, journalists-operatives were accorded elite status, a consequence of the common experience journalists shared with high-level CIA officers. Many had gone to the same schools as their CIA handlers, moved in the same circles, shared fashionably liberal, anticommunist political values, and were part of the same "old boy" network that constituted something of an establishment in the media, politics and academia of postwar America.[38]

The CIA was basically a creation of graduates from the Ivy League schools of America, like Yale (where Bob Woodward went), and would continue to be fertile recruiting grounds for decades to come.

But you might say to yourself, I understand the history of Project Mockingbird, but that ended in the 1970s, with the revelations of the Church Committee.

Or did it just go underground?

It has been said that one of the best ways to keep a secret is to pretend to tell it.

Government influence of the media may have been underground for several decades after the Church Committee hearings.

But on March 14, 2016, President Barack Obama brought it back from the supposed realm of the dead. That's when he signed Executive Order 13721, "Developing an Integrated Global Engagement Center to Support Government-Wide Counterterrorism Communications Activities Directed Abroad and Revoking Executive Order 13584. [39] This action was supposedly necessary to counter the jihadi beheading videos of the Islamic State of Iraq and the Levant (ISIL), Al-Qai'da, and other violent Islamic groups.

While many worried that this new "Global Engagement Center" might be turned against Americans, the supporters could point to express language that limited the scope of the new enterprise.

> Recognizing the need for innovation and new approaches to coun-
> ter the messaging and diminish the influence of ISIL, Al Qa'ida,
> and other violent extremists abroad, and in order to protect the
> vital national interests of the United States, while also recognizing
> the importance of protections for freedom of expression, includ-
> ing those under the First Amendment to the Constitution of the
> United States and international human rights obligations . . . [40]

This arrangement might have remained intact for several years, but in November 2016, Donald Trump was elected president, and the intelligence agency propaganda machine needed to go into overdrive.

As many have claimed, the intelligence agencies did not expect Trump to win, and they saw him as an existential threat to their survival who needed to be eliminated. If that could not be accomplished, they would do their best to hobble and wreck his presidency.

In the lame duck period of the Obama presidency, his allies in the Senate, Republican Rob Portman of Ohio, and Democrat Chris Murphy from Connecticut, proudly announced in a December 23, 2016, press release, a dramatic change to the mission of the Global Engagement Center:

U.S. Senators Rob Portman (R-OH) and Chris Murphy (D-CT) today announced that their Countering Disinformation and Propaganda Act–legislation designed to help American allies counter foreign government propaganda from Russia, China, and other nations–has been signed into law as part of the FY 2017 National Defense Authorization Act (NDAA) Conference Report.

The bipartisan bill, which was introduced by Senators Portman and Murphy in March, will improve the ability of the United States to counter foreign propaganda and disinformation from our enemies by establishing an interagency center housed at the State Department to coordinate and synchronize counter-propaganda throughout the U.S. government. To support these efforts, the bill also creates a grant program for NGOs, think tanks, civil society and other experts outside government who are engaged in counter-propaganda related work.[41]

Just at the time president-elect Trump was popularizing the expression, "fake news," the intelligence agencies working out of their new home in the State Department could start to pay "NGOs, think tanks, civil society and other experts outside government who are engaged in counter-propaganda related work."

What could be better way to counter Trump's claim of "fake news" than a new cadre of people getting a government check to engage in "counter-propaganda?"

It's almost as if government created the problem, then came up with the solution!

The Global Engagement Center is best viewed as the new and improved version of the Project Mockingbird program, updated for the twenty-first century.

And let's take a look at how Bob Woodward is probably the best example of this decades-long intelligence agency effort to manipulate the American public.

***

The last section of this chapter has the potential to either horrify, or delight both sides of the political spectrum.

There is probably no deeper divide among those who study American history than among those who admire President John F. Kennedy, and those who admire President Richard M. Nixon.

Each side sees the other as irredeemably corrupt and degenerate.

I'd like to suggest that they weren't so different, at least in the policies which they pursued, and both were similarly targeted by the intelligence agencies, one with assassination and the other by scandal. As to Nixon's view of the 1960 presidential election, and particularly the role of the CIA in handing the race to Kennedy, I quote from the 1991 book, *Silent Coup: The Removal of a President,* by Len Colony and Robert Gettlin:

> The appointment was especially puzzling in light of Nixon's deep-seated belief that the CIA had contributed to his loss in the 1960 election. Back then, Nixon told friends, the CIA had played politics with the Bay of Pigs operation, briefing candidate John Kennedy on it to the point where he was able to take a strong anti-Castro stand that Nixon did not want to take because it might jeopardize the impending Bay of Pigs invasion; the CIA had also given Kennedy ammunition for his accusations about a "missile gap" that he exploited in similar fashion.[42]

The popular account which you'll get in most history books is that Kennedy looked more glamorous in this first television debate, he'd spent a good deal of time in the sun working on a tan, while Nixon had a dark, sinister looking five o'clock shadow, refused the offer of makeup, and had recently been sick and lost ten pounds.

But what will be admitted in even the most liberal telling of the 1960 election, is that Kennedy ran to the right of Nixon in foreign affairs, accusing the Eisenhower administration of allowing the Soviets to surpass us in ballistic nuclear missiles, and that Nixon as vice president was allowing communists to establish a beachhead in the Caribbean.

Kennedy may have sincerely believed what the CIA told him, but was about to get a rude awakening, not even a month into his presidency. As recounted in a February 10, 2009, article by esteemed historian, Richard Reeves, in the *New York Times*:

On the morning of his 17th day as President, John F. Kennedy was still in bed at 8 a.m. and, as was his habit, reading *The New York Times*. One glance at the front page and he exploded, calling his Secretary of Defense, Robert McNamara and saying: "What the hell is this . . . "

"This" was a headline: "Kennedy Defense Study Finds No Evidence of a 'Missile Gap.'"

Not good. Kennedy's most powerful campaign line had been: "We are facing a gap on which we are gambling with our survival . . . " [43]

The article went on to explain that despite what had been said in the campaign, there was no missile gap, kicking out what had been one of the main claims of the Kennedy campaign. My personal feeling is that the CIA knew that after eight years in the presidency, Eisenhower (and by extension, his vice president) were deeply suspicious of the CIA and the military/industrial complex as a whole.

In fact, on January 17, 1961, Eisenhower's farewell address warned of the dangers of a growing military/industrial complex, which could pose a threat to American democracy. The likelihood is that Kennedy was badly lied to by the CIA briefers, believing he would be easier to control than Nixon, who had personally observed many of their mistakes and screwups. The scope of how badly Kennedy was deceived is staggering.

On the day before he became president, Kennedy was told by his predecessor, Dwight Eisenhower, that there was no missile gap. The United States had a huge advantage, said Eisenhower, "and one invulnerable weapon, Polaris." These were nuclear missiles aboard United States Navy submarines in the oceans off the coast of the Soviet Union.

(Later CIA reports indicated that during the 1960 campaign, the Soviets probably had only three intercontinental ballistic missiles. At the time, though, the C.I.A. estimated, incorrectly, there were about 90 Soviet ICBMs and 200 bombers capable of carrying nuclear weapons, although none of those bombers had the range to reach the United States. At the same time, the United States had 108 missiles that could reach Soviet targets and were in the process of deploying

30 more in Turkey. In addition, the United States Air Force had 600 nuclear-ready bombers capable of reaching Soviet targets.)[44]

Imagine you are John F. Kennedy, and you realize one of the central claims of the campaign that got you elected was shown to you to be false.

It was not simply a lie, but a lie which you believed.

And even worse was to come, in the form of the CIA's lies about the Bay of Pigs invasion in Cuba. Kennedy was understandably upset, but in my estimation failed to take the correct steps to remedy the situation, as detailed by Peter Kornbluth, a senior analyst at the National Security Archive in an article from December of 2014 in the *New York Times*.

> In the aftermath of the failed C.I.A.-led invasion of Cuba at the Bay of Pigs, John F. Kennedy angrily told his top aides that he wanted to "splinter the C.I.A. into a thousand pieces and scatter it to the winds." For a brief period, the president considered a State Department recommendation to strip the agency of its covert functions, reorganize, and even rename it.
>
> If Kennedy had shuttered the Central Intelligence Agency's covert operations in 1961, the United States might have been spared an unending cycle of illegal, immoral and criminal C.I.A. related scandals, among them; the infamous assassination plots against foreign leaders; the Phoenix program in Vietnam; the secret program to bring hundreds of Hitler's henchmen to America; the regime change operations in Iran, Guatemala, Brazil, Chile, and elsewhere; the domestic spying effort known as Operation Chaos; the illegal Iran-Contra operations; and now the rendition, secret detention and sadistic torture programs, which constitute nothing less than crimes against humanity.
>
> Undertaken by the C.I.A.'s directorate of operations, these covert actions have been conducted in the ostensible defense of our democratic institutions.[45]

But alas, Kennedy failed to close the directorate of operations, and his presidency ended under murky and still mysterious conditions on that fateful day in November of 1963 in Dallas, Texas.

After his death, Lyndon Johnson assumed the presidency, reversed Kennedy's executive order that would have started bringing home military advisors from Vietnam after the 1964 election, provoked and lied about the incidents leading up to the Tonkin Gulf incident, which precipitated the Vietnam War—leading to the deaths of more than 55,000 American servicemen, more than a million Vietnamese, and leading to much of the political tumult of the 1960s.

And what did Richard Nixon come to believe had happened in the 1960 election? Well, he wrote about it in his 1962 book, *Six Crises*, portions of which were excerpted in *U.S. News and World Report*.

> Mr. Nixon charges in his book that Mr. Kennedy endangered U.S. security when he urged, in a campaign speech, U.S, intervention in Cuba and aid to anti-Castro forces in that country, even though he had been briefed by the Central Intelligence Agency that U.S.-supported anti-Castro forces already were in training for an invasion.
>
> The White House and Allen Dulles, former Director of the CIA, [having been fired by Kennedy after the Bay of Pigs debacle] have denied that President Kennedy had been advised of the invasion plans before the election. Mr. Dulles said the charge apparently was the result of an "honest mistake."
>
> For the former Vice President, that incident was "the first and only time in the campaign I got mad at Kennedy–personally . . . And my rage was greater because I could do nothing about it."[46]

The Deep State did not come into being overnight. Like a serial killer might first begin his reign of terror by torturing small animals, then seeing what he can get away with and not draw unwanted attention, I strongly believe the shadow government started putting their finger on the scales of American democracy, at least as early as the 1960 election.

Nixon had spent eight years as vice president, watching the operations of the CIA, observing their strengths and weaknesses. The claim of many liberal historians that Nixon would have approved an invasion of Cuba may suggest an example of black and white thinking. Perhaps he was aware of the complexities of the situation that Kennedy was not, cognizant of the threat of communism, but also concerned that a clumsy intervention might make the situation even worse.

However, the country would have to wait eight more years to understand how Nixon might handle these challenges, three years in which Kennedy would seek to keep the peace, and five years in which President Johnson would set free the "dogs of war," and the country would be on fire, with anti-war protests and civil rights marches.

If it's true, that the Deep State took effective control of the country in November 1963 by Kennedy's assassination, it was clear by the Fall of 1968, that they had no idea how to run a democracy.

***

The 1992 book, *Silent Coup: The Removal of a President*, by Len Colodny and Robert Gettlin, presents a unique window into the Nixon administration, and Bob Woodward's role in bringing it down on behalf of the shadow government.

> Nixon's need to control his political destiny and to prevent the blunting of his agenda by bureaucrats pushed him towards the establishment of what was, in effect, a secret government. An intensely private and withdrawn man, almost the opposite of the usual gregarious politician, Nixon often recoiled from social situations and preferred to be closeted with familiar aides or sit alone with a pad and pen and jot down his thoughts. "Meeting new people filled him with vague dread, especially if they were in a position to rebuff or contradict him," Henry Kissinger observed of his former chieftain in the first volume of his own memoirs, *White House Years* ...
>
> Both Nixon and Kissinger saw the government bureaucrats as roadblocks to be circumvented. To Nixon, Congress was under the thumb of the Democrats; the Department of State and the Central Intelligence Agency were havens for Eastern Establishment liberals who hated him; and the military was full of doctrinaire, inflexible anticommunists.[47]

The claim in the book is that Nixon cloaked and hid his agenda, giving the war hawks what they claimed they wanted (secretly allowing the bombing of communist strongholds in Cambodia), while at the same time trying to negotiate arms control deals with the Soviets, and creating a diplomatic opening to China. Nixon also quietly completed the desegregation of southern schools and created the Environmental Protection Agency.

While this approach horrified those in government, it won wide approval with the public, resulting in Nixon's landslide reelection victory of 1972, in which he carried forty-nine out of fifty states, only failing to carry Massachusetts and the District of Columbia.

> But bureaucrats don't like it when they're being ignored.
>
> To the Joint Chiefs, the backchannel [to China] and Kissinger overtures to the service chiefs provided the military with special access to the commander in chief, a wondrous thing at a time when they were engaged in a war that was not being won. Yet these back-channel operations also provided the chiefs with indelible evidence that the president was circumventing other officials in the government and was probably doing the same to them.
>
> The Pentagon brass faced a dilemma. On the one hand, they approved of the president's and Kissinger's readiness to use military force in an effort to rejuvenate the United States' efforts to win the grinding, frustrating war in Southeast Asia. They secretly applauded when in March 1969 the president charged them, through back-channels, with conducting secret bombing missions over neutral Cambodia. These missions would continue over the next fourteen months and had as their target suspected North Vietnamese and Vietcong "sanctuaries" in that country.[48]

It's in this environment in which Bob Woodward enters the picture, a Navy man, tasked with overseeing Nixon's secret communications channels on behalf of the shadow government being frozen out of the decision-making process.

> The Navy brought Woodward to the Pentagon ostensibly as a communications watch officer responsible for overseeing approximately thirty sailors who manned the terminals, teletypes, and classified coding machines at the naval communications center through

which all the Navy traffic flowed, from routine orders to top secret messages. It was a sensitive position that afforded Woodward access to more than a hundred communication channels, among them, according to Admiral Fitzpatrick, the top-secret SR-1 channel through which the Navy sent and received its most important messages, for instance, those which served to operate its covert global spy unit known as Task Force 157. SR-1 was the channel that Moorer provided to the White House when Kissinger and Nixon pushed him for backchannel communications capability. When Kissinger conducted his delicate and highly secret negotiations with China during 1971, SR-1 carried Kissinger's message back to his deputy, Al Haig that the Peking mission had succeeded.[49]

The picture that emerges from Colodny and Gettlin's book is of Woodward working as one of the most trusted intelligence assets of the Navy, as well as other branches of the military, monitoring what they believe to be the Nixon threat to their power and influence.

Those fully briefed on these matters may be an extremely small group, as Admiral Thomas Moorer, Woodward's boss and Nixon's chairman of the Joint Chiefs of Staff from 1970 to 1974, readily shared with the authors his knowledge of Woodward's activities.

However, that Woodward was a briefer and that some of those briefings were to Alexander Haig can no longer be in doubt. Admiral Moorer has confirmed to us what other sources had told us, that Woodward had been a briefer and that his duties included briefing Haig.

"He was one of the briefers," Moorer told us. Did he brief Haig? "Sure, of course," Moorer said. Woodward was instructed to brief Haig, "because I was on the telephone with Haig eight or nine times a day" and there was even more to convey to Haig, so Haig could in turn relay information to Kissinger and ultimately to the president. "You don't have four-star generals lugging papers back and forth between the Pentagon and the White House," Moorer told us, "you pick up a junior-grade lieutenant and tell him to do that." But Woodward was a full-grade lieutenant, not a junior one, and especially selected for the job. What sort of briefing would Woodward normally give to Haig? "Probably the same briefing he'd just given me at nine o'clock," Moorer said, referring to the daily 9:00 a.m. briefing attended by the CNO and other flag officers at the Pentagon.[50]

When one puts the pieces together, they snap together in a satisfying (if disturbing) arrangement.

Eisenhower, the legendary World War II general and US president, understood the world that existed before the creation of the Central Intelligence Agency.

His vice president, Richard Nixon, understood the general's concerns as well, and in his eight years at Eisenhower's side, probably shared his concerns about the rise of the military-industrial complex.

When looking at the two choices in 1960, the Deep State thought Kennedy would be the one they could most easily manipulate.

After being humiliated on the "missile gap" and the chances of a successful anti-Castro revolution in Cuba, Kennedy became so irate at the CIA that he wanted to "shatter it into a thousand pieces."

Lyndon Johnson becomes president, taking the United States into the Vietnam War under false pretenses, nearly shattering the country.

Nixon becomes president in 1968, seeming to do the bidding of the shadow government and the military-industrial complex by increasing the efforts in Vietnam and bombing North Vietnamese sanctuaries in Cambodia, but he's also reaching out to the Soviet Union and China, trying to create a more stable international order.

The shadow government, composed of various military and intelligence agencies, begins to monitor Nixon, becoming ever more alarmed.

Their star agent-provocateur is Bob Woodward, Navy intelligence man, who gains inside knowledge of the workings of the White House, then when he leaves the military, obtains a position at the *Washington Post*, and just happens to be in the right place and the right time to get the first information about the former CIA agents, now Watergate burglars, when they are arrested breaking into the Democratic National Headquarters.

Woodward then gets inside information from the number two man at the FBI, Mark Felt (a.k.a. Deep Throat), who is later convicted of violating the civil rights of Americans, and also from the man he used to brief while in the Navy, White House chief of staff, Alexander Haig.

Woodward brings down the Nixon White House, writes a #1 bestselling book, *All The President's Men*, gets rewarded by having Robert Redford play him in the movie of the same name, and becomes the inspiration for countless investigative journalists, hoping to have a career of similar impact. Woodward then spends the next fifty years writing books about presidents from Nixon to Trump, the latest with a single-word title, *FEAR: Trump in the White House.*

Woodward really has had an unbelievable career.

And I'm not sure there is any of it that isn't tainted by smoke and mirrors and lies.

***

Who else working in media today might be connected to the intelligence community, like the four hundred Project Mockingbird assets, whose names remain concealed.

I can't tell you for sure, but I have my suspicions.

On September 30, 2019, I appeared on the *Ingraham Angle* with Laura Ingraham to talk about the then anonymous whistleblower alleging President Trump engaged in illegal activity in his discussion with Ukrainian President Volodymyr Zelenskyy. As I sat in the green room at the Fox News studio in Atlanta, I watched the *Hannity* show that played before Laura's show and couldn't help but notice the pin on Sean Hannity's lapel.

It was a CIA pin.

In my experience in the Agency, that was a way of broadcasting one's allegiance. When gathering one's understanding of the workings of the Deep State, it's helpful to consider their "methods" and how they have tried to deceive the public in the past.

There are only so many moves in the CIA's playbook of deception, and because of the work of many honest patriots, we've seen most of them.

Amid the tumult of news networks, from CNN to Fox News, maybe we should ask how it is that Sean Hannity, like Bob Woodward before him, manages to always stay on top?

CHAPTER TWO

A CIA OFFICER
DISCOVERS THE TRUTH

After the death of William Casey, William Webster took over as the director of the Central Intelligence Agency from 1987 to 1991, with Robert Gates becoming his deputy director.

I served as an agent on Gates's protective detail while he was deputy director and was pleased when he became CIA director on November 6, 1991. Gates was a genuine CIA man, the only director to have risen from an entry-level employee to the top position. I would also argue that the Agency was mostly run by Gates during the Webster tenure (Webster tended to be a "hands-off" boss), and it was during those years I felt the proudest of my association with the CIA. I always found Gates to be a man of tremendous integrity and intelligence, a humble man with a wonderful sense of humor.

But in a turn of events which puzzles me to this day, following the election of President Bill Clinton in 1992, and the pre-inauguration briefing he gave to Clinton, Gates resigned as the director of the CIA. I can only imagine what happened in that meeting to make the good man I knew quit the organization to which he had dedicated his professional life. I believe he saw what was coming on the horizon for US intelligence and wanted to have no part of it.

During the going-away ceremony for Gates at CIA headquarters, I met Sophia Casey and her daughter, Bernadette, giving them both a warm hug.

"Kevin, what the heck is going on around here?" Mrs. Casey asked, as puzzled as I was about the Gates's resignation, and the rumors of changes at the CIA.

"Ma'am, I don't know," I told her. "But I think it's bad."

She looked at me, knowing how dedicated I'd been to her husband, and the Agency, and said, "Well, why don't you do something about it?"

"Ma'am, maybe I will," I promised her.

My last assignment as a CIA protection agent was to participate in the installation of the new director of the Agency, John Deutch, and his team. George Tenet would take over as the deputy director of CIA, and Nora Slatkin became the first executive officer. We would take to calling them, "the bum," "the politician," and the "dragon lady," or sometimes just the "three stooges."

In his new role as the director of Central Intelligence, Deutch came to visit the CIA Counterintelligence Center (CIC) to which I'd recently been transferred. He wanted us to know how much he appreciated our work on internal espionage investigations but spoke in such a low voice that none of us could understand what he was saying. "What did he just say?" an agent sitting next to me whispered.

"I think he said what we do is important," I replied.

"That's nice," said the agent.

"Good to know the new director of Central Intelligence is filled with such . . . intelligence, right?"

In addition, Deutch was usually quite disheveled in appearance. I always found him to be deeply unimpressive, especially in comparison to the two previous CIA directors, whom I'd been able to observe at close range.

Tenet was at the opposite end of the spectrum, a glad-hander and politician, and he worked hard to raise morale at the Agency caused by Clinton's changes at the CIA, specifically, the Torricelli rule. For a time, he was successful. But when Tenet took over as director from the hapless Deutch, he became the first DCI to repeatedly invoke the "State Secrets Privilege" to shut down suits against the Agency by employees and their families, concerning things like workplace harassment, or violation of policies. The Agency that I joined prided itself on being a family, allowing vigorous dissent and disagreement inside the walls, but presenting a united front to the country and the world.

But with Tenet at the helm, the Agency was cutting off the voices of internal dissent and improvement. A *New York Times* editorial from 2009 detailed some of the harm of this policy, as well as how President Obama, despite vigorously criticizing the practice during the 2008 campaign, came to support its use once in office:

> Of the many ways that the Bush administration sought to evade accountability for its violations of the law and the Constitution under the cover of battling terrorism, one of the most appalling was its attempt to use inflated claims of state secrecy to slam shut the doors of the nation's courthouses.
>
> Sadly, the Obama administration also embraced this tactic, even though President Obama criticized the cult of secrecy while running for office, leaving it to the courts to stand up for transparency and accountability.[51]

Little did I know when Tenet assumed his office as CIA director, that I and my family would fall victim to this wretched policy.

Is it any wonder that the quality of the intelligence gathering began to suffer, leading to missed clues in 9/11, and the debacle in Iraq with the weapons of mass destruction? (More on that later.) You cannot destroy an organization from within, then expect it to function well.

Probably the worst of the group was Nora Slatkin, who was more filled with her own self-importance than any government bureaucrat I've ever met. One day when I reported for duty, I heard the gory details of how a CIA security protective officer made the mistake of stopping Slotkin and asking to see her CIA badge. (Even if you're a senior member, the rules are that if you're in CIA headquarters, your identity badge must be plainly visible.)

Despite the fact this security officer was following protocol, she loudly and publicly ripped him a new one. This only added to her growing reputation for angry and irrational outbursts, mostly centered around the idea of "don't you know how important I am?" There would eventually be a long litany of these incidents, directed against junior and senior officers.

As an example of the growing culture of "rules for thee, but not for me," in December 1996, CIA Director Deutch was accused of taking his

CIA laptop home and connecting it to unsecured sites on the internet.[52] Even for those of you with just a passing familiarity with computer security will realize that's a "bad thing" for the director of Central Intelligence to be doing.

The investigations revealed the charges were true, but of course, Clinton's attorney general, Janet Reno, announced in a letter to then director of CIA, George Tenet, that she would not be prosecuting Deutch for compromising national security.[53] If a junior officer had committed such a blunder, I can guarantee you, he or she would have been prosecuted to the fullest extent of the law, in addition to becoming a cautionary tale told to all future employees of the Agency.

During the Clinton administration, I was a manager at CIA headquarters in Langley and saw firsthand how the Agency was being ruined. Agents were resigning in droves and going into private industry. The new, seventh-floor management directed a huge demographic shift in the employee population, a precursor to the "Diversity, Equity, and Inclusion" madness, which is now bubbling through American business and education systems, with similarly toxic effects.

I had always accepted the good and healthy brand of equal opportunity and acceptance of diversity, which I believe is the key to America's past and future greatness. But what the seventh floor was peddling was not unity. It was a descent into anarchy, a Hobbesian nightmare of competing and often hostile racial and cultural groups.

Agents took assignments in the field, just to get away from these destructive policies at headquarters. Promotions were slowed down (or reduced to a glacial pace if you happened to be a straight, white male), and a freeze was put on "Exceptional Performance Awards." How can you expect exceptional performance from your employees, if you don't recognize them when they do something exceptional? The former CIA officer, Bob Baer, wrote eloquently of these problems in his excellent book, *See No Evil*, describing how the Agency would spend more money on changing the demographic of the Agency's workforce and sexual harassment workshops than on important objectives, like battling terrorism.

CIA positions, which once required passing the equivalent of the Graduate Records Exam with a 3.0 or better grade point average, were now "adjusted" and often eliminated to comply with this new demographic mandate. It's really difficult when you're an "intelligence" agency and you stop trying to recruit intelligent people. As a manager, I witnessed several employees suffer when they were denied earned promotions because they didn't fit within a certain demographic group.

In addition to the problem of the CIA recruiting dumb people, politics would intervene and declare the Agency couldn't talk to any of the bad people who might end up hurting us.

Let me explain.

Senator Robert Torricelli (the ethically challenged politician from New Jersey, who in 2002 would receive a formal letter of admonishment from the United States Senate Ethics Committee for accepting improper gifts from a campaign donor), would do enormous damage to the CIA during the Clinton Administration.

Torricelli would begin by making a number of unsubstantiated claims regarding the CIA's involvement in the death of an American hotel owner, Michael DeVine, and a Guatemalan guerilla named Efrain Bemaca Velasquez. Torricelli's tirade would lead to the Clinton administration issuing an order dictating that no CIA officer could have any contact, for recruitment or any other purposes, with a foreign national who might have any potential human rights violations. In other words, we couldn't talk to bad guys, even if we were trying to recruit them as an asset, or to switch sides.

Can we have a grown-up conversation for a moment?

That's like telling cops they can't talk to low-level Mafia guys when they're trying to bring down a crime family. It's like telling a DEA agent that he can't have anything to do with an informant who'd broken US drug laws.

How can you be expected to do your job if you can never talk to the bad guys, either to figure out what's going on, or how you might break up the organization? It was the kind of stupidity we'd come to expect from the Clinton administration.

I was in the CIA's auditorium, referred to as "The Bubble," when our disheveled and mumbling director, John Deutch, gave a speech laying out the new policy. The place was in open revolt as seasoned station chiefs and case officers booed and broke out into open laughter as Deutch tried to convey the policy. Several officers stood and said it was the worst decision they'd ever heard, and that if the policy stood, they couldn't do their job.

As a Counter Terrorism Center officer, I quickly ran afoul of this new policy. Undercover in the Middle East, I'd identified and met several times with a man I'll call, "Akhmed." He was clearly connected to terrorism, and occupied a high position in a terrorist group, but perhaps most importantly, had been able to utilize an unsuspected weakness in our systems to get close to many US embassy personnel without their knowledge. Akhmed was a trained killer, and probably could have murdered me at any time during our numerous meetings. But instead, he was interested in talking to me and continuing the relationship.

I sent an intelligence report back to headquarters documenting this potential vulnerability to embassy staff and waited for permission to proceed further.

After all, I was focused on protecting Americans.

Instead, I received a nasty phone call in which I was told, "What would the president of the United States think if he knew you had associated with a terrorist with human rights violations?"

"I think he'd want to save American lives," I replied. I also reminded this nasty official that because of my report the Agency now knew that this "terrorist with human rights violations" had been able to get close to embassy officials.

I was left alone, but my case officer was not. He was reprimanded for allowing me to take those meetings. It was especially galling to me because my case officer was among the finest men I ever worked with, had a flawless reputation throughout his career, and was one of the best operators I ever knew.

As a result of the absurd Clinton/Torricelli order, CIA station chiefs began to hide in their offices and generate shallow intelligence profiles on suspected terrorist targets, often based upon what they were able to glean from newspapers and television shows. Reporters from CNN or the *New York Times* were often able to develop better sources than the CIA.

It was comical how much the CIA was depending on sources like CNN because of what Senator Torricelli had done. As a young operational officer, I was taught that the news media was our enemy. As an example, during my training, they showed us an interview with the newsman, Brit Hume, who had once worked for the journalist Jack Anderson. (Anderson often published classified documents he'd received from whistleblowers, horrified by government abuses.) In the interview, Hume was asked if he would publish information obtained from US intelligence. Hume's answer was that publishing such information was the very nature of his job. Our instructor was horrified at this answer. (Apparently, our instructor had never read the First Amendment, or understood the role of the press in a free society.)

Little did I realize at the time that the greatest threat to me and my family would come not from foreign terrorists, or pesky journalists looking for the next big scoop, but from the CIA itself.

They would try to kill me and my family.

And even though through God's grace we escaped, we were not unharmed. Although I did my best, there were still casualties.

The depth of my anger over the attack on me and my family knows no bounds, and it informs everything I have done since that day.

***

But before I get to that story, I'd like to tell you a little more about my work as a counter-intelligence officer.

Unlike in the movies, the most important thing is not the weapons the other side may possess, but their intentions and psychology.

I want to understand how the world looks through the eyes of my adversary.

Let me give you two examples from my work against the Soviets.

On one of my early assignments, I was posted to a city that was known to have more KGB agents operating in it per capita than any other in the world. At its height, the KGB was estimated to have at least 480,000 agents, the most famous former agent being the current longtime president of Russia, Vladimir Putin.

As my partner "Brett" (pseudonym) and I moved through the city, we noticed a young blond man, wearing what looked like his Walkman "headphones," who always happened to be part of the scenery. We had found our KGB "shadow." And of course, because we weren't very creative, we nicknamed him "Boris." Sometimes, if Boris was lagging a little behind as we made our way through the city, we'd wait for him to catch up.

We'd been trained as CIA officers to never harass or confront your KGB tail, because if you did there would be swift retribution, normally in the form of broken antennas on your car, key scrapes against a door panel, or in some instances, human feces in places you didn't appreciate.

Late one evening, Brett and I went out to an Irish pub a few doors down from our hotel. The place was packed, and we were jammed in a table next to four young women who were Irish school teachers in town for a teacher's convention. As Brett and I talked and sipped on our Guiness beer, the women overheard our conversation, picked up on our accents, and started talking to us.

Aside from our accents, I've always noticed how Americans give themselves away, even before they open their mouths. Many people in that city wore jeans and khakis, but their shoes tended to be leather loafers. Only the Americans wore sneakers.

You didn't have to wait for an American to open their mouth, you just had to look at their shoes.

As we sat having a pleasant conversation with these young Irish schoolteachers, one of them turned to me and asked, "Why do you Americans hate the Soviet Union so much?"

"We don't hate the Soviet Union," I replied.

"Then why does your President Reagan call them the 'Evil Empire' and fight against them in Afghanistan?" she responded. "Why doesn't he just leave them alone? That's why people don't like Americans."

"It's really because our president is against what's happening in Afghanistan. The Soviets are intentionally leaving toy bombs on the ground in the hope the children will pick them up. They get their hands and arms blown off, often dying. That's why Reagan calls them the 'Evil Empire.'"

Although we hadn't seen him, Boris was sitting nearby, overheard what we were saying, and because he also had a good amount of vodka in his system, jumped up out of his chair, and as he advanced towards us, was shouting at the top of his lungs, "Americans! Baby killers in Vietnam! Baby killers in Vietnam!"

I first saw the look of terror in the face of the Irish schoolteachers, then quickly glanced to Brett, who was confused as I about how to respond. We weren't interested in precipitating an international incident.

Boris continued towards our table, and I stood to create a shield between him and the terrified schoolteachers. I could smell the vodka on his hot breath as he shouted, "Americans! Baby killers! Baby killers!"

My plan was to deescalate the situation. "Just calm down," I said in my most level, soothing voice. "Why don't we go outside and talk about this?"

He moved his face less than an inch away from mine. "Americans! Baby killers in Vietnam!" he said in what sounded almost like the growl of an angry dog.

Brett stood and took a position shoulder to shoulder with me. "Let's go outside, pal," my partner said. "And maybe we can talk about this as friends?"

Boris backed off a bit, looked at me and Brett, two American CIA agents, trained and ready to rip his drunken ass apart if he made the slightest move towards us. Then Boris turned, and ran out of the bar, yelling "Americans! Baby Killers! Americans! Baby killers!"

The next day as Brett and I went to the shopping mall for supplies, there was Boris again, wearing his Walkman "headphones," our little Soviet caboose. He was presumably a little hungover but doing his job in the professional manner in which he'd no doubt been trained by his spymasters back in Moscow.

***

After the fall of the Soviet Union in 1991, I spent a period of time in a formerly communist country in eastern Europe with one of their intelligence officers.

Let's call him Hans.

The idea was that former adversaries, like Hans and I, should get to know each other.

When we first met across a large walnut conference table, Hans glared at me like an enemy who had invaded his country. It was a curious and awkward feeling as neither of us trusted each other. He was the typical blue-eyed, blond-haired (but turning grey) intelligence agent of the Eastern bloc, and I was the young face of the west.

Over the next few weeks, Hans and I spent many hours together discussing not just our countries and our backgrounds, but also what it was like to work for an intelligence bureaucracy.

Ideologies may differ, but human psychology remains the same.

I came to understand what it was like for Hans to work in an organization which in many ways was the mirror of my own, complete with its own cast of heroes and villains, geniuses and idiots.

One bright and beautiful afternoon, Hans and I took a walk through a small town in his country. He amazed me with his detailed knowledge of the people in the town, the history of the area over the centuries in war and peace, watching the ideology in which he'd once so fervently believed crumble in front of him, and his surprising embrace of freedom.

There's an unusual bond I've found between people who were once enemies but discover they can be friends. In some ways, it's an even deeper connection than one might find among one's own countrymen. Maybe it's because you both realize the length of the journey you've taken to arrive at that moment.

"You know, Kevin," Hans began, "our country has left communism behind and is now a democracy."

"Yes, it's wonderful."

"But there is one thing we have learned."

"What?"

"There can be no freedom without a belief in God," said Hans. "The Bible is what makes us free. It is only by accepting that we are servants of something greater that we can find peace."

I remember feeling deeply moved in that moment. This man, who had dedicated himself to a godless system and spent decades of his life as its faithful servant, had developed a faith within him greater than almost any person I've ever known.

It was as miraculous as finding a tall tree growing in the eternal darkness of a deep cave.

And at the same time that I was amazed by Hans's faith, I worried about my own country. We were drifting away from God in so many ways. Communism had fallen because of humanity's innate thirst for genuine religion, freedom from coercion, and discovering meaning in life.

It was also doomed because people never forget evil—the imprisoning, persecution, and execution of those they held dear.

If we were drifting away from God, weren't we heading towards that same darkness from which Hans and his country had just escaped?

***

The Czechoslovakian dissident and later president of that country, Vaclav Havel, once wrote, "You do not become a 'dissident' just because you decide one day to take up this most unusual career. You are thrown into it by your personal sense of responsibility, combined with a complex set of external circumstances. You are cast out of the existing structures and placed in a position of conflict with them. It begins as an attempt to do your work well and ends with being branded an enemy of the state."

As I plan on telling you how I ran afoul of the management of the CIA, from true believer to renegade, it's probably a good idea to review the positions I held during my seventeen years at the Agency and the awards I received during that time.

I was hired by the CIA in 1985 as a security protective officer, Top Secret/Security Compartmentalized Information (TS/SCI), cleared federal police officer.

In 1986, I was promoted to the Director of Central Intelligence Security Staff (DCI/SS) and received a letter of commendation for my work.

In 1987, while I was on the Director of Intelligence Security Staff, I passed all my comprehensive exams and psychological testing and was promoted to an Office of Security (OS) staff officer, investigator, and team leader for defector protection.

From 1989 to 1996, I rotated from one assignment to another as a security officer generalist (the civilian equivalent of a military officer) and was generally rotated to a different position every two years thereafter. During this time, I passed the intensive training for the anti-terrorism assault team and was sent overseas to counter a terrorist group who had been targeting US embassy and CIA personnel. This was probably the position in which I was most vulnerable to being killed by one of our adversaries, and all of us had to take the fatalistic attitude that we might not come back from our assignment. However, our mission successfully protected American lives, we lost no members, and received a meritorious unit citation.

To give a little greater detail on my work during the years from 1992 to 1994, I was the branch chief in charge of training the CIA's federal police force, and a senior CIA briefer. In that role I was the duty briefer for everybody getting a CIA clearance, from secretaries to case officers, as well as senior officials from other agencies, like FBI, DEA, Department of State, and military brass up to the rank of general.

From 1994 to 1996, I was assigned to the Office of Security Information, Security Division, where I investigated the vulnerability of agents in the field. This got me into significant trouble at the Agency, uncovering what appeared to me to be nefarious activity.

Let me tell you how my experiences in that investigation led me to see more clearly the monster the CIA had become.

***

I want to make a point to my modern readers, which was probably something of an unspoken assumption among most people in 1985, when I joined the CIA, but may currently seem like an outdated belief.

While many might believe the CIA acted inappropriately in many of their activities abroad, the vast majority of the public thought the Agency was acting for the benefit of the United States.

Certainly, that's what I believed.

For many years in the CIA, I thought the Agency was genuinely trying its best, making its way through a forest of shadows, tyrannical governments, and groups that didn't even pretend to believe their fellow citizens had rights which came from God.

When did it start to go wrong for me?

My first wake-up call came in 1995. At the time, I was an officer in the CIA's Office of Security, performing an internal investigation on a sensitive CIA operation that had taken place overseas. Another security officer initially raised a concern about the issue, but considering she was on her way to another assignment, the problem landed in my lap.

Because of the security oaths I have signed, I cannot tell you the exact nature of the threat I uncovered. What I can say is that it involved a weakness in the embassy computer systems which might potentially enable our enemies abroad to identify our officers in foreign countries. I will give the CIA office in charge of this duty the fictitious name of the Cover Protection Division, as well as using pseudonyms for the officials involved.

I drafted a report on what I'd uncovered, then submitted it to my supervisor, whom I'll call Jack Thompson, a fair and objective professional. Jack was a brilliant, fair, and honest supervisor, and a technical expert in computer networks. He kept the report, mulling it over, and deciding what to do.

I immediately contacted the office of the chief, CPD, a GS-15, and advised his special assistant that I had possibly uncovered a serious vulnerability to our officers overseas.

A meeting was arranged with a panel of senior Agency officials, including with Charles Martin, the chief of cover protection for the CIA. I gave a slide presentation of my findings, and although at the start the atmosphere seemed suspicious, by the end I felt a sense of concealed alarm from the assembled officials. It appeared to be a state of alarm and disrespect at the same time.

Something wasn't right.

After about a week, I gave a call to the chief of cover protection, to find out if a conclusion had been reached about my findings.

The chief of cover protection's special assistant answered the phone.

"Have you had a chance to review the report I sent you?" I asked.

"What report?" she replied.

I reminded her I'd sent it to her office via internal mail, and she replied, "I don't remember seeing any report."

I advised her that was no problem and I'd resend it, which I did.

The next week I called her, and she asked, "What report?"

I reminded her of the two previous reports I'd sent to her office, but that only seemed to annoy her. She said she didn't know what I was talking about and would have to check into it.

Undeterred, I hand carried a copy of the report to CIA headquarters as well as an additional one for the Cover Protection Division front office, the third time I'd provided it. As I walked in, it seemed to me that the special assistant bristled.

"Here's the report I spoke to you about," I said as I physically handed it to her and asked that she pass it onto the chief.

"Okay," she said, glaring at me as if she was an angry cat I'd just poured a full glass of water on.

I walked out, puzzled by her behavior.

Again, I waited a week to give the chief of the Cover Protection Division time to review the document.

There was no response.

I called again and asked the special assistant if the division had reviewed the report.

"I don't remember any report," she claimed, "I must have lost it."

I could not ignore this anymore or chalk it up to the typical arrogance of senior CIA officers. This looked like a cover up.

Then things started to get really weird.

Several days later, I got a call from the chief of the Cover Protective Division, Charles Martin, to whom I'd given my second presentation. In a threatening tone he ordered me to drop the investigation, saying it was above my head.

I replied in what I thought was a respectful tone and said, "Sir, I have to tell you, there may be a serious problem here, and we need to look at it further."

"This is way above your pay grade," he said dismissively to me, knowing he was a GS-15, the highest level, while I was a lowly GS-12. "I order you to drop your investigation. Do it now."

I stewed over the problem for about two days, then made the decision that since I believed lives were at stake, I'd continue my investigation.

With the approval of my boss, Jack, I arranged a meeting with a senior officer at the Department of State, who headed the office for embassy security. Two fellow CIA tech guys accompanied me to the meeting. And of course, the special assistant for Counter Terrorism, who kept losing my memo, attended as well.

But this time when I finished my presentation, there was no concern. The State Department official in charge of embassy security told me I didn't know what I was talking about, because I was just a GS-12, unlike him, who was a GS-15. Then he said, "There is no problem here. The Department of State fixed this problem years ago. You just need to drop this and get back to your job."

I replied my findings suggested otherwise but would check my information and get back to him.

Still stinging from the meeting, I went into my office, opened up my computer, connected to the CIA server, and tried to access my memo.

It had vanished from the system.

I called the Information Technology department headquarters to see if they could retrieve the memo, but they couldn't find it anywhere in the system. Luckily, I always keep hard copies of all my work, so a few days later, I scanned it back into the computer system, with another Agency official present for corroboration.

What I'd learned more than a few times in my time at the Agency is that if you run into one roadblock, there are more than enough good people around who might be able to figure out an alternate route. This time, it was my supervisor, Jack, who summarized my findings to his old friend, Jim Callahan, a member of the Senior Executive Service, and recipient of the CIA Intelligence Medal for Heroism. Jim was old school, believed in his duty to God and country, and was a man of authentic character.

Jim called me directly a few days later and expressed alarm at what I claimed to have found. After retiring from the CIA, Jim had gone to work for the Inspector General's (IG) Office of the State Department, and since the threat I identified involved embassy employees, he could claim the authority to investigate. Jim asked for a copy of my report, and I sent him a copy via secure fax.

A few weeks later, Jim called me, told me he'd gone through my report, and was greatly alarmed. Jim set up a meeting for me to present my findings at Department of State headquarters, with him and two other Inspector General employees. At the conclusion of my presentation, they complimented me on the thoroughness of my presentation and told me they'd look into the matter. I felt a great sense of relief that my allegations would be competently investigated. I had worked with Jim several years before at the Office of Security and knew him to be a man of integrity and courage, which was why the Inspector General's office was such a good fit for him.

Afterwards, Jim warned me, "Kevin, keep your head down about this. Do not tell anyone in CIA. It'll probably take us about three months to do a full investigation. When we have the results, we'll call you."

After a global investigation, which included IG officials visiting several foreign embassies, the report was complete. Jim called me and said, "We examined the systems you documented in your report. It's even worse than you thought. In a week we'll be having a meeting about our findings at State Department headquarters. Can you attend?"

"Yes, sir," I replied. "I'll be there."

What I didn't know was that CIA officers would be attending the meeting as well. On the day of the meeting I arrived at State, was processed through security, took an elevator to the top floor, and found the office of the Inspector General. I was then led to the main conference room, where Jim was waiting for me with two senior IG officials.

"We're just waiting for CIA to join us," one of the IG officials told me.

I'm sure my eyes went wide with fear at this information, as I didn't expect them at this meeting. But I'd faced down the KGB and Islamic terrorists. Surely, I wasn't more scared of my own bosses.

But instead of Charles Martin walking through the door, it was another guy, named Bill Sullivan, who informed us he was now head of the Cover Protection Division for CIA. I noticed Sullivan seemed to be genuinely nervous, and his voice faltered as he stumbled through some small talk. We all sat down at the conference table, Jim and the IG officials at one side of the long conference table, Sullivan cowering at the other end, and I in the middle of the two groups.

"Mr. Sullivan," said the most senior IG official, "I'm sure you know why you're here."

"Not really," he replied nervously.

The most senior IG official decided to deliver the devastating news. "We've finished an international investigation into the vulnerability of the cover of CIA agents. The threat is real, you've been informed about it, and failed to act. You and the CIA are officially rebuked for intentionally covering up this issue, refusing to address it, and placing the lives of CIA officers overseas in danger for more than a decade."

The color seemed to drain from Sullivan's face. Spooks don't like being dragged out into the light. "Yes, sir," Sullivan replied.

"Consider this an official rebuke of the CIA by the Department of State, Inspector General's Office," said the senior IG official. "The results of our report will be disseminated soon to the rest of the Intelligence Community. Do you understand?"

"Yes, I do," Sullivan responded.

The IG official then dismissed Sullivan.

Sullivan rose from the table, visibly shaken, and walked out the door. When we were sure he was gone, the IG officials and Jim warmly thanked me for my work and the difference it would make to the safety of our officers.

But as I drove back to my office at CIA headquarters, I didn't feel good. I knew I'd angered the beast, embarrassing the CIA in front of the entire intelligence community. As I walked through the main lobby at CIA, I imagined a red laser dot appearing on my back, a sniper taking aim at me.

As a long-time government employee, aware of bureaucratic politics, I knew this was the time to protect myself, by keeping hard copies all important emails, performance evaluations, and summaries of my investigations.

Bill Sullivan would later reappear in my life, as the hatchet man for a curious character named "Buzzy" Krongard, who would try to destroy my career in the months before the September 11, 2001 terror attacks in New York and Washington, DC. Krongard would later be suspected of covering up vital information about the September 11 attacks, a subject which I will cover in detail in the next chapter.

After the damning IG report was published to the Intelligence Community, I received an "Exceptional Performance Award" for my investigation.

Somehow, I didn't think the award would impress my bosses at CIA or be an asset to my long-term future at the Agency.

I was an analyst for the CIA, so I can't end this section without giving my opinion as to what it might mean. Why would top officials at CIA not fix this vulnerability for more than ten years? Why make my report disappear from the CIA server? Why would multiple attempts be made to get me to stop investigating?

The only conclusion I can draw is that the CIA wanted a loophole, a problem they could blame, if a foreign Chief of Station, or an overseas agent, did not play by the rules, and the information somehow found its way into the hands of our enemies, who decided they would take it upon themselves to eliminate the troublesome agent.

That's how "plausible deniability" works.

I believe that's exactly what they did to me, putting my life directly in the hands of an Iranian assassin.

***

Four months later, I rotated to my new assignment as the CIA Enter on Duty (EOD) briefer to new employees, at all levels, from secretaries to generals.

Two months after I arrived, we got a new branch chief, whom I believe was put there specifically to harass me. In the morning, he'd give me an impossible amount of work, then check in with me on my progress in the afternoon. A few weeks later, he then wrote a performance evaluation of me which was critical of my ability to finish tasks in the time allotted.

I went directly to my division chief, Jay Thompson, and reported on the harassment. He investigated, determined I was right, and ordered the branch chief to stop the harassment, and rewrite the evaluation to reflect my abilities more accurately. Thompson took a special interest in my case, put himself in the loop to review my work, then gave me an award as a senior CIA briefer and surveillance/countersurveillance trainer.

There's a reason why so few people become whistleblowers in the CIA. The Agency has many ways to come after you, and they are nothing, if not patient.

Because of my skill in training officers in surveillance, tradecraft, firearms, and self-defense, I was then posted to the Directorate of Operations. In that position I was collecting and reporting on information from human intelligence around the world and training high level officials. You may be getting tired of me saying these things, but in this position, I received another commendation, an "Exceptional Performance Award for Timely and Relevant Human Intelligence Collection." You might say I was racking up awards as quickly as I was making enemies.

I didn't think much about it when I received an order to deploy for a few weeks to a country that had been engaged in a bloody war in which tens of thousands of people had been killed. I was supposed to provide the latest firearms training for a pro-Western group supported by our government.

I can still picture the green mountains in which I gave them their training, and how in the morning, fog would cling to the highest peaks, often hanging around until early afternoon. There was a troubling beauty to the terrain, so picturesque and yet the site of so many horrific atrocities. How could people be so terrible to each other in a landscape that was so remarkably stunning?

One of the "students" was a tall, Caucasian student with short blond hair, and blue eyes. Let's call him Amir. Amir was an excellent marksman, easily able to hit bottles with his Glock pistol at forty yards. Sometimes just the two of us went shooting in the mountains, and we often dined at night and talked about our families. His face glowed when we talked about our children.

Perhaps that is what saved my life.

I later discovered that Amir was an Iranian assassin, undercover in the country to assassinate a high government official. I also learned that while I was supposed to be undercover in the country, I was not.

The Cover Protection Division had left me in overt status, while I was conducting an operation in one of the most dangerous parts of the world.

Although I can only speculate, I often wonder how it came to be that I was working with an Iranian assassin, with no official cover.

Did he consider killing me?

Was I too unimportant a target, or did Amir respect me for the love I had for my kids? Perhaps he was impressed with my genuine concern for providing good, honest training for the students, one of whom was his close friend. Whatever the reason, despite the fact I was often alone with Amir in secluded areas of the mountains of that beautiful country, and he with a loaded Glock pistol in his hand, he never took the shot.

I am a person of deep faith, and prefer to believe it was divine protection, but I cannot tell you for certain.

In one of my favorite spy novels, John le Carré's *The Russia House*, there's a scene in which the main character, an alcoholic British publisher, Bartholemew "Barley" Scott Blair, (wonderfully portrayed by Sean Connery in the movie with the same name), is having a raucous dinner with a bunch of dissident writers at the end of the Soviet era.

In the movie version, Barley expresses great hope for the "new" Russia, which is dawning in the *glasnost* era, and at one point declares: "If there is to be hope, we must all betray our country. We have to save each other. Because all victims are equal, and none is more equal than others. It's everyone's duty to start the avalanche."

When another member of the dinner chides him for aspiring to be a hero, he responds by saying, "Nowadays you have to think like a hero, just to behave like a merely decent human being."[54]

After all my years at CIA, then the decades I've spent seeking to bring light to their actions, I often consider the obligation we owe to our fellow human beings.

It is up to all of us to start the avalanche.

***

As an officer in the CIA's Counter Terrorism Center (CIC) I knew it was taking a toll on my marriage and my kids.

I was sent on missions to twenty countries, many of them extremely dangerous. While I was on those missions, I was a different person, having to be focused with an "eye of the tiger" determination, drinking hard with potential targets, agonizing over which step to take next, a single misstep which might cause an international incident or end my life.

Although I was aware that human intelligence is critical to our nation's security, and that I gathered some of the best information which was of enormous benefit to policymakers, and received an award for doing so, the simple fact was that I was paid to drink and steal.

When I knew an assignment was coming up, I'd record hours of bedtime stories, so my wife could play them at night for our kids so they could remember the sound of my voice.

After many of these missions, I'd arrive home feeling morally bankrupt, and quickly went to church in order to reconnect with a higher power, and take something of a spiritual shower, promising myself I'd never do such things again. Eventually, when those promises had been broken one too many times, I vowed that I wouldn't live like that anymore. As much as I thought the work I was doing was unique, I knew there were several junior officers hungry to take my place.

In the spring of 1999, as I sat in my office at the Counter Terrorism Office, I got a call from the chief of counterterrorism.

The chief praised my work and offered me the opportunity to work in overseas human intelligence collection for the rest of my career. This was the moment of which many agents dream, the sign of a successful career.

I turned him down.

He asked again.

I thanked him but told him it would come at the expense of my marriage.

He asked again.

I turned him down a third time.

The chief became incensed. "Do you know what you're doing? You're ruining your career! If you don't take this job, you'll have no career in the Agency."

"Sorry, sir," I told him. "But I've made my decision."

He slammed the phone down and I felt something collapse inside me. I walked out of my office in a daze, when an older, highly respected officer came over to me and put an arm around my shoulder.

"I overheard your conversation," he said.

"Yeah, I turned down a job and took a bit of heat for it."

He gave me a fixed look, one warrior to another. "It's about time someone told the bastards no! Good job," he said.

I was immensely appreciative of the support, but worried that I'd essentially signed my discharge papers.

I was wrestling with a few realities, not wanting to be another statistic. The divorce rate in the Directorate of Operations was about 60 percent, and alcoholism was a common problem. The Agency often took the best years of your life and left you with nothing. I'd seen too many officers retire with ruined marriages and empty lives. I was aware that family and children are the only genuine wealth. Although it made others angry, I often took a coffee mug with a picture of my kids emblazoned on the side to senior meetings. The majority of the people in those senior meetings were either divorced or didn't have time in their careers to have children. That wasn't what I wanted at the end of it all.

Throughout my life there have been many miraculous events.

When I was twelve years old, I was diagnosed with a terminal illness. Both kidneys burst because of a congenital blockage in my bladder. I first knew there was a problem when I started urinating blood and was rushed by my parents to Fairfax Hospital in Virginia. The X-rays showed only a bloody mess of tissue where my kidneys should have been, and the doctors gave me six weeks to live. While I lingered for a month in the hospital, my mother, an agnostic, went to a friend who ran a small prayer group and asked them to pray for a healing.

Two weeks later, when the doctors took me for a follow-up X-ray, both my kidneys were back. Over the next few weeks, I kept getting better, the doctors removed the tubes draining my urine, took me off the medications, and my kidney tests came back normal. The doctors were still baffled by my recovery, and predicted that even with my remarkable recovery, I was unlikely to live past the age of twenty-one. Despite the doctors being shocked and overjoyed, I was told that, because of the trauma and number of X-rays, I would never be able to have children.

That was forty-seven years ago.

I mentioned in college I fell into bad habits, like drinking, smoking pot, doing crazy things, like climbing to the top of a three-hundred-foot radio tower to touch the blinking light, and casual sex. I thought my wild college days would prevent me from a career in the CIA, but found grace was offered to me by the simple act of telling the truth and choosing a different path for my life.

When I got married, and my wife and I were having trouble conceiving, I went for tests and was told I couldn't have kids.

But apparently somebody forgot to tell my wife, because we then went out and had three beautiful kids.

Maybe because I've overcome a lot of things in my life it explains why I didn't feel completely crushed by my chief's claim that I'd ruined my career at the Agency. I just had to find another path forward outside the Counter Terrorism Center.

I put my name in for several positions and a call came in from the management of the CIA Office of Security. A position had been created which was just perfect for my experience and skill set, trying to find the vulnerabilities in operational security of our agents while they were on a mission. I'd been an operational agent for many years, knew what they went through while on assignment, and could now take a twenty-thousand-foot view of how they were staying safe.

What I did not realize is that the person who would be most at risk was me, and when their planned assassination of me failed, my family.

But before I tell you that story, let me tell you what I know, and what I suspect, about the terror attacks of September 11, 2001. As a criminal and intelligence investigator, I am convinced an authentic criminal investigation of what happened on 9/11 was never done, leaving some gaping holes in our understanding of that watershed event.

I don't intend to deal with the events of 9/11 here, just my brush with a senior CIA official who engaged in some suspicious activity just before the attack. The same senior officer who tried to eliminate me following my revelations of the deadly vulnerability of our overseas officers.

His name is Alvin Bernard "Buzzy" Krognard.

CHAPTER THREE

THE CURIOUS CASE OF ALVIN BERNARD "BUZZY" KRONGARD, THE SHARK PUNCHER

On February 1, 1998, CIA Director George Tenet appointed Alvin Bernard "Buzzy" Krongard, to be his "councilor." On that same day, the *Baltimore Sun* published an article that was supposedly the last the public would ever hear of the legendary businessman before he vanished into the shadows. But the paper wanted to give this colorful character a glorious send-off, even if it did often veer into the territory of cartoonish masculinity.

The story of Buzzy Krongard would also reveal the tentacles of the intelligence octopus and how far into American life it could reach.

The next morning, Buzzy Krogard disappears.

> "Take good notes, 'cause this is the last interview I'm ever gonna give," the 61-year-old investment banker said last week, reclining in an easy chair, Cuban cigar pointed straight at the ceiling.
>
> The Baltimore native has walked away from a lucrative job as vice chairman of Bankers Trust New York Corp., the parent of BT Alex Brown Inc. and the seventh-largest bank in the country.
>
> At an age when most executives contemplate retirement. Krongard is headed to the Central Intelligence Agency.[55]

There's nothing stereotypical about a sixty-one-year-old business executive leaning back in an easy chair, smoking an illegal Cuban cigar, right? Sometimes I think fiction writers have a more difficult job because they have to create believable characters.

The reading public would never accept such an outlandish fictional character as "Buzzy" Krongard.

But the truth is he's probably one of the most consequential figures in American history of the past twenty-five years that you've never read about. The supposedly "last interview" with Buzzy Krongard continued:

> The son of a middle-class suit-maker, Krongard once punched a great white shark in the jaw. He teased a moray eel with his fingers and has a cruel scar to prove it.
>
> He is an accomplished martial artist who could kill a man as easily as he can break boards with his hands. He has dangerous fish in his basement, a meat carving set made from the shin bones of a boar, a shooting range on his 90-acre estate.
>
> He collects only guns that he can use, and he has a small arsenal. He spends the occasional weekend training with a police SWAT team.
>
> "The joke around here," said Alex Brown colleague Richard Franyo, "is that he never really worked here all along. It was just a front."[56]

The Central Intelligence Agency had been around for more than fifty years before George Tenet decided, "You know, what I really need is a Wall Street guy coming into a special position I'll create just for him." Krongard comes across as the idealized version of an adult man as might be dreamed up by a ten-year-old boy.

A "martial artist who could kill a man as easily as he breaks boards"? He has "dangerous fish in his basement" and "a meat carving set made from the shin bones of a boar"? If you were the mother of a young boy, you'd never let your son within a million miles of this guy. Instead, you'd probably report him to the local police as a possible serial killer. The glowing profile of Krongard continued:

"He will do one heck of a job for the CIA," said Robert Hammerman, chief judge of the Circuit Court for Baltimore City, who grew up with Krongard.

"He is a brilliant person, a brilliant organizer. It is the kind of thing Buzzy has been interested in all his life."[57]

Nothing like having those who know you best say you're going to do "one heck of a job," whipping the Agency into shape, like you once punched that great white shark (or maybe you'll get into trouble like when you taunted that moray eel.) For a guy who was entering the dark world of intelligence, he sure did want a lot of light shone on him.

Krongard is guarded about how he met Tenet and how long he has known him: For "centuries," he deadpanned. He said it is not unusual for them to have lunch together, either at CIA headquarters in Langley, VA, or in Washington.

It was about three months ago at a Washington restaurant, he said, that Tenet broached the subject of Krongard's coming aboard.

"We were talking," Krongard said. "It started as a lark, almost: 'Well, why don't you come down here and fix it?'"

Joining the agency was something Krongard had fantasized about, but never seriously thought he should bring up. He drew an analogy: "It's like high school, you want to ask the girl to the prom but you're afraid to ask."[58]

The CIA was Buzzy's long-held fantasy. It wasn't enough for him to conquer the world of high finance, but he was going to reshape the globe by fixing the Agency. And everybody loved good ol' Buzzy because there was nobody like him. He was the man you wanted in charge, the ultimate alpha male warrior, the scholar who would find the problem, and the general who would implement the solution.

In 1971, Krongard joined Alex Brown as a corporate finance associate.
Storming the job.
Colleagues say he ripped into the job like a jarhead storming the beach.

He got to work at 6:30 a.m. and refused to go to bed at night until every phone call was returned. He pored over complicated financial documents to understand every detail of the companies he was working with. And he developed a self-denying approach that would one day result in the official Brown mantra: "Client first, firm second, individual third."[59]

We see in Krongard the purest portrait of the corporate titan as a young man, driving himself relentlessly and selflessly on behalf of the company. He was a soldier, doing whatever it took to secure the beachhead. By 1989, Krongard was in charge of Alex Brown and Sons:

> Once Krongard became chief executive, he held the firm to his own uncompromising standards. They could be harsh. A colleague recounts how a trader who had gone over his stock-trading limit admitted it to Krongard.
>
> Krongard is said to have responded, "If you would like to be employed, you better be under your limits in 24 hours." The trader somehow did it.[60]

Further in the article, one of his associates, Mayo A. Shattuck, III (who would take over when Krongard left to take the job at CIA), was quoted as saying that Krongard "doesn't have great tolerance for stupidity."[61]

In taking the job at CIA, Krongard was giving up a $4 million dollar a year salary.[62]

But one imagines that in all those years as a corporate chieftain, he'd amassed more money than he could possibly want. But money can be a boring plaything compared to learning the secrets that other nations wanted to keep hidden and controlling the secret warriors of the CIA.

In what was supposed to be his farewell interview before he disappeared into the shadows of the intelligence world, Krongard sketched out the approach he would take to the Agency.

> "I come with no baggage, no history, no preconceived opinions, or biases. I can extract the essence of a problem, get out of it, and move on," he said.

His son Tim, who joined him in the smoking room, took his own cigar out of his mouth. "Like 'Pale Rider,'" he said—the mysterious drifter hero of one of his father's favorite Clint Eastwood movies.[63]

It's really quite a feat to have no opinions about the CIA, but to regard yourself as the hero of your own personal Clint Eastwood movie. With confidence in yourself so stratospherically high, how could anything possibly go wrong?

Another person with sky-high confidence in Buzzy's abilities was George Tenet, who in his book, *At the Center of the Storm: The CIA During America's Time of Crisis*, wrote of him:

> One person I did bring in from the outside was A.B. "Buzzy" Krongard. He had been the CEO of the investment banking firm Alex. Brown. That's heady territory, with salaries and perks to match. If Buzzy hadn't been so ready to serve his nation in a time of great need, I could never have recruited him as a special advisor. His mission was to gather the data and assemble the metrics about all of our business processes that would allow us to make the changes critical to the Agency's survival. He brought business savvy to an organization that seemed to pride itself on its unbusinesslike methods. Prior to Buzzy's arrival, the Agency was a "data-free zone." We didn't know where the money was going; we didn't know why people joined our Agency or why they left. All that would change with Buzzy's expert help.[64]

There you have it from the former director of the CIA, Buzzy was the turnaround guy, the one who would learn all the secrets of the CIA, then implement a radical restructuring of the Agency.

When one looks at the relatively peaceful world which existed in 1998, and the world which exists in 2024, a long and brutal war in Ukraine provoked by decades of US misdeeds and broken promises, a Middle East on fire as Hamas and Israel fight to the death, and brewing trouble with China and Taiwan, one can't help but wonder what part the CIA has played in either creating or failing to anticipate these problems.

***

When I was inside the CIA as an officer and heard about the Krongard appointment as Tenet's "counselor" many of us were puzzled. Why would Tenet choose an outsider with no CIA experience for such a sensitive role? Allegations would arise later that Krongard had previous dealings with the Agency, going back to the early 1990s, and possibly from his college days.

It's a little like the common joke made about the actress Doris Day, the sweet-faced, keep the knees closed, girl-next-door type from many 1950s romance movies that "I knew her before she was a virgin."

When I was undercover for the Directorate of Operations, I had a meeting with Krongard at the secret base to which I'd been assigned. I was to give him a situational update on the progress of our base. But I knew there was something he was more interested in. It was well known to all of us who trained students at covert CIA facilities that Krongard liked to pay a cordial visit to certain facilities, so that after he'd been briefed, he could spend some time on the range with some of our exotic weapons.

I took him out to the range, and he was pretty good with the weapons. The other guys liked shooting with him as well. We didn't think much about him, an interesting business guy, but mostly we thought of him as Tenet's Wall Street guy. He was gruff, but cordial. I got the feeling he wished that instead of a life in business, he'd been one of us. However, he kept things pretty close to the vest, the kind of guy you felt was checking things out but wasn't going to tell you what he was thinking.

However, I would eventually get an education in Buzzy's management style, as he would be the manager of the secret base I was living at when they tried to poison me and my family.

I would come to view Buzzy as the embodiment of everything wrong with the Agency, a callous indifference to human beings, to logic, and a supreme arrogance that could only lead the CIA and the world into disaster.

But that would be in the future.

***

Although Buzzy had supposedly already vanished into shadows of the intelligence world in 1998, on March 16, 2001, he was back in the newspapers again.

CIA Director Tenet appointed Alvin Bernard "Buzzy" Krongard to be the executive director of the Central Intelligence Agency. In this position, Buzzy was the third-highest ranking official in the Agency (just below Deputy Director John O. Brennan), and the job has been likened to that of a CEO in charge of daily operations.

The *Washington Post* gave Buzzy glowing coverage in an article entitled, "Colorful Outsider is Named No. 3 at CIA."

> A.B. "Buzzy" Krongard, a cigar-chomping former investment banker and martial arts enthusiast, was named yesterday executive director of the CIA, bringing a fast-paced management style to the agency's No. 3 job.
>
> Central Intelligence Agency Director George J. Tenet announced the appointment, saying he treasures Krongard's "wise counsel and 'no-nonsense' business-like views."
>
> Krongard, 64, former head of Alex. Brown & Co., an investment bank based in Baltimore, joined the agency three years ago as a counselor to Tenet. He switched careers shortly after helping to engineer the $2.5 billion merger of Alex. Brown and Bankers Trust New York Corp., gaining $71 million in Bankers Trust stock.[65]

That puts a little more meat on the bones of the Krongard financial situation. While one might have felt some sympathy for Buzzy losing that $4 million dollar a year salary to "serve his nation in a time of great need," that should be balanced by "$71 million in Bankers Trust stock" he got by engineering a "$2.5 billion merger" which happened shortly before he decided to join the CIA.

Nothing suspicious about that, right?

And since nothing about making $71 million in a deal just before you decide to work for the CIA is suspicious, it makes complete sense why the *Washington Post* wouldn't investigate it. Let's return to the "Colorful Outsider" article and their hard-hitting investigation of the man who would be number 3 at the CIA:

> A graduate of Princeton and the University of Maryland Law School, Krongard has a fondness for extreme military-style activities. Even

as a banking executive, he trained with SWAT teams for recreation and worked out with a kung fu master.

To impress—or intimidate—visitors, the former Marine officer would demonstrate lightning-fast moves for disabling an attacker.

The purpose of his exercise regime was not just to stay fit, he once said, but to increase toughness and discipline. To that end, he would thrust his hands repeatedly into buckets of dried rice or absorb blows to the stomach from a heavy medicine ball.[66]

In your life, how many people have you been introduced to who sought to impress you by showing off their "lightning-fast moves for disabling an attacker"? Personally, I've never met anybody over the age of twelve years old who thought that was a way to win friends and influence people.

"Gee, I'm not sure I agree with that guy's geo-political vision," you might say to yourself after an encounter with such an individual, "but I'd sure want him by my side if I get attacked by a ninja. I'm glad he's number three at CIA."

In the article, Krongard recounted his previous years at the Agency.

His rhetorical style, blunt and colorful, sets him apart on the seventh floor of CIA headquarters. In an interview yesterday, Krongard described his past duties as those of a "minister without portfolio" whom senior managers felt comfortable talking to about "sticky subjects."

"I really didn't have a dog in any fights," he allowed, "and I was allowed to broker some things."

But Krongard exhibited the requisite secretiveness when asked to explain his interest in intelligence and how he came to land a job in Tenet's inner circle. If you go back to the CIA's origin during World War II in the Office of Strategic Services [OSS], he explained, "the whole OSS was really nothing but Wall Street bankers and lawyers."[67]

Despite his claim in 1998 that he was going to vanish, Krongard kept finding his way into the public eye. It's fantastic for him to broadcast to the world that he'd been a "minister without portfolio" in the Agency, cleaning up things like a character from a Clint Eastwood western. I'm sure all those Agency personnel whose ass he kicked because he "didn't have any dog in any fights," are just thrilled that he's talking to the press about his own awesomeness.

And although Buzzy's as tight-lipped as any well-trained spy about how he got recruited, he lets you know that the forerunner to the CIA "was really nothing but Wall Street bankers and lawyers," broadcasting to any foreign power paying attention that you shouldn't trust our corporate leaders or attorneys because they might also be CIA assets. (In a strange convergence, that may be one thing that Russian president, Vladimir Putin, and the American public agree on.) As the *Washinton Post* wants you to believe, Krongard is just what the CIA needed:

> Given the CIA's insular nature, outsiders who assume top posts often arouse suspicion. That was certainly true in the case of Nora Slatkin, a Capitol Hill staffer and Pentagon official who served as executive director from 1995 to 1996 under then-CIA Director, John M. Deutch.
>
> One former agency official said that he found it "absolutely astounding" that Tenet installed Krongard in such an important job. "When you meet him, he tells you to punch him in the stomach to see how tough he is," the former official said.[68]

It's become clearer to most of the public over the past few years, how the mainstream media is constantly trying to shape the public narrative. It doesn't matter if they utilize a conservative or liberal narrative to do so. It's all in service of the continued power of the establishment. A business "outsider" sounds like music to the ears of most conservatives, and as for liberals, they've fallen in love with the intelligence agencies, and they don't need any persuading.

However, when we read their propaganda with a more discerning eye, troubling details emerge. How else is one to respond to a grown man who asks people to punch him in the stomach? I've known people who were amazing physical specimens, even trained killers, and none of them acted in the boastful manner of this man.

If you need to talk about how tough you are, you aren't tough.

But that's what we were getting with Tenet's pick for his number three guy to run the Agency. And if there was any doubt as to what effect Buzzy had on the CIA, I point to a different section of Tenet's book.

> After 9/11, making organizational changes had to be calibrated to allow men and women both to perform their mission and to continue the transformation. In the real time of the real world we operated in, the onslaught of threats and crises never abated as we tried to remake the institution. We couldn't afford pit stops. We were changing the tires as the race car was careening around the curves at 180 miles an hour. The mission had to come first. Buzzy Krongard used to say, "Country, mission, CIA, family, and self." That was the CIA I knew.
>
> The job of DCI [Director of Central Intelligence] was really two jobs—running both CIA and also the larger intelligence community, sixteen diverse agencies. One of the criticisms of not only me but all of my predecessors is that we focused on CIA to the exclusion of the fifteen other parts of the intelligence community.[69]

Do you see how in Tenet's telling of it, Buzzy Krongard was the heart and soul of the CIA? I charge Krongard with much of the misguided direction of the CIA in the years leading up to 9/11, as well as the disastrous years which followed. There was an air of make-believe about the man, the blind ambition of somebody who fervently believed that if he just worked his body hard enough, he could also transform the world in the same manner he transformed his stomach muscles so he could challenge anybody who walked through his door to punch him in the gut.

If you don't believe the CIA was engaged in make-believe during Tenet's time, look at how they describe it in their own words. They were "changing the tires as the race car was careening around the curves at 180 miles an hour."

That's not simply bad writing, it's indicative of the low quality of their thinking.

And finally, it's important for the average American to understand we don't have just one intelligence agency, the CIA, but at that time we had sixteen. (Currently, we have seventeen because along with the Space Force created by President Trump, we also got the Space Force Intelligence Agency.) Now, the CIA takes the lead position in that community (despite what the Director of National Intelligence might think), and the CIA is the only intelligence agency officially allowed to undertake missions. This makes it the tip of the spear in our dealings with other countries, and the one most likely to stir up, rather than solve problems in the world.

The intelligence community, with the CIA as its unchallenged head, has become the leviathan of our governmental system, seeking to bring more and more things under their control, silently stealing away those rights and obligations that once belonged to a free people.

***

What chain of events led me to turn renegade against the CIA?

The first was the attack on my family.

The second was my investigation of the unanswered questions about the September 11, 2001, terrorist attacks on New York and Washington, DC.

And both of these involved Buzzy Krongard.

The man certainly got around.

It's my intention to make sure he doesn't get away before you learn the truth about him.

***

In 1999, while Krongard was busy working as "minister without portfolio" at the CIA, I was assigned to a classified domestic base to ensure the security of the base and protect the cover of the base. It was the kind of job I always liked, dealing with the men and women who were willing to put their lives on the line for their country. I would find out that some of the occupants of the base boasted they were trained killers.

It was a bright, sunny June morning in The Plains, Virgina, where I lived with my wife, Lorena, and our three kids. I recall that last morning, walking out onto the porch with my usual cup of coffee, looking out at the grass still green from the April rains, and trees in the woods covered with new leaves, rich with emerald color.

I sat down on the front porch swing of our modest home, knowing I'd miss the white rambler with bordered, white wooden slats. The strawberry patch I'd planted on the hill behind the house was starting to show blossoms, the pear tree was blooming, and the small garden my children always planted down the hill near the woods lay dormant. Since we were leaving, we didn't plant our usual crop of tomatoes, beans, green peppers, yellow squash, and of course, our favorites, jalapeno and cayenne peppers.

I remained on that front porch swing for maybe fifteen, twenty minutes, finished my coffee, then went inside to rally my troops. It was an easy task, as Lorena and the kids were excited about the move. The night before I'd purchased some easy to microwave egg and bacon sandwiches so we could have a quick breakfast before getting on the road. The movers had come the day before, taking most of our possessions, so the house already felt empty, as if awaiting the arrival of the new residents.

After breakfast we loaded our remaining items into a small U-Haul we'd tow behind us, and as we stood outside our house for the last time, we said a prayer, asking God for a safe journey to our new home. We jumped into our Chevy Blazer, pulled out of the driveway, and I asked the kids and Lorena what they hoped to remember about our house.

Each kid shared a special memory, then Lorena and I shared our own. It was something I tried to instill in my kids, gratitude for what had been, and hope for what lay on the road ahead.

The journey was uneventful, but the destination turned out to be a nightmare.

If I'd known what we were all about to endure, I never would have allowed my family to step foot in that house.

***

At the CIA, I was an analyst and I'm well aware there are facts (of which one can be relatively certain), and the interpretation of such facts, which can be subject to a remarkably high degree of error.

Let me tell you some of the things which I know are facts.

Because of what I'd uncovered about the risk to our personnel overseas, I had embarrassed the Directorate of Operations for the CIA, the people who do the bad stuff, like blackmail, dirty tricks, election interference, and assassinations.

It was hard for me to forget that I'd already been sent overseas without an official cover story and placed in close proximity to an Iranian assassin, who for some reason, decided not to kill me.

Then my family and I were sent to the secret base. I'm forbidden from revealing the name of this CIA facility located on American soil, but the *New York Times* published that information on February 10, 2011. This is how the article opened:

> In many ways, the personal injury lawsuit looked routine: In late 2001, a government employee and his family sued the agency he worked for, saying it had placed them in a mold-contaminated home that made them sick and required nearly all their possessions to be destroyed.
>
> But this was no ordinary case. The employee, Kevin M. Shipp, was a veteran Central Intelligence Agency officer. His home was at Camp Stanley, an army weapons depot just north of San Antonio where the drinking water was polluted with toxic chemicals. The post includes a secret C.I.A. facility.
>
> Declaring that its need to protect state secrets outweighed the Shipps' right to a day in court, the government persuaded a judge to seal the case and order the family and their lawyers not to discuss it, and to later dismiss the lawsuit without any hearing on the merits, Mr. Shipp said.[70]

You might be asking yourself, "What does any 'state secrets' privilege by the government have to do with whether a family might have suffered from mold or any other toxic exposures?" You'd be right.

It doesn't make any sense.

But the government has been pulling this same kind of misbehavior since 1948, when the "State Secrets" privilege was first asserted. Unraveling these issues of national security can often take decades, and this situation was no different.

In 1948, an Air Force B-29 crashed near Waycross, Georgia, killing the four-man crew. On August 9, 1950, a lawyer for the widows of the three civilian engineers who died in the crash requested a copy of the Air Force's accident report to explain the incident. The government argued that the report could not be released without damaging national security. Air Force affidavits claimed that the aircraft was engaged in a "highly secret mission."

In response to the judge's request to produce the report, the assistant attorney general for the federal government stated, "We contend that the findings of the [Executive Branch] are binding . . . upon the judiciary. You cannot review or interpret it. That is what it comes down to."

The judge did not agree and found the government in default.

An appeals court unanimously agreed with the decision.

However, in 1953, the case made its way all the way to the United States Supreme Court. The court reversed the lower court's decision and for the first time, officially recognized a "State Secrets Privilege."

Fifty years later, a Freedom of Information Act request revealed that the crash had been caused by a faulty landing gear and did not involve any state secrets.

The government had simply used the privilege to cover up its negligence and the Supreme Court was only too happy to assist in the injustice.

It was ironic because our revolution against King George III was because of his arbitrary use of power against us.

The State Secrets Privilege, as it has been applied against my family, and others, is nothing short of appalling.

Let's return to that *New York Times* story which detailed much of what I and my family endured.

Mr. Shipp recently completed a memoir filled with unclassified documents that he said backed up his assertions. He says that he submitted the manuscript to the agency for the required publication review but that it blacked out swaths of information, like accounts of his children's nosebleeds, strange rashes, vomiting, severe asthma and memory loss.

Citing a confidentiality agreement he signed with the government, Mr. Shipp would not discuss where the secret facility was located, what its purpose was, which agency he worked for or what his duties were.

Still, he said, he was free to say that he worked at C.I.A. head-quarters in Langley, Va., both before and after his stint at the facility. And public documents from a separate lawsuit which he filed against his insurance carrier over a claim for his family's destroyed belongings, make clear that he was stationed at Camp Stanley.[71]

As you can clearly understand, by 2011, I'd been fighting the CIA for many years, but I was still honoring my security oaths. That was the deal I made, and I kept it. Even now that this information is in the public domain, I cannot confirm where I was stationed, and can only refer to the location as the "secret base." (I know, it doesn't make much sense, but that's the government for you!)

But let me tell you about how my family suffered during the two years we lived at that house.

My wife, Lorena, was bedridden with headaches so severe she was treated with Demerol and lost her short-term memory. Our son Joel was diagnosed by an immunologist as having a severe immune system disorder as a result of exposure to a significant toxin and eventually described his immune system as resembling someone who had been exposed to a "burst of radiation."

Mr. Shipp's ex-wife, Lorena Shipp, and one of his sons, Joel Shipp, now 28, said in interviews that the C.I.A. had assigned Mr. Shipp to a high-ranking job at the facility to uncover suspected security breaches. The family moved to an Army-owned house at Camp Stanley in June 1999 and left in May 2001.

It is not clear what took place at the C.I.A. facility. But the camp had been used as a weapons depot for generations. Joel and Lorena Shipp described bunkers and many old weapons, including Soviet weaponry. They also said that they occasionally saw officials performing tactical drills, and that sometimes items were burned or buried there.

"The house that our family was moved into was planted on top of a lot of buried ammunition," Joel Shipp said. "One time me and my little brother dug up a mustard gas shell."[72]

I understand my background as a CIA officer might make me a little more suspicious than the average person. But if I'd been handed the story of some foreign intelligence agent who'd uncovered wrongdoing in his agency, then learned he'd been sent with his family to live in a house with buried ammunition, including mustard gas shells underneath it, and they'd gotten sick, I would have reported it to my superiors as a likely assassination attempt.

The security officer on the base informed me that the house was contaminated, and he and his family had been evacuated from it due to the illness of every family member.

The CIA knew the house was contaminated when they ordered my family to live there. A base official, who had become a close friend, secretly advised me that the chief of the base paid a visit to his office and removed all the files on the contaminated house. I've often said that one of the dangers about intelligence work is that you're taught to lie so much, it eventually becomes a habit you can't turn off. You lie about everything that might be unpleasant. I joke that like an alcoholic, once you leave the CIA you have to go through a twelve-step program, and that the first six steps of that recovery are learning how not to lie.

The chief of the security guards, who had also become a confidant because of my strong support of the security guard force, came to me late one night to confide he'd found a large pile of glass ampules containing a clear liquid in a remote part of the base. His account matched that of liquid mustard gas storage ampules. Like many base employees, he lacked confidence in the leadership of the base, but was afraid to tell anyone.

The retiring chief of the secret base shared his concern that Deer gun assassination pistols (a single shot 9 mm pistol designed to be the Vietnam War's version of the World War II Liberator pistol, likely from Operation Phoenix) were buried there and beginning to percolate up to the surface. (I actually held one of them in my hand, an odd and elegant little weapon, easily concealed.) The fear was the weapons might be discovered by environmental contractors, raising some uncomfortable questions.

It was as if the earth itself was vomiting up the CIA's murderous secrets.

Whether it was the result of the buried munitions under our house or not, the house was also riddled with black mold. When the government momentarily entertained the possibility our family had been affected by something, they tended to blame the black mold, rather than the buried munitions.

When Lorena and I first saw the house, we were not enthused. It had not been lived in for years, and one of the first things we would need to do was repair it. The walls were rotten from water damage from broken pipes, there were water stains on the ceiling from roof leaks, and a long-time employee of the location advised me that at some time in the past, a pipe had burst in the house, and the incident went undetected for a month.

I reported the damage to my chief, and requested it be repaired, but the request was ignored. I asked for permission to find other housing for my family, off-base, but the request was denied.

So Lorena and I rolled up our sleeves and got to work making the house livable for our family. We painted the entire inside to cover the stains, ripped up and replaced the carpets which were covered in cigarette burns, dirt, and mildew, and had an above-ground pool installed in the backyard for the kids. The rear deck of the house overlooked the backyard and pool, and with a barbecue grill, it quickly became one of our favorite places to gather.

I had regular tea parties with my daughter, wearing the straw bonnet hat with flowers on it that she requested, and spent weekends with my sons, exploring the remote areas of the base, shooting pistols, and playing wiffle ball on the street. The extensive travel I'd taken over the years for my job had caused Lorena and I to drift apart, but with the help of counseling and a marriage support group, we again grew as close as we'd been when we were first married.

Everyone was happy.

We joined a local church and became involved as volunteers, also joining the church's Bible school in the evenings. We met and made wonderful friends.

Tragically, everything was about to change.

***

We'd been living in the house for three months when our youngest son, Bobby, came running into our bedroom, blood streaming from his nose.

He was scared, but I comforted him, applied pressure to his nose, and had him lie down until he went to sleep.

Crisis averted. Or so I thought.

Two nights later, Joel came into our bedroom, blood running from his nose. Again, I applied pressure with a cloth, told him to keep it elevated, and he went back to bed. The two incidents, occurring so close together, concerned Lorena and me, but we wrote them off as allergies, or possibly due to the new climate.

A week later, Lorena woke up with a bloody nose.

After that, Lorena began getting severe headaches, so intense that she often couldn't get out of bed. I took her to a doctor who performed an MRI, which revealed no abnormalities. In the interim, he prescribed Demerol, a strong pain medication. Even more concerning, Lorena began to lose her short-term memory, unable to recall events twenty minutes earlier. A few days later, she began to show bruises all over her body, and her gums began bleeding.

I shared this information with my neighbor across the street and he told me he was also experiencing severe headaches, but this was accompanied by episodes in which he'd lose control of the left side of his body. He went through the same routine of visiting the doctor, having an MRI performed, and being told they couldn't find anything wrong with him.

In talking about Lorena's symptoms with the chief's executive assistant who lived next door to us, she told me that her daughter had been bedridden, suffering from severe headaches, memory loss, and disorientation, and that she was unable to work. They'd taken her to a neurologist, who'd also been unable to find anything wrong, but they'd discovered a black substance growing all over their bedroom closets.

Our son Joel came into our bedroom late one night, barely able to breathe. Because I'd driven the routes to all the local hospitals as part of my job, I knew I could get us to the emergency room faster than any ambulance. Ten minutes later we were at the emergency room and the doctors immediately got to work on him, administering oxygen which brought him out of his semi-conscious state and eased his panic that he was going to die. After a long line of questioning about his allergies, examining his throat, and taking X-rays, the doctors were unable to find anything wrong with him. However, the inflammation was beginning to subside, so the attending physicians simply prescribed medicine to reduce the swelling and advised us to keep watch over him for the reappearance of any symptoms.

A few weeks later, I began waking up in the middle of the night, my lungs feeling as if they were on fire, and I'd start wheezing, as if I had asthma. Eventually, it became so bad I went to sleep in the living room so I wouldn't disturb Lorena. Finally, I went to the doctor, who diagnosed me as suffering from asthma, although I'd never had that in my life. A month later, I came down with bronchitis.

Late one afternoon when I arrived home, Joel ran up to me excitedly and said, "Dad, look what I found!"

I looked down to see he was holding the fragment of a military shell, clearly labeled "mustard." That stood for mustard gas, one of the most potent chemical weapons ever devised, not the condiment you put on your hot dog.

"Throw that away and never touch it again!" I ordered him.

This was getting to be too much. I needed to take this up the chain of command. And to whom did my request go? It went to the man at the CIA responsible for the secret domestic base to which I'd been deployed.

That man was Buzzy Krongard.

***

We had discovered the black mold underneath our house and in our air ducts, which meant that all our items were contaminated. After four requests to CIA headquarters to get my family out of the house, and due to refusals and commands not to disclose it, I made my case to CIA management, citing all the evidence I'd uncovered.

The chief of the base ordered me to use my American Express government credit card to pay for all the evacuation expenses, including moving my family back to Virginia. That order was likely given by Buzzy Krongard. My wife, Lorena, was present at the meeting. Twice, we asked the chief of base for his order in writing, and he refused both times.

Because of the widespread contamination, the cleanup company, Servpro, removed all of our possessions: furniture, clothes, children's toys, baby pictures, everything had to be taken out and burned. My children sat in shock as their toys were taken away from them. They still suffer from the trauma.

Because my wife had several priceless heirlooms, I had Servpro remove them for quarantine and decontamination.

It was only after I'd contracted Servpro that a series of events unfolded which made me question the basic decency of the Agency. When the Servpro technician first went into our house, she told me her tongue swelled up so much she had to leave the house, clear evidence of an environmental hazard. However, before she could start work, she'd received a call from another company, Raba Kistner, the CIA's environmental contractor on the base, offering her a job with a boost in salary so significant she had to take it. In her words, they "gave her an offer she couldn't refuse."

Money is power with the CIA, and it throws around its secret budget with impunity.

A week later, we received a certified letter from our family doctor, whose office was near the facility, explaining she could no longer see our family, but not providing an explanation for our termination.

When I received a letter from an environmental expert at Texas Tech University regarding my situation, I discovered it had already been opened. (I guess that's one of the perks of being under surveillance. Your mail comes to you pre-opened and pre-read! How thoughtful!)

Under my desk in the main building, I found wire clippings, a sign that a listening device had been installed.

A base official slipped and mentioned details about the suspected toxins that my wife had only discussed in the privacy of our bedroom.

Several times I saw a black sedan parked in the driveway across from our house with unknown individuals inside it. I can tell you now that I was the executive officer at the base, also in charge of any and all security, as well as responsible for any emergencies. Although I was in charge of knowing who had access to the base, the chief of base never answered my questions as to their identity. It was clear to me the black sedan was a listening post and I was the target. The fact that I could plainly see them was also part of the intimidation.

The chief of the security guards advised me that my family was being spied on by a group of individuals hiding in the woods across from our house. While on deployment in foreign countries, I expected to be under the gaze of intelligence services. But never in my wildest dreams did I expect to be under surveillance by my own Agency.

Lorena and the kids were terrified, and it only strengthened my resolve to protect them.

The second night I was back in Virginia, I received a call from Servpro, telling me I had to pay their entire $15,000 fee within twenty-four hours, or else they would put my wife's priceless furniture on the curb.

It was clear the CIA had gotten to them.

The noose was tightening around my neck.

Back in Washington, DC, a day later, I was called into a mandatory meeting. My polygraph division supervisor, obviously under orders, got into my face, and tried to anger me. They could not get me on anything, so they started to ratchet up the accusations, push my buttons, hoping I'd start shouting back at them, giving them the pretext to say I was being insubordinate.

I kept my cool.

I knew their tactics.

I was one of them.

As soon as my lawsuit hit the courts, containing the environmental evidence and toxic blood results, I was ordered to a meeting with the new chief of the polygraph division and ordered to report to the CIA officer of medical services for blood and psychological testing.

The trick was an old one and I knew it.

The Office of Medical Services would falsify a diagnosis that I was paranoid and that the blood tests had revealed nothing. Sadly for them, I already had reports from third party environmental experts and immunologists who'd examined me and my family and had documented our toxic exposures.

I respectfully declined but told them I would pass the request onto my lawyer, and if his opinion differed from mine, I'd happily comply.

Even in that moment of stress, I thought of that humorous moment from the Jim Carrey movie, *Liar, Liar,* when after telling all the members of his law firm what he really thinks of them, says, "See you later d***heads!"

My attorney thanked me for keeping those thoughts in my head and walking quietly out of the meeting and the building.

Next, I was called into the CIA outer building under orders to meet with a security officer. Sadistically, they picked an officer who was a close friend of mine.

The security officer told me Buzzy Krongard had ordered my blue badge be taken from me and all access to CIA buildings be terminated because I had misused a government credit card.

I was walked out of the building in front of the security protective officers, many of whom I had trained when I was chief of CIA police training.

I could see what was coming. As long as I remained with the Agency, I was under their control. I submitted my resignation, giving them thirty days' notice, and felt a freedom I hadn't felt in years, a freedom to fight back.

Several years later, at a corporate program manager's off-site facility, I was approached by a former official for the Inspector General's Office of the CIA, who had been hired by the same company as a program manager. He told an interesting story. He claimed the Inspector General's Office had been ordered by the director of Central Intelligence, George Tenet, and his executive officer, Buzzy Krongard, to take me down because the CIA didn't want their chemical and other illegal weapons program which they'd run at the secret base to be exposed. He profusely apologized for being a part of it.

Unfortunately for me, it was a little too late, as the CIA had already intentionally injured me and my family, and tried their best to avoid responsibility.

As CIA Director George Tenet had written in his book, it was Buzzy Krongard's new and improved CIA and I had just made a powerful enemy.

But the same toughness I'd learned with the CIA would serve me well in my five-year battle against the Agency.

***

Let me quote from one of the many medical reports we received as we were trying to heal ourselves from these events, after I'd left the CIA. Using the State Secrets Privilege, the CIA, and their accomplices at the Department of Justice placed this and other medical records under seal for several years, preventing me, my wife, and my family, under threat of jail, from discussing our medical problems. To me, this was a greater assault than any English king had ever visited upon the American citizenry. If such policies are allowed to stand, we no longer live under a Constitution, but under effective martial law.

September 8, 2003

To whom it may concern:

The following is a brief summary of my therapeutic involvement with the Shipp family. I opened cases on both Joey, as well as his mother, Lorena. Separate cases began because of the possibility that they would need medication management from our agency, but their family physician was willing to provide psychotropic medications.

The entire Shipp family was (is) profoundly impacted not only by their exposure to mold, but to the treatment that the family received by the government agency that Mr. Shipp was formerly employed by. I have met all five members, in various configurations, and all of them are consistent in their report that prior to their exposure, family relationships and individual functioning was not problematic. As a result of their exposure, all members have been traumatized, taking somewhat different forms for each member. As a family, they were experiencing significant daily turmoil. Living arrangements caused much hardship, and their inability to receive any significant responses to their concerns caused much frustration. At various times, each member of the family experienced, in addition to medical/somatic problems, anxiety and depression, as well as PTSD symptoms.

Mrs. Shipp has experienced on-going depressive symptoms that have interfered with her daily role as a mother and wife. Her depression often takes on a vegetative variety in which she has great trouble motivating herself to do anything. She feels that she is to blame for not having protected her children, although she clearly did so. She has had suicidal tendencies, and I am aware of one incident in which she was restrained by her husband from acting on suicidal impulses. There is no evidence of any pre-existing depression or suicidal tendencies.

Joey Shipp has displayed a great deal of emotional instability and volatility, that according to him and both parents was not present prior to their exposure to mold and subsequent treatment by his father's employment agency. He has clear PTSD symptoms, including flashbacks. He is quite convinced that he will never be better, and as a result experiences suicidal ideation as well as occasional homicidal.

Although I had less contact with Bobby and Carly, they participated in family sessions and could verbalize without any coaching just how unsettling matters had (have) been. The loss of their toys and familiar surroundings were especially difficult for them due to their age. Carly still manifests clinging/dependent behaviors that did not exist to any such degree prior to the events.

Mr. Shipp has consistently tried to be protective of and responsive to his family despite going through a great deal of turmoil himself. Although he tries to present in a stoic manner, he suffers from anxiety and depression. He not only lost his career as a result of these events, but his reputation has been questioned. Although he is very self-effacing, he believes he was an excellent employee of the agency he worked for and could not believe he would be treated in such a manner. When this examiner met with a representative of the agency that Mr. Shipp worked for, I was asked, and it was implied that others felt Mr. Shipp to be possibly "paranoid." I find no evidence whatsoever of this impression.

This therapist was not given clearance for an extended period of time which impacted the sessions, in that Mr. Shipp could not discuss certain particular issues nor could I inquire.

Because of financial strain, the Shipps had to make decisions as to whom needed sessions and often it became a choice of having one session, as opposed to building in two sessions that would have been therapeutically called for. The medications that they were treated for are also costly, which created more strain for the family, in particular, Mr. Shipp.

I find the Shipps, as individuals and as a family unit to be honorable and straightforward people. There was never one time in my dealings with them that I questioned their veracity or truthfulness. They very much want to go forward with their lives and believe that it has been next to impossible to do so in light of their having been rebuffed time and again when they have brought up the issues that have so profoundly effected them. They have suffered from serious psychiatric problems that appear to have been due purely to situational stressors. Although I have attempted to have them see their future as relatively optimistic, further work sessions will still need to occur to have them recover from a situation, not of their making, that led to life-threatening conditions, at worst, and constant family anxiety and depression at a minimum.

Very truly yours,
Ronald Schmal, Ph.D.
Licensed Clinical Psychologist[73]

It's said that a man's self-esteem is closely tied to his job and career, and when that is damaged, it extracts an enormous toll on him. I found that to be true for myself, but I also had a mission. I needed to get my family better, and I was fighting for the truth to be revealed about what had happened to us.

How badly did the CIA want to keep the truth hidden?

For four years, the CIA threatened me and my family with prosecution if we talked to the news media, immediate family, or anybody else. The Agency had persuaded a federal judge into issuing a "gag order" which sealed all information pertaining to our case so that we were even unable to share any information with our medical doctors.

The judge had initially ruled in our favor for the personal injury lawsuit against the CIA, and planned to hear the case in his court.

We were later told that the Agency asked for and received a secret meeting with the judge, which our attorneys were not allowed to attend. My main attorney, Clint Blackman, was incensed, saying he'd never had that happen with a client before.

After that meeting, the judge issued a gag order on every member of my family, instructing us not to use our real names when discussing the case, even with our attorneys or government representatives.

They did let us use fake names, however.

We were given the names, John, Ann, Johnny, Mark, and Barbie Doe.

I guess that's what passes for humor at the highest levels of the CIA.

***

However, as the 2011 *New York Times* article demonstrated, I didn't give up. I wrote a manuscript about what I'd experienced, submitted it to the CIA for its required review, and they blacked out large portions of it. So, I published it anyway, with the blacked-out portions exposed, and eventually some of the truth came out.

> Camp Stanley has a troubled environmental record. In August 2001, according to local news reports, military officials began distributing bottled water to residents nearby after it was discovered that toxins from the camp had polluted an aquifer in the area contaminating the drinking water.
>
> The Shipps said they were twice evacuated from the house after expressing concern about their sudden health troubles. But, Kevin Shipp said, his supervisor played down the problems, declaring that the house was fine after its air was tested, although the windows and doors were open at the time, Mr. Shipp said.
>
> Suspicious of a cover-up, Mr. Shipp said he sent samples from the house to a scientist at Texas Tech University. His manuscript includes a Texas Tech report showing that the samples tested positive for toxic mold.[74]

These test results were sealed by the CIA using the State Secrets Privilege.

The country learned that my secret base had environmental problems, the drinking water was contaminated, and that the samples from my house had toxic mold. What else did the country find out?

They found out how the CIA acted in bad faith towards its employees with complaints. Because my evidence against the CIA was so strong, according to my attorney, Clint, the federal district judge told the CIA representatives, "Well, it looks like Mr. Shipp has you over a barrel." The *New York Times* article continued, noting that the CIA had been ordered into mediation, a $400,000 settlement had been proposed to and agreed upon, but that the government had withdrawn the offer and invoked the State Secrets privilege.[75]

In other words, when you're the government, it's a case of "heads I win, tails you lose." The government is like the casino where they make sure the rules are always stacked in their favor. But they don't hold all the cards because if we have the courage to say what we think, it's a difficult thing to stop us.

I'm often asked why there aren't more whistleblowers like me.

The answer is that it can take an enormous toll on a person.

And you need to be ready to pay the cost.

This is what you need to understand.

Every secret operational program of the United States government has a secrecy oath they require their employees to sign, even nowadays, the Weather Service. (You might ask yourself, what could possibly be secret about the weather? Maybe the actual temperature readings, or some geo-engineering projects?) Originally these agreements protected legitimate sources and methods, as well as military technology or the location of troops in the field.

We can all understand that.

But that legitimate use of a secrecy oath has been taken and turned into a monster whose only purpose is to intimidate well-intentioned government employees. When you sign a form like that, here's what you give up:

Your right to a jury trial.

Your right to any trial.

Your right to sue the government in any forum for exposure to a toxic substance.

Your right to due process.

It's a science to destroy a whistleblower, and the government has come close to perfecting the recipe. They might first go to your supervisor, encouraging him or her to deny you earned promotions, or give you embarrassing or menial assignments. They'll want your fellow employees to see you being punished, as a warning not to pursue a similar path.

If you persist, they'll ratchet up the pressure, by maybe raising the interest rate on the loan you took out from that government credit union. You might try to pull some money out of your retirement account to help with those increased interest rates, only to find that your access to that account has been blocked as well, which is a felony under US law.

But the CIA doesn't care about US law.

It doesn't matter that these actions are against the law, especially when you control the judges who run the courts.

If they never prosecute those who violate them, it's as if these laws don't exist.

But don't despair. God tells us that no evil thing can remain hidden.

But enough questions have been raised about Buzzy Krongard and his work at the CIA, that I'm hopeful, that like that mustard shell which surfaced in my yard and was picked up by my son, long buried secrets will always come to light.

***

It's interesting that some of the first questions raised about the September 11, 2001 attacks involved Buzzy Krongard and secrets he might have been trying to bury.

One of the first anomalies noted was a large amount of short selling of United stock in the days before the attacks on New York and Washington, DC (two of the hijacked planes were owned by United Airlines, and the other two were owned by American Airlines), as reported in the *San Franciso Chronicle* on September 29, 2001.

> Investors have yet to collect more than $2.5 million in profits they made from trading options in the stock of United Airlines before the Sept. 11 attacks, according to a source familiar with the trades and market data.
>
> The uncollected money raises suspicions that the investors—whose identities and nationalities have not been made public—had advance knowledge of the strikes . . .
>
> The source familiar with the United trades identified Deutsche Banc Alex. Brown, the American investment banking arm of the German giant Deutsche bank, as the investment bank used to purchase at least some of the options. Rohini Pragasam, a bank spokeswoman, declined comment.

Investigators' attention previously had been drawn to Germany because of the residence there earlier in the year of some of the principal suspects in the Sept. 11 attack and unusual patterns in the short selling of insurance, airline and other financial company stocks prior to the attacks.[76]

Normally, if somebody has a financial windfall by betting on/or against a company, there's a rush to cash in on the proceeds. But for some reason those who purchased these stock options weren't interested in collecting their cash.

Maybe like bank robbers who stowed their loot in a storage locker, they didn't want to venture there again because they thought the authorities might be watching them. Although the *San Francisco Chronicle* noted that the speculators hadn't picked up their money by late September, the situation was still the same in mid-October, prompting this article from the British publication, *The Independent*:

Share speculators have failed to collect $2.5m (1.7 million pounds) in profits made from the fall in the share price of United Airlines after the 11 September World Trade Center attacks.

The fact that the money is unclaimed more than a month later has reawakened investigators' interest in a story dismissed as coincidence . . .

Further details of the futures trades that netted such huge gains in the wake of the hijackings have been disclosed. To the embarrassment of investigators, it has also emerged that the firm used to buy many of the "put" options–where a trader, in effect, bets on a share price fall–on United Airlines stock was headed until 1998 by "Buzzy" Krongard, now executive director of the CIA.

Until 1997, Mr. Krongard was chairman of Alex Brown, Inc, America's oldest investment banking firm. Alex Brown was acquired by Bankers Trust, which in turn was bought by Deutsche Bank.[77]

It's certainly an odd occurrence, and we shouldn't forget that the 9/11 Commission looked into these allegations and dismissed them as a "coincidence." However, as criticism of the 9/11 Commission Report has mounted in recent years (particularly their concealment of Saudi support and contact with many of the hijackers), the question is whether the 9/11 Commission will join the Warren Commission investigation into the assassination of President Kennedy as an object of ridicule by the public and widely disbelieved.

We may end up having more questions about Buzzy Krongard in the future as more information comes to light.

However, in the excellent book, *Black 9/11, Money, Motivation, and Technology*, author Mark H. Gaffney, makes a number of assertions about Krongard at odds with the official narrative.

> George Tenet writes in his memoirs that in February 1998 he recruited Buzzy Krongard to become his councilor, in which capacity Krongard probably served as Tenet's personal liaison to Wall Street. Krongard's known ties to the CIA, however, go back at least as far as 1992. In the mid-1990s Krongard had served as a consultant to CIA director James Woolsey. Then he returned to finance and was named chairman of America's oldest investment banking firm, Alex Brown and Sons, Inc., which in 1997 merged with Bankers Trust. In 1999, BT Alex Brown was in turn acquired by Deutsche Bank, the firm that placed the UAL [United Airlines) put options.[78]

When dealing with the intelligence agencies it can be like peeling back the layers of an onion. There's the "official" story, the one printed in the pages of the *Washington Post* or the *New York Times*, and it's important to read those stories, because they'll often let slip important facts. I often read such stories through a different lens, asking myself, what are they trying to broadcast to other members of the intelligence community? The other question I usually ask is, where do they want my attention to go, and what questions are they steering me away from asking?

I often think of the quote attributed to Sigmund Freud that, "He that has eyes to see and ears to hear may convince himself that no mortal can keep a secret. If his lips are silent, he chatters with his fingertips; betrayal oozes out of him at every pore."[79]

This is what comes through loud and clear to me in the information about Buzzy Krongard in both the mainstream media and alternative voices: The CIA utilizes the top people in the business world to accomplish their objectives. If you think there's a division between the intelligence world and the American corporate world, you might be in for a rude surprise.

We need to ask ourselves, what particular skill set did Buzzy Krongard provide to the CIA? *Black 9/11* provides a possible answer:

> In 1998, BT Alex Brown refused to cooperate with a Senate subcommittee that was conducting hearings on the involvement of US banks in money-laundering activities. At the time, BT Alex Brown, like other large US financial institutions, was in the business of private banking, meaning that it catered to unnamed wealthy clients, often for the sole purpose of setting up shell companies in foreign jurisdictions, such as on the isle of Jersey, where effective bank regulation and oversight are nonexistent. According to Michael Ruppert, Krongard's last job at Alex Brown was to oversee "private client relations," meaning that Krongard personally arranged confidential transactions and transfers for the bank's unnamed wealthy clientele.[80]

I'll make that last paragraph easier to understand. When you investigate the intelligence world it's akin to learning a foreign language. You just have to understand what the words mean, and you'll make out fine. Whenever you hear the expression "private banking" I want you to translate that in your mind as "possible money laundering operation."

As Gaffney goes onto explain, private banks are able to set up multiple offshore accounts in different locations, using different organizations and names, which allows the quick and confidential transfer of money across international borders.[81] Many of these private banking havens have laws that do not permit the bankers to know much about the accounts they set up, which gives the banks a layer of plausible deniability. Some have suggested that the intelligence agencies have been instrumental in setting up these banking havens for just such a purpose.

It's much easier to win the game when you're the one who made the rules.

The investigation of Buzzy Krongard continued in *Black 9/11*:

After Buzzy Krongard's departure to the CIA, his successor at BT Alex Brown was his former deputy Mayo Shattuck III, who had worked at the bank for years. In 1997, Shattuck helped Krongard engineer the merger with Bankers Trust, and he stayed on after Deutsche Bank acquired BT Alex Brown in 1999.

According to the *New York Times*, Bankers Trust was "one of the most loosely managed [banks] on Wall Street," and during the 1990s was repeatedly rocked by scandal. In 1994, clients and regulators accused the bank "of misleading customers about its risky derivative products." The case went viral when tape recordings were made public that showed bank salesmen snickering about ripping off naive customers.[82]

One of the great things about utilizing a "loosely managed" bank like Alex Brown and Sons, Inc. is that it's much easier to cover up bad things when they come to light. You can simply blame it on something like "failure to supervise" or a "few, rogue employees" rather than the entity being set up specifically for a nefarious purpose.

The world simply shrugs its shoulders and moves on.

The saga of Alex Brown and Sons, Inc., as it was sold to Bankers Trust, then to Deutsche Bank continued:

In 1999, BT Alex Brown pled guilty to criminal conspiracy charges, after it was revealed that top-level executives had created a slush fund out of at least $20 million in unclaimed funds. The firm had to pay a $63 million fine and would have been forced to close its doors but for the fact that it was purchased, just at this time, by Deutsche Bank, Europe's largest. According to the *New York Times*, Mayo Shattuck III stayed on and was named "co-head of investment banking in January [2001], overseeing Deutsche Bank's 400 brokers who cater to wealthy clients. Shattuck himself reportedly handled the private accounts of such dubious notables as Saudi financier Adnan Khashoggi and Seagram's owner Edgar Bronfmann. His sudden unexplained resignation immediately after the 9/11 attacks must therefore be viewed as highly suspicious.[83]

I think a couple things in the previous paragraph bear comment. While the CIA and other parts of the intelligence community may hold significant power, it's not absolute. Other parts of the government interested in law enforcement, will often trip over these secret activities, and while they may not find the ultimate source behind these crimes, they may be able to punish the intelligence agency cut-outs (as I suspect Alex Brown and Sons, Inc. to be).

And I also think it's important to note that the intelligence agencies may also keep many of their partners in the dark about their ultimate intentions. One wonders what happened to Mayo Shattuck III, in light of the 9/11 attacks and the revelation that his company had executed significant "put options" on United and American Airline stocks, the two airlines utilized by the hijackers in their attack. Did he simply say to himself, "I can no longer be a part of this?" Or did he fear prosecution, and think it was time to move out of the line of fire?

Or was his life in danger?

This is speculation and conjecture but seems reasonable given the facts.

As early as 1974, credible accusations were being made that the CIA was involved in the stock market, specifically in a book called *The CIA and the Cult of Intelligence*, written by Victor Marchetti, a former CIA analyst, and John D. Marks, who worked at the State Department. As Gaffney wrote in *Black 9/11*, about Marchetti and Marks's book:

> The authors assert that with the approval of top CIA leadership a small group of senior officers for years played the stock market using the CIA's "employee retirement fund, certain agent and contract-personnel accounts, and the CIA credit-union's capital." In more recent years, the assets likely included slush funds (that I will discuss in a subsequent chapter) generated from the illicit sale of arms, possibly kickbacks from the drug trade, plus assets derived from a vast quantity of Japanese gold seized after World War II.
>
> Initially, the CIA played the markets through a Boston-based brokerage house. But eventually the Agency economists, accountants, and lawyers concluded the Boston brokers' investment strategy was too conservative, and that they would do better on their own.[84]

My point in citing this work is not to prove the truth of the assertion, but to acquaint you with some of the robust questions which have been raised about the CIA since the 1970s, and how many of the questions remain unaddressed to this day.

As an example of asking the "wrong" question, the 9/11 Commission expressly asked whether Al-Qaeda was manipulating the stock market in the days before the attack.

The question NOT ASKED was whether Americans connected to intelligence agencies could be linked to these trades. Endnote 130 of the 9/11 Commission Report contains this passage:

> Highly publicized allegations of insider trading in advance of 9/11 generally rest on reports of unusual pre-9/11 trading activity in companies whose stock plummeted after the attacks. Some unusual trading did in fact occur, but each such trade proved to have an innocuous explanation. For example, the volume of put options—investments that pay off only when a stock drops in price—surged in the parent companies of United Airlines on September 6 and American Airlines on September 10–highly suspicious trading on its face. Yet, further investigation has revealed that the trading had no connection with 9/11. A single U.S.-based institutional investor with no conceivable ties to al Qaeda purchased 95 percent of the UAL puts on September 6 as part of a trading strategy that included *buying* [Commission's emphasis] 115,000 shares of American on September 10. Similarly, much of the seemingly suspicious trading in American on September 10 was traced to a specific U.S.-based options trading newsletter, faxes to its subscribers on Sunday, September 9, which recommended these trades.[85]

As a former CIA investigator, let me tell you what's so wrong about this information. The US-based institutional investor who purchased the put options on United on September 6, and the US-based options trading newsletter that suggested shorting the American Airlines stock on September 10, were the same company, the former Alex Brown and Sons, Inc., which at that time had been acquired by Deutsche Bank, and had previously been run by none other than Buzzy Krongard.

Any sophisticated corporate criminal, seeking to cover his tracks, would have laid a false trail, such as having his company place what looks like a counter-bet. Would our corporate criminal care if his company lost some money, as long as he escaped with his money?

The 9/11 Commission Report seemed like a joke to me, specifically in their failure to look more deeply into the insider trading allegations against the former Alex Brown and Sons, Inc.

In the years since 9/11, I've looked at many of the claims, such as the unexplained collapse of Building 7, and other anomalies, and I am convinced that many of the questions remain unanswered.

But in my mind, the most dramatic set of accusations swirl around the role of Buzzy Krongard, the executive director of the CIA at the time of the attacks, whose former company placed bets against the two airlines which the Al Qaeda terrorists hijacked to stage their day of terror.

**

If such accusations cause you to immediately recoil, certain that nothing even remotely like what I'm asserting has been done in America over the past decades, we can back off for a moment.

Let's imagine this is all taking place in a fictional country.

Just for argument's sake, let's call this country, Hopelandia.

The Hopelandians are a hardworking, God-fearing people, but they worry about their enemy, the inhabitants of the far-away land of Stalinista.

Stalinista is a genuinely bad country, banning private property, it has leaders who shout and often don't bathe for days, doesn't allow their citizens to criticize their government (lest they be deemed "insurrectionists"), and have a special hatred for anybody with religious faith.

The Hopelandians know the Stalinistas will try to take advantage of the freedoms of Hopelandia, so they make an exception, and create the Guardians.

The Guardians are the very best people of Hopelandia, graduates of the top universities, pure of heart and free from any venality, and it's for this reason the Hopelandian Parliament grants the Guardians special rights. The Hopelandians will not be able to see anything the Guardians do, even if it's alleged that the Guardians killed their President while he was riding in an open convertible in Dallas, Texas.

In addition, the Guardians have a secret budget, and it can never be audited.

Even with the best of intentions, what do you think Hopelandia would look like after seventy-five years of this arrangement?

It would probably look a lot like Stalinista.

Even the best of the Guardians can't be trusted with absolute power, given unlimited money, and left in darkness for decades.

But let's leave our mythical Hopelandia behind and get back to America.

***

Even though he liked to talk a lot, it still seems Buzzy Krongard had a few secrets.

Sometimes other people would share Buzzy's secrets, like Ed Hale, the former chairman of the board of the Bank of Baltimore, who in his 2015 memoir, spun a remarkable tale.

> **In your new memoir, Hale Storm, you disclose that you worked for the CIA for about a decade. How and when were you recruited?**
> I was recruited in 1992 by Buzzy Krongard, who was the chairman of [investment bank] Alex. Brown at the time. I was chairman of the board of the Bank of Baltimore and we happened to be in the same building.
>
> **What was Mr. Krongard's relationship to the CIA at the time?**
> I'm not sure exactly. I don't think it was official. But eventually, he became the number three person in the CIA under George Tenet. But at the time I don't think he had any official position.[86]

The easy way the intelligence agencies work together with the very top of American businesses is displayed in this account. Two top executives start talking, one revealing his work for the CIA, and it's relatively easy to recruit the other executive. Hale's account suggests the almost frictionless manner in which American intelligence and American business can work hand in glove with each other.

So how did it work?
[The CIA] would either send me a resume or the handlers would come over with people who were to be given credentials by me, HaleTrans, Baltimore Blast–I would hand them shirts, hats, cards, and they were sent on their way. They were not [my] employees. They were, in fact, paid by the agency. That's how their compensation was, so it didn't get too complicated. I would just give them identities that these people were employed by me, as opposed to somebody who was a "military attaché" or a "cultural attaché" to an embassy over in Libya. Everybody knew you were a spy. In this case, it was undetectable . . .

Did Mr. Krongard or anyone else at the CIA ever explain why they picked you?
They could have gone to any number of people, and I'm not aware they went to anyone else, maybe they did. But I was the one that was most plausible because I was in international shipping. I had tugboats and barges. They would go to the Mediterranean. They would go into Alexandria, Egypt, to Cyprus. They would go to all these, you know, maybe unfriendly countries, and there was a reason for me to send people to go and make sure everything was being transacted properly, and that the vessels arrive on time, and things like that.[87]

In other words, Hale had an extremely effective cover story for the countries in which he operated. When Hale's book came out, reporters questioned Krongard about the assertions, but he kept a stony silence.

Hale's 2014 book had some interesting details about why Krongard had picked him.

Later, Hale was also told his help was desperately needed because of problems the Agency was having deploying operatives due to the so-called "Torricelli Principle," named after New

Jersey's controversial Democratic Congressman, Robert, "The Torch" Torricelli.[88]

Have we answered the question of whether the CIA uses leading American businessmen to conduct its operations? I think we have.

> Hale was now part of the shadowy CIA substratum of agents given non-official cover–known as NOCS and pronounced "knocks"– who typically posed as business executives. For the next nine years, Agency operatives purportedly working for him were dispatched to Uzbekistan, Cyprus, Egypt, Lebanon, and Jordan, among other countries where terrorists were known to operate.[89]

This arrangement worked out well for the most part, except for the time he was in Israel and interrogated by agents of the Shin Bet, Israel's internal security service, who were suspicious of some of his activities.

However, the attacks of September 11, 2001, changed his status with the Agency, as they finally had the justification they needed to take more extreme measures, without having to use people like Hale as a cut-out for their activities. As Hale recalled in his book:

> "The gloves were off then," he said. "The thinking (in the intelligence community) was: 'They killed 2,000 of our people? We're going to get them. And we don't care what anybody thinks, whether it's Mr. Torricelli or whoever. We're going after them.' That was the end of my career there."
>
> The Agency would call again a few years later, asking if Hale would return in a similar role. But he declined after talking with Maryland Sen. Barbara Mikulski, who advised him that the climate in the Agency had changed and that NOCS were no longer receiving the support they had in the past."[90]

Of course, when asked about it, the Democratic Senator of Maryland, and then chairwoman of the Senate Appropriations Committee says that she only has some vague knowledge of Hale's work with the CIA and "that's all I know"[91] I mean honestly, if you hear anything else in her words, you

THE CURIOUS CASE OF ALVIN BERNARD

must be a conspiracy theorist. It's interesting, though, how in the same paragraph, Mikulski could be both "circumspect," and ignorant.

That's a tough combination to pull off.

But while Senator Mikulski was apparently both circumspect and ignorant, Buzzy Krongard certainly wanted to talk about what he'd done. After all, the "shark-puncher" had spent a lifetime creating his own legend, sharing it with anybody who cared to listen.

As Freud said, nobody can keep a secret. Human beings want to share who they are. If we listen closely, we will learn exactly who they are. Around 2018, Buzzy did a video interview with his granddaughter who was working on a family history project, and his granddaughter posted it on the internet.

The story he tells is remarkable, of being recruited by the CIA from Princeton University in 1958, and for many of those years living a double life, a mystery even to his family. He explained that he was recruited by the dean of students at the university, and was working for the CIA even while he was at Alex Brown.[92] He goes on to explain that this was in the context of the Cold War and that when he officially joined the Agency it was like, "divorcing his wife and marrying his mistress."[93]

It's a pretty clear story that Krongard tells his granddaughter. The best colleges and universities in the 1950s had "talent scouts" for the CIA, who found promising talent, brought them into the office, and made an offer.

Once recruited, these top students would go into business, academia, maybe even the media, and try to rise to the top. All that time they're on the payroll of the CIA.

You may have thought there were only spies in the intelligence agencies.

But they might be anywhere.

The president of your local bank.

The professor at that prestigious Ivy League college.

The corporate CEO of that company in which you invested part of your stock portfolio.

Maybe that well-known political commentator or journalist who always seems to get the biggest scoops?

If you ran the CIA and wanted to control the United States, does this chapter suggest a way you might have done exactly that?

CHAPTER FOUR

I HAVE MY OWN PERSONAL EXPERIENCE WITH "PROJECT MOCKINGBIRD"

After nearly ten years of trying to get justice for my family and the health problems associated with living at the secret base, I'd had enough.

I recall the date I reached the end of my rope, the moment I realized there was no way of resolving this problem through the system, because the system was designed to prevent these kinds of problems from ever being solved.

That date was February 11, 2011.

It took me a while to get there.

Here are a few things that happened along the way.

In 2003, a federal district judge ordered the CIA to a mediated settlement on my claims, meaning the CIA had to submit their evidence to an impartial arbitrator, respond to my evidence, and accept the verdict of the arbitrator.

I would later learn that before the issuance of this order, the CIA asked for and received a "secret meeting" with the judge, without my lawyer present. They wanted to shut my case down.

But the judge wasn't having any of it. My lawyer later told me that the judge had told the CIA in that meeting, having already reviewed my evidence, "Well, it looks like Mr. Shipp has you over a barrel." Following the court ordered mediation and my presentation of the evidence of what my family and I had suffered, the CIA offered a $400,000 settlement offer, prior to the arbitrator issuing his ruling. I reproduce that settlement agreement below:

IN THE MATTER OF THE MEDIATION OF JOHN DOE, ET AL V. UNITED STATES OF AMERICA, W.D. TEX., NO. SA-02-CA-573-OG

Settlement Agreement in Principle

1. Pursuant to the Order of the Court dated December 2, 2003, this matter was mediated before Harold Himmelman. The parties have reached a full and complete settlement of all disputes between them, subject to the final approval of the United States, which approval must be provided no later than noon, Tuesday, December 16, 2003. Upon the approval of the United States, the parties shall execute a definitive settlement agreement on or before January 5, 2004.

2. The United States shall pay to Joel S., the sum of $175,000 and shall pay to Lorena S. and Kevin S. together the sum of $225,000. These payments shall be made within thirty days of the execution of the definitive settlement agreement.

3. The United States shall provide to Joel S. a letter of apology for the events that gave rise to this matter.

4. The United States shall provide to Joel S. and the Kevin S. and Lorena S. a letter assuring them that they are not under surveillance and that the United States has no intentions of placing them under surveillance.

5. The United States shall provide a letter to Kevin S. rolling back his cover to his date of entry on duty, subject to appropriate protections regarding the two years of his service in the matter leading to this litigation.

6. The United States shall provide a letter of commendation to Kevin S.

7. The parties will maintain in confidence the financial terms of this settlement agreement, except as to family members, tax, legal, and accounting advisors.
SO AGREED this 12th day of December, 2003.[94]

When your family has been harmed, as mine was, I don't think any amount of money can be thought of as genuine compensation for what they endured.

But it was a chance for the truth to be acknowledged, the war to be over, and we could begin to move on with our lives and have a couple dollars in our pockets.

We all signed the settlement agreement.

In an unprecedented move, three weeks later, I was told that CIA leadership refused to abide by the settlement agreement, invoking the "State Secrets" privilege to seal the evidence and witness testimony. In addition, they threatened my family and our attorneys that we would be sent to prison if we talked about it to anybody. I can only conclude this order came from the director of the CIA, George Tenet, as he was the listed defendant in the documents we filed with the court. And in the final meeting after I'd filed my suit, the security officer told me that the executive officer, Buzzy Krongard, had instructed her to take my security badge.

All along, I knew that Tenet and Krongard would be the eventual arbiters of my fate, but never imagined they would resort to such blatantly unjust tactics.

And of course, they offered a new settlement agreement, which was a fraction of what had been agreed to in the mediation, as well as removing the promises we would not be under further surveillance and that my service record would be cleaned up.

This is part of the letter from the US Department of Justice to my lawyer, sent on January 29, 2004, making the new offer as well as invoking the State Secrets privilege (referred to as "evidentiary privilege motion") in the document:

> [I]n the interests of settling the Doe case and relieving all parties of the burden, uncertainties, and expense of additional litigation, the United States extends a final settlement offer of $100,000 plus an additional $5,000 per year for ten years payable to the four remaining Plaintiffs in the cause. The Plaintiffs would be paid $150,000 by the government in addition to the $60,000 which they previously received from their insurer in the settlement of their state court case, thus their combined recoveries in the matter would total $210,000 exclusive of whatever health insurance benefits have

paid their medical bills. The parties must also agree to maintain in confidence the financial terms of the settlement, except to family members, tax, legal, and accounting advisors.

In order to allow you a reasonable time to communicate this offer to your clients, I seek your concurrence for the United States to move the Court for a one-week extension of the discovery stay until February 9, 2004. Please be advised that our office has received the appropriate authorization from the Justice Department and the client agency [CIA] to file the ***evidentiary privilege motion*** [bold and italics added by author] referenced in the Defendant's Unopposed Motion to Stay Discovery (filed on January 5, 2004).[95]

It's been my experience that most people can't believe that our own CIA would act in such a cavalier fashion to one of its own employees. Which is ironic, considering they're fine to believe the CIA could assassinate foreign leaders and overthrow governments.

But not take care of one of its own agents?

Inconceivable! The wall of stars in the lobby of the CIA is supposed to broadcast that even if an agent is gone, they are not forgotten.

I was the original straight-arrow, Johnny Patriot kind of officer, and even when the government harmed my family, I made sure to follow the letter and the spirit of the law, even if my superiors did not. Remember, one of my jobs at CIA was to assist in the declassification of sensitive material. I understood what could be declassified and what could not. When the government asserted the State Secrets privilege against my claim, my lawyer responded. This is part of what he wrote:

> Defendant is creating a "cover-up" of the evidence and cloaking the injury by claiming "National Security." In no other area of American jurisprudence is a defendant allowed to conceal the facts of a claim from a Plaintiff.As legal professionals we are bound to follow authorities and precedent, but for this situation there is no authority, no precedent, no guidance other than our knowledge that the decision made in this case will decide the future of "National Security." If a government defendant can stop a civil personal injury claim using National Security where will "the slippery slope" take

our jurisprudence? Will National Security trump a future conspiracy claim? What about a crime that occurs at the Location? What about a murder that occurs? Plaintiffs argue the courts must find a way to see that justice is served for both the injured citizen as well as the government. Our Constitution was drafted to protect the rights of the individual over the government. This case should be heard and the damages determined by the Court.

For these reasons, Plaintiffs ask the Court to deny Defendant's Assertion of State Secrets and other privileges, deny its motion, and set this case for trial.[96]

What was most remarkable about the assertion of the State Secrets Privilege was that from June 17, 2002, when we filed the case, until February 11, 2004, the CIA did not make an assertion of the State Secrets Privilege. There would later be accusations that CIA Director George Tenet was using the privilege to shut down any and all legal cases against the CIA, whether it be for personal injury or equal opportunity.[97]

Like a scene from *The Godfather,* you could say, "it wasn't personal," that Tenet was just trying to throw my case out along with all of the other trash, but for me it was intensely personal.

Despite the wonderful response of our attorney, the government triumphed in its assertion of the State Secrets Privilege against my case. We couldn't even talk to our representatives in Congress because the CIA issued an order making it illegal for Congress to talk to us as well.

While this fight was going on, I retained one of the best constitutional lawyers in the country, the famed Jonathon Turley, from George Washington University. But any possibility that I might use the services of this constitutional law expert were dashed in a March 26, 2004, letter from Assistant U.S. Attorney Glenn W. Taggart to one of my attorneys, G. P. Hardy III, which read in part:

Dear Mr. Hardy:

On behalf of the United States government and in light of your recent John Doe case filing of the Plaintiff's Motion to Allow Specialized counsel to Assist the Plaintiff's Response, I write to remind you and your clients of your obligations not to disclose any classified information to Mr. Jonathon Turley or any other third party unless and until the U.S. government has expressly authorized such persons to have access to classified information in this case. This is not to suggest or otherwise imply that you have or intend to make such disclosures.

In its discretion, the U.S. government has made certain accommodations to you regarding access to limited classified information in connection with this case. In return for these accommodations, you have agreed to abide by certain restrictions in the handling of classified information. I respectfully write to remind you of those restrictions and to provide you specific guidance so that you do not inadvertently commit any unauthorized disclosures of classified information. Therefore, you may not disclose any of these unclassified documents in their current form to Mr. Turley or any other third party in any manner associated with this civil action.

As you know, appropriate U.S. government authorities determined that you could maintain certain unclassified documents in your office so long as these documents were stored separately from and were not in any way associated with this case. When associated with this case, those documents contain information that becomes classified.[98]

That decision nearly broke me, and I do blame it for the break-up of my marriage to Lorena. I had dedicated my life to an organization which had hurt me and my family, and I couldn't do a thing about it.

Late one night, I lay in bed exhausted, drained from my battle with the CIA, feeling I could not go on. I believed the Lord had forsaken me and was on the verge of renouncing my faith. But like Jacob wrestling with the angel, I took one final shot. I raised my right hand and prayed, "Lord, please help me. I have no strength left and cannot do this anymore."

I got up the next morning as a man without faith. Just because of habit I decided to open the Bible one last time, my eyes falling on Isaiah 41: 10-13. I shuddered, feeling as if God was directly answering my prayer:

Fear thou not; for I am with thee: be not dismayed for I AM thy God: I will strengthen thee; yea, I will help thee; yea, I will uphold thee with the right hand of my righteousness.

> *Behold, all they that were incensed against thee shall be ashamed and confounded: they shall be as nothing; and they that strive with thee shall perish.*
>
> *Thou shalt seek them, and shall not find them, even them that contended with thee: they that war against thee shall be as nothing, and as a thing of nought.*
>
> *For I the LORD thy God will hold they right hand, saying unto thee, Fear not; I will help thee.*[99]

Three months later, George Tenet resigned from the CIA, ostensibly to spend more time with his family. But even NBC News couldn't cover up the disasters which had unfolded on Tenet's watch. They wrote:

> CIA Director George Tenet has resigned as director of Central Intelligence for "personal reasons," President Bush said in a surprise announcement. A government source told NBC news that the agency's director of operations, James Pavitt, would also announce his resignation on Friday.
>
> Although the resignations were said to be unrelated, the changes will bring a significant new look at the top of the CIA, which has been under fire for the way the agency monitored terrorist activity before Sept. 11, 2001 and for intelligence failures leading up to the war in Iraq.[100]

Let me give you a peek behind the curtain of official Washington. When a top official suddenly resigns to "spend more time with their family," you can be certain that's not the reason. Most of the time the family absolutely hates the son of a bitch, and they're secretly whispering to each other, "What the hell are we going to do with him home?"

More often than not, though, the family doesn't have to worry.

There's usually a cushy, well-paid consulting job waiting for them with a military-defense contractor to cushion the fall from power. The *NBC News* article put the final nail in the coffin of Tenet's reputation:

> During his seven years at the CIA, speculation at times has swirled around whether Tenet, 51, would retire or be forced out.

Even when his political capital appeared to be tanking, Tenet managed to hang on with what some said was a fierce loyalty to CIA personnel and to Bush, whose father was a predecessor in the post. A likeable, chummy personality also helped him become the second longest serving CIA director in history–only Allen Dulles stayed longer, from 1953 to 1961.[101]

It may sometimes take a while, a terrorist attack which kills three thousand Americans, and wrongly invading a country based on faulty claims of weapons of mass destruction, but eventually incompetence catches up to you. Tenet spent seven years as head of the CIA, and even *NBC News*, the most reliably pro-intelligence agency news network around, could only rouse itself to say Tenet had a "likeable, chummy personality?"

Where was the praise for his intellect, his judgment, his strategic vision?

They couldn't because even the Mockingbird media knew that was a lie too big to sell.

But even though God may have removed one obstacle, the road to justice for me and my family still had many miles for us to travel.

***

Thomas Jefferson once wrote, "When injustice becomes law, resistance becomes duty."

If I'd had any illusions that the CIA had gone rogue, their actions removed any lingering doubts for me. In my mind, the CIA, especially the Directorate of Operations, which I'd so long and loyally served, had become a criminal entity, able to control Congress and the courts. I'm not sure it's possible for people who have never been in such a no-win situation to understand how a single event so clarifies your thinking.

I recalled an adage I'd heard long ago, and it rang true for me: "You can mess with the man, but you don't mess with his family."

How many levels of guilt did I have as to what I'd put my family through in the past ten years?

Level one was the guilt of how I'd been a ghost to them for years when I was working as an undercover operative.

Level two was the guilt I felt over how in my effort to reconnect with them I was responsible for the move from our idyllic home in Virginia, to the toxic waste dump of a home at that secret base, sitting on top of mustard gas shells, and God knows what else.

Level three was the guilt I felt over the two years we lived in that house, the nightly terrors my children experienced, and the days when my beautiful wife could not get herself out of bed.

Level four was the guilt I felt over the fact that the CIA, where I had worked for seventeen years (and where my father had also worked), did nothing to take care of us, and actively sought to block us from any hope of financial or physical recovery.

Level five was the guilt I felt over the realization that the system, as designed and implemented by people like CIA Director Tenet, and his loyal lieutenant, "Buzzy" Krongard, did not care that we had been injured in the service of our country. Instead of honoring that sacrifice, they tried to throw us away in the garbage like a set of broken tools.

The truth is that for several years I wallowed in despair, bravely trying to put one foot in front of the other. While my case was working its way through the corrupt courts, I worked at the CIA as a polygraph examiner. When I was harassed on that job, I submitted a letter of resignation and got a job with the State Department, supervising the activities and safety of personnel overseas.

I might have been blackballed in the CIA, but in the relatively less corrupt State Department, I was something of a hero.

In September of 2007, I learned I had a partial blockage of one of the coronary arteries in my heart and needed surgery. I thought this was God offering me one last chance to save my family. I wrote a detailed memorandum of the events that had occurred, made sure all the information was unclassified, and sent it to every member of the House Permanent Committee on Intelligence (HPCI) and the Senate Select Committee on Intelligence (SSCI).

I survived the surgery without any complications, but my faith in Congress was a casualty. Nobody on either committee ever responded. (The one Congressman who did respond was Frank Wolf, my own representative, and he listened to our case and tried to get the Agency to respond. They never did.)

In early 2011, I contacted a *Washington Post* reporter. (I will protect his name for the sake of his career as I believe he is an honest reporter. What happened was not his decision.) I'd lost my fear of being prosecuted by the Agency.

In working on my story, I was careful not to violate any of my security oaths. When one realizes that a lot of information eventually becomes public, you can talk a great deal about a situation, while avoiding very specific questions.

It took four weeks for the *Washington Post* reporter to get all the facts right. Day after day the reporter contacted me, trying to get me to answer questions which would reveal classified information.

It appeared to me the questions were coming directly from his editor at the *Post*, whom I assumed was Bob Woodward, given the fact I'd gone onto the *Post* website and found he was the editor assigned to the national security beat. What I was told was that the reporter's editor would not let him publish the story until I provided what I knew to be classified information.

Finally, I'd had enough. I was not going to give the *Washington Post*, and by extension, the CIA, the ammunition that they would use against me. I told the reporter that he had all the information he needed, and if he didn't publish it in its current version, I'd go to the *New York Times*.

The reporter was panicked and begged for more time. I gave him a week, then called Charlie Savage, the national security reporter for the *New York Times*, who immediately began his own investigation.

The story was finished and published within a matter of days.

I believe that Bob Woodward was in place at the *Washington Post* as part of the modern iteration of Operation Mockingbird, to monitor and kill stories like mine that painted the intelligence agencies in a bad light.

What exactly is Operation Mockingbird?

I'm so glad you asked.

***

For those unfamiliar with the story of Project Mockingbird, let me quote from a 25,000-word essay written by Woodward's fellow Watergate journalist, Carl Bernstein, in October of 1977 and published in *Rolling Stone* magazine.

I've often wondered why Bernstein became so interested in the story of the CIA's collaboration with journalists, which they named "Project Mockingbird." Was it because Bernstein was worried he had been the victim of just such a campaign, when he'd been paired with first-year *Washington Post* reporter, Bob Woodward, who seemed to have all these amazing sources, and got the biggest scoops, that somebody like Bernstein, several years into the business, couldn't dream of getting?

Did it get under his skin that in the movie version of their book, *All the President's Men*, Woodward was portrayed by Hollywood heartthrob Robert Redford, inspiring generations of journalists, while Bernstein was portrayed by diminutive actor Dustin Hoffman, best known for male victim roles: being seduced by Anne Bancroft in *The Graduate*, left by his wife Meryl Streep in *Kramer vs. Kramer*, or being plagued with autism and abandoned in an institution by his family in the movie *Rainman*? In other words, Hoffman, while always bringing great humanity to his roles, was usually a sucker.

This is from Bernstein's article, an atonement, perhaps, for his work with Woodward:

> The history of the CIA's involvement with the American press continues to be shrouded by an official policy of obfuscation and deception for the following principal reasons:
>
> - The use of journalists has been among the most productive means of intelligence-gathering employed by the CIA. Although the Agency has cut sharply back on the use of reporters since 1973 (primarily as a result of media pressure), some journalist-operatives are still posted abroad.
> - Further investigation into the matter, CIA officials say, would inevitably reveal a series of embarrassing relationships in the 1950s and 1960s with some of the most powerful organizations and individuals in American journalism.[102]

How do people who study human psychology predict whether individuals will engage in certain behaviors? The simplest way to predict human behavior is to ask whether the behavior is beneficial to the person involved, or whether there will be a significant cost associated with it.

It's just a case of incentive and deterrence.

If the benefit outweighs the cost, it's a good bet the behavior will occur. We know that the Agency itself admitted to Bernstein that the use of journalists was "among the most productive means of intelligence-gathering" and that they were loath to reveal a "series of embarrassing relationships" with the top journalists of the time.

However, what was admitted by Agency officials, was truly mind-boggling.

It brings to mind the story of how easily Bank of Baltimore CEO, Ed Hale, was recruited by Buzzy Krongard, at the time the CEO of Alex Brown and Sons. It's as if the alpha males of American capitalism can't wait to add "CIA spy" to their resumes. This is more of Bernstein's article from *Rolling Stone* magazine.

> Among the executives who lent their cooperation to the Agency were William Paley of the Columbia Broadcasting System [CBS], Henry Luce of Time Inc., Arthur Hays Sulzberger of the *New York Times*, Barry Bingham Sr. of the *Louisville Courier-Journal*, and James Copley of the Copley News Service. Other corporations which cooperated with the CIA include the American Broadcasting Company [ABC], the National Broadcasting Company [NBC], the Associated Press, United Press International, Reuters, Hearst Newspapers, Scripps-Howard, *Newsweek* magazine, the Mutual Broadcasting System, the *Miami Herald*, and the old *Saturday Evening Post* and *New York Herald Tribune*.
>
> By far the most valuable of these associations, according to CIA officials, have been with the *New York Times*, CBS, and Time, Inc.[103]

Since we're talking about the CIA, we have to consider the possibility that they're lying. Maybe instead of believing the best allies of the CIA in journalism were the *New York Times*, CBS, and Time, Inc., we should be open that the biggest suck-ups to the CIA were actually the *Washington Post*, NBC, and maybe *LIFE* magazine. I'm not saying that's true. It's just that when dealing with an "admission" from the CIA, perhaps we should consider they're not telling us the whole truth. As an example, let's look at how Bernstein described the CIA strategy with journalists.

To understand the role of most journalist-operatives, it is necessary to dismiss some myths about undercover work for American intelligence services. Few American agents are "spies" in the popularly accepted sense of the term. "Spying"–to acquisition of secrets from a foreign government–is almost always done by foreign nationals who have been recruited by the CIA and are under CIA control in their own countries. Thus the primary role of an American working undercover abroad is often to aid in the recruitment and "handling" of foreign nationals who are channels of secret information reaching American intelligence.

Many journalists were used by the CIA to assist in this process and they had the reputation of being among the best in the business. The peculiar nature of the job of foreign correspondent is ideal for such work; he is accorded unusual access by his host country, permitted to travel in areas often off-limits to other Americans, spends much of his time cultivating sources in governments, academic institutions, the military establishment, and the scientific communities.[104]

We now understand that for the most part, CIA "agents" are foreign nationals, and the critical role of a CIA officer is to contact and "handle" the agent. But a problem might develop because the intelligence agency of the target country may already be aware of the identity of CIA employees with an interest in the country. The target country might be watching, hopeful that the CIA handler may try to contact his foreign "source" or "agent." The description of how a journalist might serve the CIA as a "handler" of foreign agent, thus avoiding this problem, continued:

> "After a foreigner is recruited, a case officer often has to stay in the background," explained a CIA official. "So you use a journalist to carry messages to and from both parties."
>
> Journalists in the field generally took their assignments in the same manner as any other undercover operative. If, for instance, a journalist was based in Austria, he ordinarily would be under the general direction of the Vienna station chief and report to a case officer. Some, particularly roving correspondents or U.S.-based

reporters who made frequent trips abroad, reported directly to CIA officials in Langley, Virginia.[105]

It can be a little sickening to realize how extensively the intelligence agencies have compromised journalists in the past, and the illusion most people have had regarding our "free press." The claims of dictators when they arrest our journalists as "spies" seems to have a little more merit than many are comfortable to admit. While for the most part their job consisted of being the "eyes and ears" of the CIA, they sometimes took on more extensive operations.

> On other occasions, their assignments were more complex: planting subtly concocted pieces of misinformation; hosting parties or receptions designed to bring together American agents and foreign spies; serving up "black" propaganda to leading foreign journalists at lunch or dinner; providing their hotel rooms or bureau offices as "drops" for highly sensitive information moving to and from foreign agents; conveying instructions and dollars to CIA controlled members of foreign governments.[106]

Ask yourself whether the CIA teaching journalists the skills of spies is an effort we should encourage. Bernstein's article details that the Agency was teaching journalists how to place "misinformation" into the public debate, serve up "black propaganda" (fake documents or reports which appear to originate from the group you are targeting), and how to bribe public officials.

With the collapse of public confidence in the American media taking place so quickly, one wonders if the answer can be found in the CIA using these same methods a few too many times to undermine American democracy with phony journalism, in the same way they have so often practiced in foreign countries. How are we to determine which stories are "misinformation," whether supposed evidence against an individual or political group was in fact "manufactured" by the CIA, and who in the public might be receiving under the table payoffs from the intelligence agencies?

One would hope the media isn't as willing a partner in this cloak and dagger game as the alpha males of American capitalism. With that in mind, Bernstein paints a picture of a more subtle approach used by the CIA in its seduction of journalists.

> Often the CIA's relationship with a journalist might begin infor-
> mally with a lunch, a casual exchange of information. An Agency
> official might offer them a favor—for example, a trip to a country
> difficult to reach; in return, he would seek nothing more than the
> opportunity to debrief the reporter afterward. A few more lunches,
> a few more favors, and only then might there be mention of a for-
> mal arrangement—"That came later," said a CIA official, "after you
> had the journalist on a string."[107]

They say the devil never forces you to do something, but persuades you with clever lies, and appeals to your vanity. It starts as an innocent flirtation, the exchange of favors, then into an "arrangement," and the next thing you know, you're setting up a meeting with a government official to betray his country, and letting the CIA use your apartment to consummate the deal.

As a former CIA officer, I have a great deal of sympathy for what a typical journalist might have been experiencing. The public at large generally holds the intelligence agencies, whether that by CIA, the FBI, or others, with a great deal of respect. If you doubt me, think what you would do if you heard a knock on your door, opened it to find a well-dressed man and woman, one of them flipped open their wallet and presented you with identification, and said, "We're from the FBI/CIA, and wanted to ask you a few questions. Is it all right if we come in?" Even now, I think ninety-five percent of the public would say, "Well, I guess so. Come on in. What's this about?"

I'm here to tell you that if such a thing ever happens, your proper response is, "No thank you. If you have any questions to ask me, that will happen in the presence of my lawyer."

Then you close the door and lock it.

You are an American and you have rights, but you have to assert them.

If the intelligence agencies are coming to talk to you, it's likely that they don't have your best interests at heart.

Look what happened to General Michael Flynn, Trump's pick in 2017 for the director of National Intelligence, who wanted to reorganize the intelligence agencies in a manner more consistent with their original mission. He said yes when two agents from the FBI sent over by FBI Director James Comey, asked to question him in the hopes that the general would say something they could call a lie and charge him. The agents knew Flynn should have had his lawyer present for any interview, but wanted to quickly remove, if possible, what they perceived as the greatest threat to their corrupt establishment.

And in case you forgot, it worked.

It's important to understand the past in order to create a successful future.

Let's return for a final time to Bernstein's article about the CIA and the media, for a more complete picture of how this monstrosity was created:

> Many journalists who covered World War II were close to people in the Office of Strategic Services [OSS], the wartime predecessor of the CIA; more important, they were all on the same side. When the war ended and many OSS officials went into the CIA, it was only natural that these relationships would continue. Meanwhile, the first postwar generation of journalists entered the profession; they shared the same political and professional values as their mentors. "You had a gang of people who worked together during World War II and never got over it," said one Agency official. "They were genuinely motivated and highly susceptible to intrigue and being on the inside. Then in the Fifties and Sixties there was a national consensus about a national threat. The Vietnam War tore everything to pieces–shredded the consensus and threw it in the air."[108]

With the collapse of the national consensus brought about by the Vietnam War, as well as other social problems, the media, after decades of debauchery because of their association with the intelligence agencies and hoodwinking the American public, suddenly declared themselves "born-again virgins" dedicated to holding the powerful to account.

But the joke was on us.

The puppet-masters in the shadows are still pulling the strings.

***

Poor Congressman Mike Johnson, the former Speaker of the House of Representatives, will one day have written in his obituary that he was the biggest chump of the intelligence agencies.

All in all, Johnson seemed a decent enough guy, a family man, a dedicated Christian, and most importantly for this story, a strong critic of the Foreign Intelligence Surveillance Court, developed as a result of the Foreign Intelligence Surveillance Act (FISA).

The wake-up call for many Americans came during the 2016 presidential election when candidate Donald Trump made what seemed like an insane claim, that his campaign was being surveilled by the intelligence agencies. Was that the first time the intelligence agencies intruded into our politics, or was it the first time they so clearly showed themselves? And if they'd been in our politics in 2016, were they still there today?

In December 2019, the Office of the Inspector General for the US Department of Justice under Michael Horowitz released what for many was a definitive answer to the question of whether the 2016 Trump campaign had been spied upon by our intelligence agencies.

The answer was clearly "yes," and the question was whether the surveillance had been legally authorized, and the appropriate laws had been followed. The background of the executive summary detailed what had led to the investigation:

> The Department of Justice (Department) Office of the Inspector General (OIG) undertook this review to examine certain actions by the Federal Bureau of Investigation (FBI) and the Department during an FBI investigation opened on July 31, 2016, known as "Crossfire Hurricane," into whether individuals associated with the Donald J. Trump for President Campaign were coordinating, wittingly or unwittingly, with the Russian government's efforts to interfere in the 2016 U.S. presidential election. Our review included examining:
>
> • The decision to open Crossfire Hurricane and four individual cases on current and former members of the Trump campaign, George Papadopoulos, Carter Page, Paul Manafort, and Michael Flynn; the early investigative steps

taken; and whether the openings and early steps complied
with Department and FBI policies;

- The FBI's relationship with Christopher Steele, whom the
  FBI considered to be a confidential human source (CHS);
  its receipt, use, and evaluation of election reports from
  Steele; and its decision to close Steele as an FBI CHS;

- Four FBI applications filed with the Foreign Intelligence
  Surveillance Court (FISC) in 2016 and 2017 to conduct
  Foreign Intelligence Surveillance Act (FISA) surveillance
  targeting Carter Page; and whether these applications
  complied with Department and FBI policies and satisfied
  the government's obligations to the FISC;

- The interactions of Department attorney Bruce Ohr with
  Steele, the FBI, Glenn Simpson of Fusion GPS, and the
  State Department; whether work Ohr's spouse performed
  for Fusion GPS implicated ethical rules applicable to Ohr;
  and Ohr's interactions with Department attorneys regarding
  the Manafort criminal case; and

- The FBI's use of undercover employees (UCEs) and CHSs
  other than Steele in the Crossfire Hurricane investigation;
  whether the FBI placed any CHSs within the Trump
  campaign or tasked any CHSs to report on the Trump
  campaign; whether the use of CHSs and UCEs complied
  with Department and FBI policies; and the attendance of a
  Crossfire Hurricane supervisory agent at counterintelligence
  briefings given to the 2016 presidential candidates and
  certain campaign advisors.[109]

One of the things which I've found most conservatives don't fully appreciate is how there are many parts of the government that are trying to do the
right thing, such as the Office of the Inspector General.

Conservatives and liberals should love the Office of the Inspector
General, because for good or ill, they seek to find the truth, no matter
where it leads. When it comes to the government, it's important to realize
that powerful institutions create their own rules, and then often see how
close they can come to bending, without breaking them. The investigation

into Crossfire Hurricane shows a clear attempt to walk up to that line, per-haps not violating the letter, but certainly the spirit of that law. It should also be concerning to the public how often members of the intelligence community, which initiated Crossfire Hurricane against the Trump cam-paign, pled a poor memory in response to the most important questions, in a style not much different than a common criminal.

This is what the report had to say about Christopher Steele, the author of the infamous "Steele Dossier," which was the document that allowed the Crossfire Hurricane investigation to be approved. (Steele was a former British intelligence officer who joined their Secret Intelligence Service in 1987 and ran the Russia desk at MI6 headquarters in London from 2006 to 2009.)

> As we describe in Chapter Four, Steele is a former intelligence offi-cer [BLACKED OUT] who, in 2009, formed a consulting firm specializing in corporate intelligence and investigative services. In 2010, Steele was introduced by Ohr to an FBI agent, and for sev-eral years provided information to the FBI about various matters, such as corruption in the International Federation of Association Football (FIFA). Steele also provided the FBI agent with reporting about Russian oligarchs.
>
> In 2013, the FBI completed paperwork allowing the FBI to des-ignate Steele as a CHS [Confidential Human Source] However, as described in Chapter Four, we found that the FBI and Steele held significantly differing views about the nature of their relationship. Steele's handling agent viewed Steele as a former intelligence officer colleague and FBI CHS, with obligations to the FBI. Steele, on the other hand, told us that he was a businessperson whose firm (not Steele) had a contractual arrangement with the FBI and whose obligations were to his paying clients, not the FBI.[110]

Most chilling of all, CIA Director John Brennan leaked the Russian collusion story to the mainstream media,[111] calling it "intelligence." Brennan knew exactly which Mockingbird outlets would run with it.

And if you want further evidence of the collusion between the CIA and the Department of Justice, I suggest you'll find our expose of two-time attorney general of the United States, William "Bill" Barr, to be very illuminating. His smooth, pontificating style is the perfect cover for a closet representative of the national security state.

Sometimes it's helpful to have a former analyst for the CIA to help you wade through all the deception.

One of the concepts helpful to have in mind is that people can be criminal in their actions, and ALSO stupid.

There are a few evil geniuses in the world, and you can marvel at the sophistications of their plans, but most of the chaos agents you come across function at barely above idiot level.

Let's go through all the problems associated with letting Christopher Steele, the former British intelligence officer, become such a critical part of the American political process.

The first warning flag is that he was an intelligence agent for a foreign power. (Yes, I understand it was for jolly, old England, but our interests may not always align. Remember the Revolutionary War, for instance?)

The second is that he worked the Russia desk from 2006 to 2009, which means that by 2016 the Russians had certainly identified him, and thus any information he received from his Russian "sources" would have to be considered potentially suspect.

The third concern is what Steele has really been doing in the seven years since he allegedly stopped working for British intelligence. (It's common to say there's no such thing as a "former" intelligence agent, regardless of the country. Maybe you'll give me a little more latitude since the Agency tried to kill me and my family.) The big scoop he'd been able to provide was to show corruption in professional soccer and pass some information on Russian oligarchs to the FBI.

The fourth, and possibly most concerning problem, is that the FBI and Steele had vastly different views of their relationship. The FBI considered him one of the team, a "former intelligence officer colleague" and CHS.

But Steele didn't consider himself that way at all.

In his mind, he had no allegiance to the FBI, and it was simply his firm that had an obligation to his paying clients. (And as has been revealed, the ultimate source of the funds to hire Steele was Hillary Clinton, Trump's democratic opponent in the 2016 presidential election.)

In a later section of the report, it details how Steele, the former British intelligence officer, was able to easily insert himself into the media, showing that at the very least, the operational protocols of Project Mockingbird were still in place.

> However, as we describe later, as the FBI obtained additional information raising significant questions about the reliability of the Steele election reporting, the FBI failed to reassess the Steele reporting relied upon in the FISA applications and did not fully advise NSD or OI officials. We also found that the FBI did not aggressively seek to obtain certain potentially important information from Steele. For example, the FBI did not press Steele for information about the actual funding source for his election reporting work. Agents also did not question Steele about his role in a September 23, 2016 *Yahoo News* article entitled, "*U.S. Intel Officials Probe Ties Between Trump Advisor and Kremlin*," that described efforts by U.S. intelligence to determine whether Carter Page had opened communication channels with Kremlin officials. As we discuss in Chapters Five and Eight, the FBI assessed in the Carter Page FISA applications, without any support, that Steele had not "directly provided" the information to *Yahoo News*.[112]

Here's how this CIA analyst interprets the actions of my domestic intelligence agency brethren at the FBI. They wanted to get Trump, and decided that if they got caught, they could simply plead that they did a bad job at verifying the allegations. After all, government officials don't get fired for incompetence. Some would say it's in the job description, right?

And for those who might question whether Steele's reporting was critical to the opening of the investigation, this is what the report found: "We determined that the Crossfire Hurricane team's receipt of Steele's election reporting on September 19, 2016 played a central and essential role in the FBI's and Department's decision to seek the FISA order."[113]

No Steele dossier bought and paid for by Hillary Clinton and no Russia collusion scandal, General Michael Flynn gets to work reengineering the intelligence agencies, maybe we get peace in North Korea, the Middle East moves toward peace with Israel signing more treaties with their neighbors, the war plans of Iran die for lack of money, and Russia never invades

Ukraine because Trump knows that pushing Ukraine towards NATO membership is a red line for Putin.

I think that's what a Trump first term would have looked like if it hadn't been hobbled by the Russia collusion hoax.

But let's jump back to the inspector general's report on the Russian collusion story and specifically, the work of Christopher Steele.

> FBI efforts to verify information in the Steele election reports, and to learn about Steele and his source network continued after Steele's closure as a CHS. In November and December 2016, FBI officials travelled abroad and met with persons who previously had professional contacts with Steele or had knowledge of his work. Information these FBI officials obtained about Steele was both positive and negative. We found, however, that the information about Steele was not placed in his FBI CHS file.
>
> We further learned that the FBI's Validation Management Unit (VMU) completed a human source validation review of Steele in early 2017. The VMU review found that Steele's past criminal reporting was "minimally corroborated," and included this finding in its report to the Crossfire Hurricane team. The determination of the VMU was in tension with the source characterization statement included in the initial FISA application, which represented that Steele's prior reporting had been "corroborated and used in criminal proceedings." The VMU review also did not identify any corroboration for Steele's election reporting among the information that the Crossfire Hurricane team had collected.[114]

This is where it gets difficult for me to restrain my anger. The investigation of a suspected crime, especially one that involves our election system, is of the highest importance. Let's assume for the sake of argument, that the initial suspicions of the Trump campaign colluding with Russia were well-founded.

I don't think the evidence suggests that, but let's say it did.

Every investigator has drilled into them the perils of tunnel-vision, accepting facts that fit your narrative, and disregarding those which do not.

That's why it's important to have a different set of eyes reviewing your work, like the Validation Management Unit, and including their work as part of the record. An investigator never omits critical information simply because it goes against his narrative.

What I see in the inspector general's report makes me angry because I know there are good people in government who are trying to do their job with integrity. They are real, they work hard, and for the most part, you will never know their names.

Christopher Steele's work was of questionable quality. That fact is undisputed. It's what the inspector general's report found. And yet, it was relied upon to continue the investigation into Trump. When one sees such a violation of procedure, the assumption has to be that the reason given for continuing the investigation is suspect.

Let's investigate the facts regarding the first person who was the subject of a FISA warrant, Carter Page, who was suspected of being a Russian agent. In retrospect, the claim was comical because Page had actually been an asset for the CIA against Russia. But of course, such information was omitted from the FISA request.

> Omitted information the FBI had obtained from another government agency [CIA] detailing its prior relationship with Page, including that Page had been approved as an "operational contact" for the other agency from 2008 to 2013, and that Page had provided information to the other agency concerning his prior contacts with certain Russian intelligence officers, one of which overlapped with facts asserted in the FISA application;[115]

How outlandish was this chain of events?

The FBI said they needed a FISA warrant on Carter Page because he might be a Russian asset.

But in fact, it turns out he was an asset for our CIA against the Russians and the FBI knew this information. It's like saying black is white, day is night, and water is dry.

Okay, you might be saying to yourself, the FBI made a major mistake in their FISA application to surveil the first person on the Trump campaign, Carter Page.

But you're sure that's probably the only significant mistake they made.
Nope.
Not even close.

We identified at least 17 significant errors or omissions in the Carter Page FISA applications, and many additional errors in the Woods Procedures. These errors and omissions resulted from case agents providing wrong or incomplete information to OI and failing to flag important issues for discussion. While we did not find documentary or testimonial evidence of intentional misconduct on the part of the case agents who assisted OI in preparing the applications, or the agents and supervisors who performed the Woods Procedures, we also did not receive satisfactory explanations for the errors or problems we identified.

In most instances, the agents and supervisors told us that they either did not know or recall why the information was not shared with OI, that the failure to do so may have been an oversight, that at the time they did not recognize the relevance of the information to the FISA application, or that they did not believe the missing information to be significant. On this last point, we believe the case agents may have improperly substituted their own judgments in place of the judgment of the OI, or in place of the court, to weigh the probative value of the information.[116]

How did the agents and supervisors keep their jobs? Seventeen significant errors or omissions with the Carter Page applications, which is what opened an intelligence agency investigation on a presidential candidate and sitting president of the United States? If this happened in a foreign country, we'd be imposing sanctions on them for violating the principles of a democracy.

How were charges not brought against these government employees, if for no other reason than to get to the bottom of their completely inadequate responses, not being able to remember information, or failing to "recognize the relevance of the information," or the weaselly excuse that "they did not believe the missing information to be significant?"

For the life of me, I cannot understand the restrained language of the inspector general's report, pointing out to everybody who has the slightest amount of sense and ability to read, that this was nothing less than a "hit job" on Donald Trump.

Were these appalling lapses in judgment and procedures limited just to the FBI's investigation of Donald Trump?

If so, that might provide some solace to the general public, which would rightfully condemn the attack on a political figure but might think of these actions as an aberration.

However, inspector Michael Horowitz continued his investigation of the FBI's use of the FISA process for surveilling Americans in twenty-nine applications, chosen at random, and reported those findings in March of 2020.

> Horowitz says the FBI could not locate that supporting documentation, known as a Woods File, in four of the 29 cases. In three of the instances, the IG says, the FBI did not know whether the files ever existed.
>
> In every case in which the FBI could locate the Woods File, the IG found significant problems with the documentation.
>
> "Our testing of FISA applications to the associated Woods Files identified apparent errors or inadequately supported facts in all of the 25 applications we reviewed," the inspector general says.
>
> "At this time, we have identified an average of about 20 issues per application reviewed, with a high of approximately 65 issues in one application and less than 5 issues in another application."[117]

How was the sloppiness of the FISA application process not one of the biggest stories of the year? Maybe it had something to do with the fact that a little thing called COVID-19 was in the middle of shutting down the country? How fortunate that timing was for the dark side.

But a virus will come and go.

What about a permanent threat to American liberty, as I believe the Foreign Intelligence Surveillance Act (FISA) to be? A secret court, convened without the knowledge of the accused, a judge and no jury, violating the privacy of the accused without a warrant, and unleashing the awesome power of the national security state on an American citizen. In what world in which human beings exist, can this be anything other than a horrible idea?

However, in order to understand how things go from bad to worse, let's do a case study of a relatively obscure congressman, Mike Johnson, who has recently found himself thrust onto the public stage. We'll show how Johnson went from being a FISA critic as an unknown congressman, to being the Speaker of the House and casting the deciding vote in reauthorizing the FISA law for another four years, and removing the need for the intelligence agencies to get a warrant at all.

And it's all because the intelligence agencies whispered in his ear.

Mike Johnson even admits it.

***

When Mike Johnson became Speaker of the House on October 26, 2023, after a no-confidence vote for the previous Speaker, Kevin McCarthy, many were hopeful that the country now had a strong constitutional conservative who would rein in the excesses of the surveillance state.

If there were those with any doubts, they need only read a joint letter that Johnson, then the ranking member of the Subcommittee on the Constitution, Civil Rights, and Civil Liberties, drafted with Congressman Jim Jordan on January 27, 2022, to the director of the FBI, Christopher Wray. In one section, Johnson and Jordan wrote:

> Section 702 authorizes the Attorney General and the Director of National Intelligence, subject to limitations, to jointly authorize warrantless surveillance of non-U.S. persons reasonably believed to be located outside the United States. In November 2020, the Foreign Intelligence Surveillance Court (FISC) issued a memorandum opinion and order finding that the FBI had committed "apparent widespread violations" of privacy rules in conducting surveillance under section 702 of FISA.
>
> In addition to those documented concerns raised by the FISC, the DOJ's Office of Inspector General (OIG) has issued troubling reports over the last several years suggesting a pattern of abuses and deficiencies in the FBI's internal FISA process. Most recently, in

September 2021, the OIG issued a detailed report–confirming its March 2020 initial findings–of widespread noncompliance with Woods Procedures, which are an internal FBI process to minimize factual inaccuracies in FISA applications by requiring the FBI to maintain supporting documentation for each factual assertion in the application. The September 2021 report documented over 400 instances of non-compliance with the Woods Procedures in connection with 29 FISA applications. The OIG also found that out of over 7,000 FISA applications approved between January 2015 and March 2020, there were 183 FISA applications for which the Woods File was missing in whole or in part. This lack of documentation suggests, at best, the FBI maintains sloppy oversight of its use of warrantless spying authorities. At worst, it suggests the FBI holds a cavalier disregard for the fundamental protections enshrined in the Bill of Rights.[118]

There can be no doubt that Congressman Johnson was aware of the problems with the FISA process and its numerous violations of the "fundamental protections enshrined in the Bill of Rights." Remember, when the inspector general examined twenty-nine random FISA applications, they found an average of twenty factual errors in each application, in addition to three applications in which there was no supporting Woods Procedure fact file. How forgiving do you think the IRS would be if you averaged about twenty errors every year when you submitted your taxes to them?

Protecting the freedoms enshrined in our Bill of Rights should be the hill that any politician, regardless of their political philosophy, should die on, right? However, if one followed the debate, you got the sense that there was some enormous, unseen force, like a massive black hole in the center of our political community, pulling politicians away from doing what they knew to be right, and handing over even more power to the intelligence community.

And it isn't as if Johnson didn't have strong support from the public. From a December 13, 2023, article in *Newsweek*:

> U.S. House Speaker Mike Johnson will feel the wrath of his party if he pushes warrantless surveillance, according to former National Security Agency intelligence contractor Edward Snowden.

Johnson, who has been in his role for about two months following the ouster of Speaker Kevin McCarthy on October 3, could face a similar political fallout based on his approach to defense spending and including an extension of the Foreign Intelligence Surveillance Act (FISA) within the National Defense Authorization Act (NDAA), an annual bill that is instrumental to authorizing funding for the Department of Defense (DOD).

A list of internal talking points obtained by Axios shows Johnson being compared to ex-Republican House Speaker John Boehner, including one memo that refers to this year's NDAA as "an utter disaster for House Republicans and a massive unforced error from leadership."[119]

For those who believe "things just happen," it's interesting to see how early into Johnson's speakership he was considering betraying his previously stated position about FISA.

When one considers the enormous amount of criticism heaped upon the FISA court and the way the FBI was cavalierly trampling on the Bill of Rights, it would seem there would be two reasonable responses.

The first would be to let the FISA authority expire. The FISA court had been established in 1977 and it certainly hadn't stopped the September 11th attackers in 2001.

The second would be to pass FISA with additional protective provisions and strong punishments for violations.

The *Newsweek* article continued:

U.S. intelligence officials argue that FISA Section 702 allows their agencies to conduct warrantless surveillance of non-American citizens outside the U.S. during investigations.

However, privacy concerns exist among many Americans and some members of Congress based on information collected on U.S. citizens that could be stored in the form of various communications for a number of years as part of a wide-ranging database.

Other vocal house Republicans chastising Johnson included Georgia Representative Marjorie Taylor Greene, who on Wednesday claimed collusion between Johnson and Democrats based on multiple measures included in the final draft of the NDAA.[120]

Again, for my tastes, this take is far too soft on the intelligence agencies. They are spying in a wholesale manner inconsistent with the Fourth Amendment guarantees of privacy from unreasonable searches, and the *Newsweek* article portrayed the case as if a person accidentally stepped on somebody's toes while waiting in line for coffee at Starbucks. Give me Edward Snowden every time for telling the public just what's at stake.

> "If Mike Johnson (@SpeakerJohnson) abuses the NDAA to smuggle into law an extension of the warrantless surveillance regime (FISA 702) that the FBI exploited to spy ON AMERICANS more than TWO HUNDRED THOUSAND times in JUST ONE YEAR, he should be dumped just like McCarthy," Snowden, who remains exiled in Russia after leaking classified documents in 2013, wrote on X. "No excuse."[121]

However, much worse was to come.

And the powers that be would try to explain Johnson's flip-flop as an "evolution" rather than a betrayal of the American people. This is how Johnson's change of heart was described in an April 11, 2024, article in *The Hill*:

> The battle over the nation's warrantless surveillance powers is highlighting the evolution of Speaker Mike Johnson (R-La.) a one-time critic of the foreign spy program who's now fighting to usher its renewal through his warring GOP conference.
>
> It's a role that put Johnson at odds with both former President Trump and his former colleagues on the House Judiciary Committee, where like other GOP members he could be counted on to blast what they see as government overreach.
>
> "These were views that the Speaker deeply held, like 20 minutes ago," Rep. Matt Gaetz (R-Fla.) said Wednesday shortly before leading an effort to tank a procedural vote that would have kicked off debate on the broader FISA reform bill.[122]

To what can we attribute this massive change in Johnson's opinion? In the view of political commentator Tucker Carlson in an interview for the Joe Rogan podcast in April of 2024, Carlson expressed the view that when one is an "empty vessel," as is the case with most politicians, including Mike Johnson, it's easy for evil to get a foothold in their soul.

The move also seemed puzzling to Johnson's former colleague on the Judiciary Committee, Texas congressman Chip Roy.

> The whole lead-up prompted lawmakers like Rep. Chip Roy (R-Texas) to accuse Johnson of tipping the scales against his former Judiciary colleagues.
>
> "What we ended up with was a bill that didn't have the warrant protections in the bill. It was going to be force added as an amendment. And then the Speaker of the House put his finger on the scale against the amendment. And that pretty much is the story," said Roy.[123]

The amendment being considered was that the FBI would need to get a warrant to look at the communications of any American swept up in the communications of a foreign individual. Civil libertarians were concerned that this innocuous sounding problem was an exception through which the intelligence agencies would use as wide-scale justification for spying on any American they wanted.

And what was Johnson's stated reason for changing his position on this issue? Thankfully, he tells us, but his answer raises even more troubling questions.

> "When I was a member of the Judiciary, I saw all of the abuses of the FBI–there were terrible abuses, over and over," Johnson told reporters in the Capitol on Wednesday evening.
>
> "And then when I became Speaker, I went to the SCIF and got the confidential briefing from sort of the other perspective on that, to understand the necessity of Section 702 of FISA and how important it is for national security. And it gave me a different perspective," he continued, using an abbreviation for sensitive compartmented information facility (SCIF).[124]

Here's what's so deeply wrong with Johnson's statement, which no matter how you interpret it, states clearly that the intelligence services control the United States government.

The intelligence agencies bring you into the SCIF and tell you their "secrets," like maybe they've used FISA to disrupt four potential nuclear attacks on the United States.

You don't know if the claim is true, and can't do the slightest amount of investigation, or tell a single person what you heard, or else you have broken the law.

Whether you believe this is a good arrangement, or a terrible one, you have to admit that it means the intelligence agencies are controlling our government.

Whether the intelligence agencies are lying or telling the truth, they're controlling our government.

I think this is a terrible arrangement, not just because I distrust the intelligence agencies, but because I have an appreciation of human nature. If you tell people they will never be challenged for telling lies, you will get people telling a lot more lies.

Since both Mike Johnson and the intelligence agencies are comfortable allowing this black box situation to exist, where we, the public, don't even get a sanitized version of the information discussed, our imaginations run wild with all sorts of scenarios.

All of us are in the dark with this secrecy.

And that is the problem.

***

When the powerful interests win, perhaps the only thing one can do is document the record for history. Senator Rand Paul was one of the first voices against the decision of Speaker Johnson, and he wasted little time in telling Fox host, Maria Bartiromo, that the Republican Speaker was little different than a Democrat. The military-intelligence-industrial complex which controls both parties had won again:

> "Speaker Johnson was incredibly wrong," Paul said in a "Fox News Sunday" interview. "He broke the tie. He voted with the Democrats. Here we have the leader of the Republicans in the House votes with the Democrats against a warrant requirement."

"We also have Speaker Johnson voting for the spending package [$95 billion for Ukraine, Israel, & Taiwan] once again with a majority of the Democrats," he continued. "As I see it now, I'm not sure there's a difference between Mike Johnson being in charge and the Democrats being in charge."

The FISA amendment vote was bipartisan, with 86 Republicans–including Johnson–and 126 Democrats voting against it. Paul, a libertarian-minded conservative, was a major Senate backer of the FISA amendment.[125]

Polls clearly showed that voters did not want these programs, but the permanent establishment Deep State and the intelligence community blob did want them. So, the measures passed.

It doesn't take a CIA analyst to realize that when there is such an enormous gulf between what the public wants, and what our politicians give us, that some unseen force, more powerful than the citizenry, is acting upon the country. Congressman Thomas Massie and others were even more eloquent as to what was being done.

Massie wrote: "This is how the Constitution dies. By a tie vote, the amendment to require a warrant to spy on Americans goes down in flames. This is a sad day for America. The Speaker doesn't always vote in the House, but he was the tie breaker today. He voted against warrants."

. . . "Today is a dark day for America," Rep. Troy Nehls (R-TX) said in a written statement after the vote. "It is no secret that the DOJ and FBI have used and abused FISA to spy not only on the greatest president of my lifetime, Donald J. Trump, but spy on everyday Americans. I could not, in good conscience, vote to give our nation's weaponized DOJ the power to mass surveil the American people without significant reforms, such as a warrant requirement."[126]

I know that, for many, these developments will seem overwhelming and leave you in a state of hopelessness. However, I see this as a remarkable development, proving to me that every day the shadow government is losing more power.

Why do I say that?

Because it's only in the shadows that one can exert their malign influence and get the public to ignore what you're doing. When you step into the light so boldly, people start to take notice.

The original Patriot Act in 2001 passed 98-1 in the Senate.

We believed that the intelligence agencies would protect us.

That understanding no longer exists.

I entered the CIA in the 1980s when the Cold War was in full swing, and the Soviet Empire looked invincible. However, we would learn that what looked like a crack-down, was the beginning of a crack-up.

The jewel of the Soviet Empire in Eastern Europe was undoubtedly East Germany.

In 1989, East Germany, with a population of a little more than sixteen million people, had an estimated two million people working as collaborators for their intelligence service, the dreaded and brutal Stassi.

And yet the Berlin Wall still came down on November 9, 1989, with East and West Germans breaking down sections of that dreaded barrier with sledgehammers to reunite their people in a celebration of freedom.

In East Germany, at the time the wall fell, one out of every eight people was likely to be informing for the government. That doesn't seem to make sense.

We mistakenly believe that the more people working for the government as spies, the stronger the government would be from challenges to its authority.

However, once the Rubicon of absurdity has been passed, the number of people secretly working for the government has an inverse effect, creating additional challenges. You can't hide in the shadows when you're bringing so much attention to yourselves. It's as if the CIA has been possessed by the braggart soul of Buzzy Krongard, and can't stop talking about how important they are, how their secrets can only be entrusted to certain people, then turn around and say they're defending democracy.

This is the thing that the intelligence agencies, with their lies and likely bullying of Speaker Mike Johnson, don't understand.

You can't avoid the attention of the public when you take the Speaker of the House into a secret facility, tell him secret things, then say this representative of the people can't say those secret things, and then get Johnson to be your sock puppet when he says the citizens just have to trust him.

People will accept a lot of lies, but that one goes just a little too far.

The shadow government will collapse when it's clear to a majority of Americans that they only have the power we give them.

And like smelling rain in the air and seeing dark clouds on the horizon, I'm sensing that time is nearly upon us.

***

CHAPTER FIVE

THE DEADLIEST MAN IN THE CIA: TED SHACKLEY – EASTERN EUROPE TO THE KENNEDY ASSASSINATION

"We've finished an internal investigation into the vulnerability of the cover of CIA agents," said Jim Callahan, the investigator for the Inspector General's Office, former CIA agent and recipient of the CIA Intelligence Medal for Heroism. I felt like one of the knights at King Arthur's table. I was sitting on one side of a long table with a clutch of executives from the IG's office, while the acting head of the Operations Directorate of the CIA, William Sullivan, sat cowering at the other end.

The senior inspector general official stood up and in a strong voice said, "The threat is real, you were informed about it, and you failed to act. You and the CIA are officially rebuked for intentionally covering up this issue, refusing to address it, and placing the lives of CIA officers overseas in danger for more than a decade."

As you know, I reached this moment in 1998 only by going around my superiors, enlisting help from outside the CIA, and even though I would receive a commendation for my work, I knew there would be a target on my back.

But little did I know the targeting would likely come from the CIA's most notorious assassin.

After the bombshell report I'd authored on the CIA's intentional negligence was published to the entire intelligence community, I received a call from the Directorate of Operations.

I was advised that the legendary spymaster, Ted Shackley, wanted to talk with me about how the Agency was going to deal with my report.

How do I justify calling Ted Shackley a "spymaster"? Well, you don't have to believe me. You just have to look up the title of Ted's own posthumously published autobiography, entitled *Spymaster: My Life in the CIA*.[127]

Some may wonder where Ted Shackley is in the afterlife.

I'm reminded of the last reported words of CIA counterintelligence chief, James Jesus Angleton, as he lay dying: "The better you lied and the more you betrayed, the more likely you would be promoted. If you were in a room with them, you were in a room full of people that you had to believe would deservedly end up in hell. I guess I will see them there soon."

The foreword to Ted's book, written by B. Hugh Tovar, a former member of the Office of Strategic Services in the China Burma India theater of World War II and thirty-year veteran of the CIA, sets out what Shackley hoped to achieve with his story.

> The late Ted Shackley's life as a "spymaster" in the CIA could have made a great novel. But he was much too serious about life to have written one. Life to him meant work. During the three decades of his career in the Central Intelligence Agency, he stands out as one of a comparatively small group of men who have had a significant impact on the agency's clandestine operations.
>
> The title of this book, especially his use of the word "my," suggests that he was writing an autobiography or perhaps a memoir in the classical vein. Not so; this book offers very little insight into his own background. Instead, it is an effort to distill from Shackley's own experience in the intelligence business the kernel of knowledge that he deemed essential. Wearing his instructor's hat, and with no preliminaries, he launches the reader into a systematic examination of what the old master Allen W. Dulles called the "craft of intelligence."[128]

Let me tell you how this former CIA intelligence officer and trained analyst interprets that opening. The writer is telling you quite clearly he's going to avoid the controversial parts of Shackley's career, such as his role in running the operations against Castro, establishing the Phoenix assassination program in Vietnam, estimated to have killed perhaps forty thousand Vietnamese, the Kennedy assassination and the Watergate scandal, the part he played in the Iran-Contra scandal which nearly brought down the Reagan administration, or his suspected organization of what famed constitutional lawyer, Danny Sheehan, called "The Secret Team," a band of mercenary CIA assassins for hire to dictators around the world and other unsavory characters.

But just because you won't be getting certain truths from this account, doesn't mean there's nothing of value to be found in reading through Shackley's manual for clandestine operations overseas and at home. In fact, at CIA we were taught to focus intensely on such writings of a target individual, for as Freud believed, despite our best efforts, we long to tell the truth about ourselves. Let's look at what Shackley inadvertently reveals when he puts on his "instructor's hat" to tell us about the CIA's clandestine operations overseas, and how they need to manipulate the American public at home in the chapter entitled, "Knavish Tricks":

> Turning to examples close to home, compare two CIA-sponsored invasions; first of Guatemala and then of Cuba at the Bay of Pigs. The important things to remember in this context are that (1) the U.S. government heartily endorsed and supported the Guatemalan operation, whereas the Cuban operation enjoyed only a grudging acquiescence by the administration that inherited it; (2) the American press was friendly in the first instance and hostile in the second; and (3) we succeeded in the first and failed in the second.
>
> Covert action operations can be as deceptively peaceful as a letter-writing campaign or as flagrantly violent as a guerilla uprising. In every case, though, the instigating government must make at least a token effort to hide its hand. The flood of letters inveighing against the neutron bomb during the Carter administration and apparently sent by simple, peace-loving citizens would have been ineffective had they been signed by the KGB's Yuri V. Andropov. Here the need for tight cover by the Soviet sponsors of the letter campaign was imperative.[129]

Shackley is telling you exactly what is necessary for the CIA to pull off a successful operation overseas. The elected government must be behind it, and the press in the United States must be in favor of it as well. The reader is left wondering two questions:

1. What might the CIA do to a president who doesn't show the requisite enthusiasm for their planned operations, and,
2. What might the CIA do to generate the desired support in the American media?

I encourage you to look at recent American history, starting with the Kennedy assassination in 1963, to the 1968 assassinations of Martin Luther King Jr. and Robert F. Kennedy, to the modern day, through the lens of these two questions.

Perhaps I'm reading between the lines, but it doesn't seem as if Shackley was pleased with the Kennedy administration's lack of enthusiasm for the Agency's Cuba plans. Shackley continued with his instructions for the would-be clandestine operative.

> For simplicity's sake, we classify covert-action tactics under the general headings of psychological warfare, political action, and paramilitary, but in doing this we risk muddling strategic thought because the lines between these pigeonholes are not always sharply defined. For example, influencing public opinion clearly falls under the heading of psychological warfare, but how about influencing a government? Changing a government through elections is undeniably a form of political action, but what about changing it through terrorism? And how clearly drawn is the line between terrorism and guerilla warfare? In what follows, I will use these three "P" words many times, but the reader should be warned that not all of my examples will fall neatly into one category or the other.[130]

The fatal flaw of most secret organizations is that they're staffed by human beings. If we do not tell the truth, it makes us physically ill at some level. That's why so many agents of any intelligence agency end up as burned-out

THE DEADLIEST MAN IN THE CIA

drunks, drug addicts, hollow shells of the idealistic people they might have once been.

If you want to enjoy robust health, try practicing radical honesty.

Why do I think Shackley was being so honest about his philosophy as he was dying? Because it felt good to finally tell the truth, as horrible as it was. He did not see himself as the monster he appears to us. But even with the realization many might see him as a villain, it felt better than hints of his great adventures in the shadows.

And what monstrous truths did the legendary spymaster reveal?

Shackley gave us the menu of dirty tricks by the CIA.

There's "psychological warfare," which can include influencing a country or a government.

There's "political action," which can include changing a government.

And finally, there's "paramilitary," which occupies a murky area somewhere between guerilla warfare and terrorism.

Shackley instructs us, though, not to have such sharp distinctions between the three, as any operation in the real world is likely to contain elements of all three, in varying degrees. One might think of the three as consisting of an escalation protocol.

First, see if "psychological warfare" can persuade the target country to voluntarily accept your desired actions. An "influence" campaign, if you will, with carefully chosen "influencers."

Second, if your psychological warfare has been unsuccessful, one is likely to proceed to "political action," and change the government by any means necessary, but preferably in the least visible way possible.

Third, if the first two strategies have failed, one proceeds to violent, kinetic action, accepting that the line between guerilla warfare and terrorism is very thin, if it exists at all.

The great trick of the CIA over the years has been to fool the public as to the rules by which they play the game. To the public it appears as if "things just happen," whether it be an unstable political challenger who may have had some reasonable criticisms, but apparently had some substantial personal failings that rendered him or her unsuited for leadership, or some political group that fell apart due to internal fighting.

The illusion that the CIA and other intelligence agencies are neutral in the affairs of the United States is a necessary fiction. The agencies need the public to believe that narrative if they are to have any hope of maintaining their power.

Let's go to what Shackley describes as "psychological warfare," specifically the shaping of public opinion when it comes to media and books.

> Newspapers have been another favorite medium for the CIA, just as they have been for the KGB. In the early days we tended to go whole hog, acquiring entire newspapers by funding them at the top—but we gradually learned—just as the KGB did—that it was usually more effective to have a relationship with an individual and to get our messages into print through the stringer, the staff writer, or the editor. An apparent violation of this rule was our funding of the Chilean newspaper *El Mercurio*, but our purpose in that case was to keep the newspaper alive as a symbol of resistance as well as a vehicle through which to surface anti-Allende material.[131]

I hope it's obvious to the reader, but the CIA views free speech, in other countries, as well as our own, as just another tool they can exploit for their own benefit. It has been one of their operating principles from the very beginning.

And the best influence campaign is the one where you do not believe you are being manipulated.

Is this game still being played? And if the CIA was willing to make an exception in Chile to buy an entire newspaper, might they do the same in the United States? And if so, which would be the best value, combining the lowest price with the greatest possible impact? It's one thing to have Bob Woodward at the *Washington Post*, killing stories that put the Agency in a bad light, as mine did, but what if you could buy the whole paper?

That may be exactly what they did in 2014 with the purchase of the *Washington Post* by Amazon CEO, Jeff Bezos. An opinion piece from 2014 entitled "Why the *Washington Post's* New Ties to the CIA are So Ominous," raised the possibility in the following fashion:

> American journalism has entered highly dangerous terrain.
>
> A tip-off is that the *Washington Post* refuses to face up to a conflict of interest involving Jeff Bezos—who's now the sole owner of

the powerful newspaper at the same time he remains Amazon's CEO and main stakeholder.

The Post is supposed to expose CIA secrets. But Amazon is under contract to keep them. Amazon has a new $600 million "cloud" computing deal with the CIA.[132]

Just so you keep the players straight, Jeff Bezos is the owner of Amazon. The CIA awarded Amazon a $600 million dollar cloud computing contract to host their information. Bezos then went out shortly afterwards and bought the *Washington Post*, which had been famously losing money for years.

Isn't that a curious "coincidence"?

Many have suggested that the CIA is the world's largest creator of "coincidences."

The article continued with the possible conflict of interest when a billionaire's company is working for the CIA, while at the same time, that same billionaire owns a newspaper that is supposed to report on the wrongdoing of the CIA.

The *Washington Post*'s refusal to provide readers with minimal disclosure in coverage of the CIA is important on its own. But it's also a marker for an ominous pattern—combining denial with accommodation to raw financial and governmental power—a synergy of media leverage, corporate digital muscle and secretive agencies implementing policies of mass surveillance, covert action, and ongoing warfare.

Digital prowess at collecting global data and keeping secrets is crucial to the missions of Amazon and the CIA. The two institutions have only begun to explore how to work together more effectively.

For the CIA, the emerging newspaper role of Mr. Amazon is value added to any working relationship with him. The CIA's zeal to increase its leverage over major American media outlets is longstanding.[133]

The next time you see another flattering media portrayal of Jeff Bezos, maybe you should ask some questions. Like the 2021 Netflix series *Shatner in Space*, where Bezos gives a free ride on his rocket to the famed actor, William Shatner, best known for his portrayal of Captain Kirk on the classic TV show and series of movies, *Star Trek*. In one scene, the two men are riding their horses, talking about life, just like two regular guys. A viewer might wonder, "Is that a real story or a CIA production?"

The best influence campaigns are the ones you don't realize are an influence campaign.

Perhaps the viewer is thinking to himself, "That Jeff Bezos sure is a great guy giving the actor who played Captain Kirk a real chance to go into space. And when Shatner returned to Earth and broke down crying, saying how beautiful and fragile our planet looked from space, well, it made me love that billionaire Bezos even more."

But as our instructor in clandestine operations, Ted Shackley, tells us: The CIA's psychological operations aren't just limited to newspapers and traditional media outlets. For the more discerning among us, they can also include books.

> To get its message out to book-reading audiences, the CIA has inspired the writing of some books and assisted in the distribution of others. When in 1954 the Yugoslav communist cadre Milovan Djilas broke with the party and subsequently wrote a book in which he denounced the corruption and privilege of Yugoslavia's new rulers, the CIA saw to it that his effort reached the widest possible readership.
>
> We have also written some books ourselves. The Russian agent Oleg Penkovsy used to speak at length in his debriefing sessions about the injustices of the Soviet system and his wish that the Russian people might someday enjoy the many freedoms taken for granted in the West. When he was arrested and executed in 1963, there was no longer any reason to keep his views from the public. The CIA therefore arranged for a careful culling and editing of his operational file and had the book published under the title *The Petrovsky Papers*.[134]

If you were a regular consumer of newspapers, the CIA knew how to get information into your hands with Project Mockingbird. If you were more of the bookish sort, they had that avenue covered as well.

How might today's intelligence operatives go about influencing the public, who by and large don't get physical newspapers, or read as many books, but certainly consume vast amounts of social media about their favorite celebrities?

Maybe use a rock singer as an agent of influence?

An article in *Vanity Fair* from February of 2024 responded to this possibility:

> In a statement, Deputy Pentagon Press Secretary Sabrina Singh told *Politico*: "To set the record straight–Taylor Swift is not part of a DOD psychological operation. Period." While conspiracy theories surrounding Swift reached a fever pitch this weekend after her boyfriend's football team clinched its spot in the Super Bowl, the arguably most deranged moment came last month when a Fox News anchor [Jesse Watters] went on the air, and declared, not a joke, "Around four years ago, the Pentagon psychological operations unit floated turning Taylor Swift into an asset during a NATO meeting."[135]

What do I think about such a claim?

I have no information which would allow me to confirm or deny it.

However, as a former intelligence operative, I'd say to myself, "If you could pull that off, it might just work." Who would seriously consider a singer whose biggest audience is adolescent females who've probably never had a serious boyfriend as an intelligence asset? It's only a little less believable than using the head of a local bank or the CEO of America's oldest investment banking firm.

With this story, I'd suggest putting a pin in it, and coming back to it in five years and see if you have a different opinion.

Stranger things have been known to happen.

***

Certainly, one of the strangest things that happened to me during my time at the CIA was being told to report to Ted Shackley for a discussion of my report which had so thoroughly embarrassed the Directorate of Operations.

I figured the old spook had retired years ago. For God's sake, he'd enlisted in the Army in October of 1945, recruited into Army's Counterintelligence Core in 1947 because of his fluency in Polish, then assigned in September 1951 to the CIA.[136] What was the man still doing at the CIA in 1998, especially since he'd been so publicly linked to the Iran-Contra scandal in 1987, not to mention his association with the Phoenix assassination program during the Vietnam War? The official record states Shackley "retired" from the CIA in 1979, but nearly two decades later it seemed he was still in residence.

Shackley was nicknamed "the blond ghost," because of his pale complexion. As remembered by somebody with whom he worked during the Vietnam War:

> "Oh man, was Shackley weird," a CIA officer who was in Laos recalled, providing a slightly exaggerated description of his chief. "Tall, thin, real tall. And cold, man, real cold. Calm, quiet, he just kind of looked at you in this weird way. And real white skin, real white. He never went out in the sun, man, he never went out in the sun."[137]

Shackley's office was in a part of the CIA building I'd never visited. I pushed open the door to see a large room with empty walls, and a large desk in the center, with the tall, pale Shackley standing in front of it.

"Kevin," he said loudly as I walked in the room. "The CIA is going to do something about this! Do you understand the CIA is going to do something about this?"

For a report with such importance as mine, I would have expected to meet with the director of Central Intelligence, his executive officer, or the director of security, at the very least. But here I was talking to one of the most disreputable characters in the history of the CIA, accused of everything from gun running, to drug trafficking, and assassination.

"Yes, sir," I said in stunned reply.

"That will be all," said Shackley, concluding what was probably the shortest meeting I've ever had with a CIA official.

Was that "something" which Shackley promised, sending me and my family to live on top of a toxic waste dump at that secret base where some of Shackley's secrets were buried?

I believed my report had put a target on my back, but I hadn't expected the Agency would enlist its most legendary assassin to take me down.

And to this day, I'm puzzled why he summoned me to his office for such a brief meeting. Was Shackley "old school" in that he wanted to look me in the eye before deciding to kill me?

The question fell moot as I'm still above ground and Shackley is not.

And while in Shackley's own book he did not want to reveal all of his secrets, other writers were interested in digging them up.

***

One of the most authoritative books on Shackley is *Blond Ghost: Ted Shackley and the CIA's Crusades*, by David Corn, a former Washington editor of the left-leaning publication, *The Nation*, and published in 1994. In the opening of the book, Corn describes Shackley in the following manner:

> Ted Shackley, like most CIA people, was no James Bond. He was a manager, and in that sense, a representative of a certain breed of intelligence officer, an intellicrat. He made decisions and participated in actions with life and death consequences, but usually from behind a desk. For many CIA employees during the Cold War, the real drama in the intelligence business did not come from face-to-face confrontations with an armed KGB officer. It was found in the office—in headquarters or a base overseas—where a U.S. government employee decided which foreign national would be enticed to become a spy, how to handle a defector, where to land a sabotage team, what village or area should be targeted for bombing. Shackley was a government bureaucrat who did all this.
>
> He was an organization man, a spy in a gray flannel suit. Through decades of the Cold War, Shackley took orders that came from the White House and the CIA's top command and turned them into reality. People like Shackley were the heart and soul of the Agency, the ones who saluted sharply and made concrete the abstractions of the Cold War, the people who guaranteed that the dirty work got done.[138]

I think Corn's book is an excellent work of scholarship, although it does have significant limitations. As Corn admits in his "Note to the Reader," he was only able to obtain one interview with Shackley, and although he talked with more than a hundred former CIA officers, they were still under secrecy oaths "pledging not to reveal Agency information."[139]

In addition, the book was published in 1994, four years before I would be told to visit with Shackley to discuss my report. Writing about a public figure while that person is still active is a little like trying to build a plane while flying it.

However, even if one may not be able to tell the whole truth, many truths will inevitably be revealed, and Corn's book does an admirable job of sketching out the arc of Shackley's career. Corn also strikes me as a certain type of liberal, almost extinct in modern America, one who was distrustful of the intelligence agencies, and a staunch defender of the Constitution as well as the ideals of representative government.

Corn also comes across to me as a man aware of his own biases, and in the America which used to exist, worried that such bias might possibly skew his coverage. Corn gives the reader the information that he can verify, often leading right up to the brink of what many would consider illegality or treason, but does not cross that line. In most instances it's because such information has been classified under the cloak of "national security."

More than a quarter of a century later, many Americans have adopted a different standard when it comes to the intelligence agencies. Instead of adopting a position that "no such evidence exists," when that evidence has been hidden under the veil of national security, the more discerning citizen has concluded that if the intelligence agencies do not answer legitimate questions of culpability, it's because they're "guilty of significant wrongdoing."

The only thing we're missing are the specific details.

I don't claim this standard will be accurate in all instances, simply that it's a better reflection of the likely reality.

In looking at the trajectory of Shackley's career, and how it reflects the broader history of the Operations Directorate of the CIA, we will cover six specific areas.

First, Shackley's early CIA years dealing with Poland in the early 1950s.

Second, his work as the CIA station chief in Miami in the early 1960s, dealing with the campaign against Fidel Castro's Cuba. Personnel from the Miami CIA station would later be accused of being involved in the assassination of President Kennedy, and some of the same members would be convicted of being involved in the Watergate break-in that brought down the Nixon administration.

Third, Shackley's role as the head of CIA operations in Vietnam and association with the Phoenix assassination program.

Fourth, his retirement (firing?) in 1979 from the CIA by Admiral Stansfield Turner.

Fifth, his central role in what would later blossom into the Iran-Contra scandal that threatened to bring down the Reagan administration.

And finally, Shackley's alleged role in the creation of a "Secret Team," which was an off-the-book group of former CIA assassins, available for hire to dictators and democracies around the world.

***

In seeking to understand Ted Shackley, perhaps it's worthwhile to understand that his first intelligence mission was an absolute failure and embarrassment.

In 1952, the director of the Central Intelligence Agency was Walter Bedel Smith, and the man he'd tasked with CIA operations in Western Europe was named Frank Wisner, who was tasked with preventing a Soviet takeover. As detailed in the 2007 National Book Award winner, *Legacy of Ashes: The History of the CIA*, author Tim Weiner detailed what some of those plans entailed:

> While the war in Korea still raged, the Joint Chiefs commanded Frank Wisner and the CIA to conduct "a major covert offensive against the Soviet Union," aimed at "the heartland of the communist control system." Wisner tried. The Marshall Plan was being transformed into pacts providing America's allies with weapons, and Wisner saw this as a chance to arm secret stay-behind forces to fight the Soviets in the event of war. He was seeding the ground all over Europe. Throughout the mountains and forests of Scandinavia,

France, Germany, Italy, and Greece, his men were dropping gold ingots into lakes and burying caches of weapons for the coming battles. In the marshes and foothills of Ukraine and the Baltics, his pilots were dropping agents to their deaths.[140]

To put it bluntly, the Western intelligence agencies, the Americans, the British, and the French, were losing badly to the Soviets. A trusted three-star general, Lucian K. Truscott, was sent to take over Wisner's operation in Germany and find problems with the program. He found plenty, including a system of secret prisons.

The agency had set up clandestine prisons to wring confessions out of suspected double agents. One was in Germany, another in Japan. The third, and the biggest, was in the Panama Canal Zone. "Like Guantanamo," Polgar said in 2005. "It was anything goes."

The zone was its own world, seized by the United States at the turn of the century, bulldozed out of the jungles that surrounded the Panama Canal. On a naval base in the zone, the CIA's office of security had refitted a complex of cinder-block prison cells inside a navy brig normally used to house drunk and disorderly sailors. In those cells, the agency was conducting secret experiments in harsh interrogation, using techniques on the edge of torture, drug-induced mind control, and brainwashing.[141]

The use of drugs in interrogation began in 1948, and the first name given to the effort was Project Artichoke. It would later be renamed Project Ultra, then in its final iteration became known as Project MK-Ultra.

The problem the Agency had was that many of the Russian and East German agents turned out to be failures, raising the question of whether they had been compromised, or were double agents for the Soviet Union from the start. The need to find a fool-proof interrogation method to smoke out suspected double agents became of paramount importance to the Agency.

On May 15, 1952, Dulles [Allen Dulles, who would later be named Director of the CIA on February 26, 1953] and Wisner received a report on Project Artichoke, spelling out the Agency's four-year effort to test heroin, amphetamines, sleeping pills, the newly discovered LSD, and other "special techniques in CIA interrogations." Part of the project sought to find an interrogation technique so strong that "the individual under its influence will find it difficult to maintain a fabrication under questioning." A few months later, Dulles approved an ambitious new program code-named Ultra. Under its auspices, seven prisoners at a federal penitentiary in Kentucky were kept high on LSD for seventy-seven consecutive days. When the CIA slipped the same drug to an army civilian employee, Frank Olson, he leaped out the window of a New York hotel.[142]

The CIA seemed to love its secret prisons and drug programs from the very start. And these programs were just as disastrous for everybody involved from the beginning as they have been shown to be today. When you wonder if the intelligence agencies might be using a rock star like Taylor Swift for an influence campaign, just compare that to the image of the CIA slipping LSD to prisoners and some of its own employees during the supposedly squeaky-clean 1950s.

This is the CIA which Ted Shackley joined, and he would soon have his own similarly spectacular failure in Poland, with a phantom army of freedom fighters.

Toward the end of 1952, in the last months of Smith's tenure as director of central intelligence, more of Wisner's hastily improvised operation began coming apart. This fallout left a lasting impression on a newly anointed CIA officer named Ted Shackley, who started a supercharged career at the agency as a second lieutenant shanghaied from his job training military police in West Virginia. His first assignment was to make himself familiar with a major Wisner operation to support a Polish liberation army, the Freedom and Independence Movement, known as WIN.

Wisner and his men had dropped roughly $5 million worth of gold bars, submachine guns, rifles, ammunition, and two-way radios into Poland. They had established trusted contacts with "WIN outside," a handful of emigres in Germany and London.

They believed that "WIN inside" was a powerful force–five hundred soldiers in Poland, twenty thousand armed partisans, and a hundred thousand sympathizers–all prepared to fight the Red Army.[143]

And yet it was all part of a cleverly crafted illusion created by Soviet and Polish intelligence services. Instead, what was happening is that patriots outside of Poland (or communist double agents) were parachuting into the country where they'd be quickly picked up by Polish and Soviet intelligence. With their drops of ammunition and money, the CIA was actually funding and arming the local communist groups.

> The Soviet and Polish intelligence services had spent years setting their traps. "They were well aware of our air operations. When we would drop our agents in," McMahon said, "they would go out and make contact with people we knew who would be helpful to us. And the Poles and the KGB were right in back of them and would mop them up. So it was a well-thought out plan, except we were recruiting agents of the Soviet Union. It turned out to be a monumental disaster. People died." Perhaps thirty, maybe more, were lost.
>
> Shackley said he never forgot the sight of his fellow officers realizing that five years of planning and millions of dollars had gone down the drain. The unkindest cut might have been their discovery that the Poles had sent a chunk of the CIA's money to the Communist Party of Italy.[144]

The communists in Europe were simply better at the intelligence game than their western counterparts. The OSS had been very successful putting agents into Western Europe against the Nazis, but the CIA was having little success against the Soviets in Eastern Europe after the Second World War.

This frustration seemed to generate a certain kind of paranoia among early CIA officers, the sense that their assets in the field might not be trustworthy.

Ted Shackley was among that number who saw how badly the West was doing in its battle against the communists and was determined to start getting some wins.

***

The next significant posting for Shackley would be as head of the CIA station in Miami, Florida, where the campaign against Cuban leader Fidel Castro was being run. From the book, *Blond Ghost: Ted Shackley and CIA's Crusades*:

> On April 21, 1962, Bill Harvey, the gruff, gun-toting CIA man, was in Miami. He had not come to Florida to relax. The Agency's no-too-covert war against communism had shifted to a new locale. Forget Europe, the Reds were now in Cuba, less than one hundred miles away, truly in the backyard. Harvey, no longer in charge of the Berlin base, had been entrusted with perhaps the most sensitive assignment in the Agency. He was to arrange the assassination of Fidel Castro, the Marxist leader of Cuba, whose demise was an obsession of the Kennedy administration.
>
> Harvey arrived in Florida carrying four poison pills concocted by chemists of the CIA. As part of the scheme, Harvey was to provide $5,000 worth of explosives, detonators, rifles, handguns, and boat radar to a leader of Cuban exiles in Miami. In return, this exile would smuggle the death pills into Cuba. Harvey ordered the Agency's Miami station—codenamed JMWAVE—to procure the equipment. The man in charge of rounding up the lethal goods was the officer Harvey had handpicked to head the JMWAVE station and serve as the field commander for the crusade against communists of Cuba, Ted Shackley.[145]

I think it's important for the modern reader to fully understand the range of activities with which the Agency was involved in Cuba. First, because the historical record is so abundantly well-documented, and second, it provides a framework for how the CIA operates as an entity when it identifies a target it wants to destroy. A common expression goes that "integrity is who you are in the dark, when nobody is watching."

In order to understand the true nature of at least some parts of the CIA, we must ask ourselves the question of what they have done when we have allowed them to operate under the cover of darkness.

I believe it's also critical to understand how Ted Shackley was often the tip of the spear for the most aggressive actions of the CIA, even though he liked to hide behind the façade of a scholarly middle-manager type. It also explains why Shackley was still hanging around the CIA in 1998 when I was called into his office. When you have committed acts which you hope will never come to light, it's a good idea to have somebody in place who knows where the secrets are buried.

And as I would later discover, some of Ted Shackley's secrets were buried at the secret base to which he had sent me, and I had tripped over them.

Let's return to the Cuba operation and look at some of the CIA's partners in their effort to oust Castro.

> Harvey and Shackley drove an arms-filled U-Haul truck through the wet streets of Miami to a drive-in restaurant parking lot. Harvey passed the keys to a mob-linked hoodlum named John [Johnny] Rosselli, who was supposed to transfer the weapons to Cuban exiles. Fearing a double-cross, Harvey and Shackley kept the parking lot under surveillance until the Cubans arrived and drove the truck away. The CIA, as part of an unholy trinity that included the Mafia and right-wing Cuban expatriates, was a step closer to murder. A short time later, the Cubans returned the truck empty, and Harvey and Shackley brought it back to the rental office. Then for the spymaster and his young associate, it was onto more official U.S. government business.[146]

For those who may not be familiar with the background and importance of the "mob-linked hoodlum," Johnny Rosselli, a little background is probably necessary. Perhaps the best place to begin is the end, namely, how Rosselli died, fourteen years after taking the keys to that U-Haul truck full of weapons from Ted Shackley's hands.

On July 28, 1976, "Handsome Johnny" Roselli, a mobster who rose up the ranks with Al Capone, had brunch with his sister in Miami before borrowing her car and driving to the marina. There, he boarded a private boat with two men, one of them an old friend. But when they got to sea, the third man–someone Rosselli didn't know from Chicago–strangled the 71-year-old gangster to death. He wasn't even on the vessel an hour and he was dead, rubbed out by a Mafia hitman who sawed off his legs, stuffed his body into a 55-gallon drum, and threw the barrel overboard in Dumfoundling Bay.[147]

It's a bad day when all you wanted to do was go fishing, but instead you end up strangled, your legs sawed off, placed in a fifty-five-gallon drum, and dumped over the side of the boat.

But one couldn't say Rosselli hadn't had a good run in his time, working in Hollywood, Las Vegas, and with the CIA in Florida.

Part of Rosselli's "assignment" in Los Angeles was to cultivate relationships with the film industry hierarchy. He knew everybody, dated movie stars, played golf with studio heads. His closest industry friend was the boss of Columbia Pictures, Harry Cohn. They socialized together, and Johnny was often at the studio advising the mogul on his gangster pictures. When Cohn needed a large loan in a hurry it was Johnny who put him together with East Coast mobster [Abner Zwillman.] This had its own complications, as the mobster maintained his secret piece of Cohn's studio for many years, until he died suddenly, tortured to death or by his own hand, depending on whose story you believe.[148]

Accounts like this start to put questions in your mind. The mob had influence in Hollywood. The CIA and the mob worked together to get rid of Castro (and also during World War II in the invasion of Sicily and mainland Italy.)

One wonders if the CIA was as interested in influencing Hollywood as the mob?

However, we can't forget Rosselli's time in Las Vegas, or his appearance before Congress:

As the virtual godfather of Las Vegas in the 50s and 60s, Rosselli knew most of the big showbiz stars who played the showrooms. Sinatra and Dean Martin were personal friends. Frank and Dean sponsored Johnny's membership in the Friar's Club . . .

The Kefauver Hearings in the early 1950s was the first in-depth government investigation of nationwide organized crime. Few people in America knew just how far-reaching was the spread of what was known as the Mob and the Syndicate, corrupting every area of the country. The Kefauver group from Washington hauled in every top gangster, including Johnny Rosselli. Unlike most of the mobsters, who tried to play it tough and not say anything (and some went to jail for it), Rosselli answered every question, but with a strategic skill that gave nothing away.[149]

Roselli was one cool customer, his nickname being the "gentleman gangster." So maybe it's not surprising that even though he was a known criminal figure because of his appearance in the 1950s before the Kefauver hearings, that the CIA would recruit him in the 1960s, and put him to work with Shackley.

And when Roselli was slain in 1977, the *New York Times* conducted a hard-hitting investigation to determine who might have been behind the crime. It seems everybody was under suspicion.

Early speculation that the C.I.A. or Cuban agents might have been involved in the Roselli murder centered on the fact that another participant in the Castro assassination plots, Sam Giancana, a former Mafia boss of Chicago, had been murdered in his home a year earlier. Mr. Giancana was killed shortly before he was to be summoned before the Senate Committee on Intelligence.

Mr. Roselli himself testified for the committee three times, the last a secret appearance three months before his death, when he was questioned about the assassination of President Kennedy.

The CIA may have been involved, according to one theory, because it feared further damaging revelations about its Mafia connections. The Cuban agents may have been involved, according to another theory, because they sought to retaliate for the plots to kill Mr. Castro.[150]

Let's just take a step back from this *New York Times* article to make sure we understand the situation. One of the major players in the CIA/Mafia alliance, the "former Mafia boss of Chicago," Sam Giancana, was murdered a year earlier in his home, shortly before he was to testify before the Senate Committee on Intelligence.

Did nobody think that Rosselli might be in similar danger, given his continuing testimony?

The *New York Times* wants us to believe there are three possible suspects, the Cubans, the CIA, and the mob. And they're going to do their best to find out who it was, because after all, the American people deserve answers.

> "If Cubans had killed Rosselli, they would have shot him down in the street or blown him up in his car to make a point, not stuffed him in a barrel and thrown him in the bay," said Detective Julio Ojeda, a member of the Miami homicide team investigating the Rosselli murder, who is himself of Cuban origin.
>
> The Cuban retaliation theory is also discounted by authorities because Robert Maheu, the most important figure in the plots against Mr. Castro and later a chief aide to the late Howard R. Hughes, has not been touched. "I think Castro is sophisticated enough to know the historical context in which those things [the plots on his life] were done," and forget about them, he said in an interview.[151]

This is what passes for investigative journalism at the *New York Times*? The Cubans are in the clear because some Cuban guy said, "That's not the way we'd do it?" And do we really trust Robert Maheu, described by the *Times* as "the most important figure in the plots against Castro and later a chief aide to the late Howard R. Hughes"? In other words, Maheu was CIA, then went to work for one of the richest men in the United States.

Sounds like yet another connection between Big Intelligence and Big Business.

Say we assume the Cubans are in the clear, a question remains. What about the CIA?

If you really want the truth, it's probably best to ask a CIA guy for answers. And that's exactly what the *Times* did.

The possibility that the C.I.A. may have had Mr. Rosselli killed to keep him from disclosing damaging facts about the agency is discounted by those who knew him best, including his closest friend, Joseph Breen, who was his partner in the gift shop at the Frontier Hotel in Las Vegas, which provided Mr. Rosselli's only source of income—$60,000 a year–at the time of his death.

Mr. Breen said the C.I.A. would not have killed Mr. Rosselli over his Senate committee testimony because he had checked with the C.I.A., including Bill Harvey–his C.I.A. contact–prior to his appearance, and they told him to tell whatever he knew "because it was going to come out anyway." The agency he said, "would have no reason to kill him."[152]

Can we perhaps look at the facts as stated by the *New York Times* in a little more skeptical light? Your business partner is strangled, cut-up, and put in a fifty-five-gallon drum by parties unknown. Do you finger the likely killer? Or are you afraid that if you do, you'll meet the same end as your friend and Sam Giancana?

And I'm unaware of any criminal investigator, anywhere in the world, who thinks that if you ask a suspect if they were involved in a crime, and they deny it, you close the case. And that's exactly what the *New York Times* reporter did with Shackley's good buddy, the gift shop owner at a Mob casino, and Rosselli's CIA handler, Bill Harvey,

Hey, CIA, did you have anything to do with this guy being killed?

Nope, not us.

Okay, thank you. You can go now.

And to make things even more suspicious, Rosselli, wasn't pointing his finger at the CIA either, although the story he was telling seemed to be falling apart, as detailed in the *New York Times* article about his death.

Three months before his death on April 23, 1976, Mr. Rosselli was questioned about the Kennedy assassination by representatives of the Senate intelligence committee, including Senator Richard S. Schweiker, the Pennsylvania Republican, in secret session in a suite of the Carroll Arms Hotel.

The transcript of Mr. Rosselli's testimony has been classified "top secret" but a copy of it was examined by The Times.

Mr. Rosselli testified that he had told some people he believed that Fidel Castro was behind the Kennedy assassination. When asked by Michael Epstein, a member of the committee's staff, if he had "any facts" to back up his supposition, he replied: "No facts."[153]

Rosselli was caught in a trap. He'd been trained as an assassin and our president had been assassinated. He was exactly the kind of person with the needed skill set to execute such an operation.

And perhaps most importantly, he was doing a bad job of pointing the finger of blame at somebody else. His good looks weren't getting him out of this situation.

But the New York Times wants us to believe it's all about the Mafia, conveniently forgetting that the entire Cuban operation was a CIA/Mafia operation. Is it inconceivable that the CIA and the Mafia would have a mutual interest in keeping Giancana and Rosselli from testifying? It's funny how that possibility is never raised in the article.

Mr. Giancana was killed because he tried to reassert his authority in Chicago after a 10-year absence. "Sam thought nothing had changed, but everything had changed," the Mafia figure said. The task of killing Mr. Rosselli proved difficult because he was a cautious man. Nevertheless, his pursuers were persistent. "They would watch his movements for a couple of weeks, leave him alone for a few months, then go back and watch him some more," the Mafia figure said. "Rosselli was careful, but nobody can be that careful. When the decision is made to hit you–you're dead no matter how long it takes."[154]

Isn't it interesting how a New York Times reporter can get a "Mafia figure" to talk quite openly about the killing of two men, and yet the law enforcement authorities will never make an arrest in either of the cases? It should have made the public wonder if they were being played. Is this a real Mafia figure, introduced to the Times reporter by his CIA handler who has vetted the story, or is it just one of the CIA's colorful cast of characters impersonating a Mafia figure?

Perhaps it is just as it appears, a Mafia figure genuinely wanted to set the record straight for America, and the *New York Times* reporter did his journalistic duty by protecting the identity of his source.

But I won't be betting any money on it.

***

Did the CIA lie in what was perhaps one of the most important investigations in history, the Warren Commission investigation into the assassination of President John F. Kennedy?

You might be surprised to know that even the CIA admits it lied to the Warren Commission. An article from 2015 in *Politico* reveals what the Agency found in its own investigation:

> John McCone came to the CIA as an outsider. An industrialist and an engineer by training, he replaced veteran spymaster Allen Dulles as director of central intelligence in November 1961, after John F. Kennedy had forced Dulles out following the CIA's bungled operation to oust Fidel Castro by invading Cuba's Bay of Pigs. McCone had one overriding mission: restore order at the besieged CIA. Kennedy hoped his management skills might prevent a future debacle, even if the Californian—mostly a stranger to the clubby, blue-blooded world of the men like Dulles who had always run the spy agency—faced a steep learning curve.
>
> After JFK's assassination in Dallas in November 1963, President Lyndon Johnson kept McCone in place at the CIA and he became an important witness before the Warren Commission, the panel Johnson created to investigate Kennedy's murder.[155]

The *Politico* article did a fine job of setting the stage for McCone's lies but omitted one very crucial fact.

The head of the Warren Commission was Allen Dulles, the former head of the CIA, who'd been fired by President Kennedy. In any legal investigation, that would be known as a glaring conflict of interest. You are not supposed to have had a prior relationship with the individual which might in any way influence your objectivity. You do not get to investigate the murder of a man who fired you.

As the former head of the CIA, Dulles was also likely to know what McCone was concealing. However, instead of asking questions about Dulles, the article focused on McCone.

> But did McCone come close to perjury all those decades ago? Did the onetime Washington outsider in fact hide agency secrets that might still rewrite the history of the assassination? Even the CIA is now willing to raise these questions. Half a century after JFK's death, in a once secret report written in 2013 by the CIA's top in-house historian and quietly declassified last fall, the spy agency acknowledges what others were convinced of long ago: that McCone and other senior CIA officials were "complicit" in keeping "incendiary" information from the Warren Commission.
>
> According to the report by CIA historian David Robarge, McCone, who died in 1991, was at the heart of a "benign cover-up" at the spy agency, intended to keep the commission focused on "what the Agency believed at the time was the 'best truth'–that Lee Harvey Oswald, for as yet undetermined motives, had acted alone in killing John Kennedy."[156]

I'm always a little suspicious when government agents start using weasel words to describe what in the rest of the civilized would be described as lying. If those same government agents were sitting across a table from us, asking us questions, and we answered as they did, they'd call "perjury" and likely prosecute us. You weren't "complicit" in keeping "incendiary" information from the government.

You lied.

There's no defense to perjury called the "benign cover-up," and when one raises their hand in a legal proceeding you don't swear to tell the "best truth." It's "the truth, the whole truth, and nothing but the truth."

There really isn't a lot of wiggle room.

The most important information that McCone withheld from the Commission in its 1964 investigation, the report found, was the existence, for years, of CIA plots to assassinate Castro, some of which put the CIA in cahoots with the Mafia. Without this information, the commission never even knew to ask the question of whether Oswald had accomplices in Cuba or elsewhere who wanted Kennedy dead in retaliation for the Castro plots.[157]

It also meant people like Miami CIA station chief, Ted Shackley, would not come to the attention of congressional or other law enforcement agencies who might want to dig a little deeper in the details of that relationship.

The report identifies other tantalizing information that McCone did not reveal to the commission, including evidence that the CIA might somehow have been in communication with Oswald before 1963 and that the spy agency had secretly monitored Oswald's mail after he attempted to defect to the Soviet Union in 1959. The CIA mail-opening program, which was later determined to have been blatantly illegal, had the codename HTLINGUAL. "It would be surprising if the DCI [director of central intelligence] were not told about the program," after the Kennedy assassination, the report says. "If not, his subordinates deceived him. If he did know about HTLINGUAL reporting on Oswald, he was not being forthright with the commission–presumably to protect an operation that was highly compartmentalized and, if disclose, sure to arouse much controversy.[158]

When dealing with the CIA, it often seems that their answers only generate more questions. Although it's been covered in many fine books, as well as Oliver Stone's masterful movie, *JFK*, it's probably worthwhile to review a few odd facts about Lee Harvey Oswald, the man fingered in the Warren Commission report as being Kennedy's lone gunman assassin.

At the height of the Cold War, Oswald, who had been a radar operator at an air base in Japan which launched U-2s over Russia, defected to the Soviet Union in 1959. He tried to join Soviet intelligence while in Russia, promising to reveal information about the U-2s, but the Russians thought he was a fake defector. When Oswald returned to the United States, he was not prosecuted, but given money and aid by the State Department, later raising suspicions that he might have been an intelligence asset of some sort.

He spent some time in the summer of 1963 in New Orleans, the home territory of Mafia boss, Carlos Marcello, became associated with radical pro-Castro groups, got into a well-publicized fight with an anti-Castro group, appeared on a local radio show praising Castro, and struck up an unlikely friendship with an older wealthy man, George de Mohrenschildt, a petroleum engineer, and occasional CIA field agent. He got a job at the Texas Book Depository in Dallas, which overlooked Kennedy's motorcade route, where depending on who you believe, he did or did not participate in the assassination.

He was arrested that day by the Dallas police for murdering the president, famously declared he was a "patsy," then got gunned down in police custody by Jack Ruby, a nightclub owner who claimed he did it because he wanted to spare Jackie Kennedy the trauma of a trial. Credible allegations would later be made that Ruby worked for the Chicago and New Orleans mob.

And even though the CIA in 2013 wanted the American public to believe they were revealing all they knew about the Kennedy assassination, there were still secrets being kept.

> The declassification of the bulk of the 2013 McCone report might suggest a new openness by the CIA in trying to resolve the lingering mysteries about the Kennedy assassination. At the same time, there are 15 places in the public version of the report where the CIA had deleted sensitive information—sometimes individual names, sometimes whole sentences. It is an acknowledgment, it seems, that there are still secrets about the Kennedy assassination hidden in the agency's files.[159]

Somebody who clearly didn't believe the Warren Commission's conclusions about the Kennedy assassination was President Richard M, Nixon, and he wanted his CIA Director Richard Helms to know it, as revealed by one of the most infamous of the Watergate tapes:

> "We protected Helms from one hell of a lot of things," Nixon growled on the tape. "You open that scab there's a hell of a lot of things, and we just feel that it would be very detrimental to have

this thing go any further. This involves these Cubans [ex-CIA man and Watergate burglar Howard] Hunt, and a lot of hanky-panky that we have nothing to do with ourselves.

Nixon advised chief of staff H.R. Haldeman on how to get the CIA director to kill the FBI's probe.

"Say, 'Look, the problem is that this will open the whole, the whole Bay of Pigs thing, and the President just feels that, ah, without going into the details . . . don't . . . don't lie to them to the extent to say there is no involvement. But just say that this is sort of a comedy of errors, bizarre, without getting into it. The President believes that it is going to open the whole Bay of Pigs thing up again."[160]

The "Cubans" that Nixon is referring to in this tape are the group of Cubans and their assorted allies who were being run out of the Miami CIA station by Shackley. Shackley could count the alleged assassins of Kennedy, as well as the convicted members of the Watergate burglary team as his former employees, which must be some kind of historical record for "coincidences." And it seems as if Nixon's reference to the "whole Bay of Pigs thing" was a lightly disguised code for CIA operations against Castro, and how that might have resulted in Kennedy's assassination.

> Haldeman suggested that Nixon used the phrase, "the whole Bay of Pigs thing," as a coded reference to the assassination of President John F. Kennedy on Nov. 22, 1963. It was, he wrote, "the president's way of reminding Helms, not so gently, of the cover-up of the CIA assassination attempts on the hero of the Bay of Pigs, Fidel Castro, a CIA operation that may have triggered the Kennedy tragedy and which Helms desperately wanted to hide.[161]

The question would be, "which group from the anti-Castro efforts," the anti-Castro Cubans, the Mafia, or the CIA, would be most likely to have participated in the Kennedy assassination, and why? (Note how far we are from any discussion of the possibility that Lee Harvey Oswald was a lone, deranged gunman, acting without support from any other groups.)

Let's look at this question through the lens of power.

Which group might expect to commit such a crime and get away with it? The anti-Castro Cubans, given their recent arrival in America and dependence on the CIA, would have the least hope of getting away with such a heinous act. The Mafia might have a little more power, but given their tenuous position in American life, probably wouldn't take such an action on their own. (They might, I just think it's unlikely.)

My opinion is the group which would reasonably believe they'd have the best chance of getting away with it would be the CIA. (It doesn't mean it's true, it's just the most likely answer.) If you look at other opinions, I encourage you to determine whether those authors stated it as simply as I just did.

> Haldeman's take on "the whole Bay of Pigs thing" lived on in Oliver Stone's 1995 biopic "Nixon." The film depicted an ominous exchange about the Bay of Pigs in which Helms (played by the chilly Sam Waterson) condescends to Nixon (played by Oscar-winning Anthony Hopkins). In articulating his dream of détente with China and Russia, Nixon says, "Cuba would be a small price to pay." Helms replies, "So President Kennedy thought." Spliced with film footage of JFK's assassination, the exchange implied enemies of Kennedy's Cuba policy were behind his assassination.[162]

While Nixon did want détente with China and Russia, and didn't want to end up like Kennedy, he also wanted the CIA to know he wasn't going to air their dirty laundry. By the time of Nixon's presidency, he considered Cuba to be a dead issue. They were not going to dislodge Castro.

In other words, Nixon might be moving in a new direction, but he didn't want the CIA to think he was going to be digging up old secrets. In another tape, Nixon laid out his thinking to CIA Director Helms, reflecting a recent discussion he'd had with John Ehrlichman.

> "Now to get to the dirty tricks part of it," Nixon went on. "I know what happened in Iran [a CIA-sponsored coup in 1953]. I also know what happened in Guatemala [a CIA-sponsored coup in 1954], and I totally approve both. I also know what happened with the planning of the Bay of Pigs under Eisenhower and totally approved of it."

Nixon wanted to talk about what he saw as JFK's failure, namely his refusal to authorize air support for the CIA-backed rebels when Castro's forces pinned them down on the beaches of the Bay of Pigs.

"The problem was not the CIA," Nixon said. "The problem was that your plan was not carried out. It was a goddamn good plan. If it had been backed up at the proper time. If he'd just flown a couple planes over that damn place . . . "[163]

The narrative of American power, both covert and overt, should be clear in Nixon's statement. Just as the communists were trying to overthrow governments around the world, we were doing the same thing. That's what led to the Korean War, the Vietnam War, and nearly a war in Cuba. The question which might have been asked in the early 1970s, given that nearly thirty years had passed since the end of the Second World War, was what was the path forward? Kennedy had wanted to de-escalate the East-West conflict in the 1960s and may have paid the ultimate price for it.

In the early 1970s, Nixon seemed to prefer a similar approach. If we look at Watergate as something of a one-two punch by the Deep State— the CIA supplying the incompetent burglars, the FBI pretending to do a serious investigation of the crime—it would appear we have our answer.

But the false trail kept being laid, with either the Cubans working with the Mafia, or the Mafia working on its own. The well-known (and usually accurate) political columnist, Jack Anderson, thought he had the Kennedy assassination figured out in 1988, and published his claims in the *Washington Post*:

> The killers were hand-picked by Santo Trafficante, who had been the Mafia boss in pre-Castro Havana. After six hit teams failed, the CIA reportedly learned that Trafficante had tipped off Castro. The CIA cut the Mafia out, but continued.
>
> Without Trafficante's help, Castro no longer knew when or where the CIA would strike. In September 1963, he publicly warned that if the CIA continued its attempts to kill "Cuban leaders," then "American leaders would no longer be safe."
>
> Participants in the plot against Castro claim that Castro then enlisted Trafficante to turn the Mafia against President Kennedy.

Trafficante allegedly got the assistance of two other Mafia godfathers, Sam Giancana and Carlos Marcello, who hated Kennedy for his crackdown on the mob.

For such a crime, the Mafia needed someone to divert suspicion from themselves. They allegedly were led to Lee Harvey Oswald, a political crackpot who once defected to Russia.[164]

It's a powerful claim, and maybe it's true, but let's first kick the tires of this theory to determine if it makes sense.

Castro kicks the mob out of Cuba when he comes to power by taking away their casinos.

The Mafia and the CIA collaborate in getting rid of Castro because they each have their own reasons to hate the communist regime.

The CIA and the Mafia sent in six assassination teams, all of which failed. We don't know why they failed.

The claim is that Trafficante has secretly made a deal with Castro, over the CIA.

Trafficante then enlists the aid of two other mob godfathers, Sam Giancana and Carlos Marcello, both of whom live in the United States, not Cuba, to kill the president of the United States.

And of course, they need a fall guy ("a patsy"), so they choose Lee Harvey Oswald, and the entire US government goes along with this Mob fiction in the Warren Commission report.

Does it make sense that these three powerful Mafia dons would have risked the wrath of the United States government by such an action?

Let's have just a little skepticism as we continue with Jack Anderson's article.

The CIA veteran who directed the abortive attempt to assassinate Castro, William Harvey, told his superiors that the operation had backfired against President Kennedy, associates said. Then-CIA Director John McCone shared this shocking report with Robert F. Kennedy and the new president, Lyndon B. Johnson, our sources said.

In the 1970s, a congressional committee investigated CIA's use of Mafia hit men to kill Castro. Senate investigators asked questions about whether Castro used the Mafia to retaliate against Kennedy. The committee subpoenaed Santo Trafficante, Sam Giancana, and the Mobster who worked with Harvey, Johnny Rosselli.

Trafficante fled to the Caribbean, our sources said. But before Giancana and Rosselli could say anything that might link Trafficante to Dallas, they were slain. Police concluded from the evidence that the men were hit by Trafficante. Trafficante, who died in 1987, refused to answer committee questions.[165]

It's all a tight little package, until you realize the CIA, and particularly, Ted Shackley's boss, William Harvey, was in charge of all parts of the narrative. It's Harvey who picked Shackley to head the Miami CIA station in charge of going after Castro, it's Harvey and Shackley who handed over a U-Haul full of guns and ammunition to Rosselli, and it's Harvey who told his bosses, "Sorry guys, our Mafia buddies got out of hand, turned traitor with Castro, and killed the president."

Let's just imagine for a moment that this scenario is true, and that there would be good reasons to hide it from the public.

In the shadows, don't you think the CIA and the FBI would absolutely rip the Mafia apart?

Are we genuinely supposed to believe that in the immediate aftermath of the Kennedy assassination in 1963, the CIA knew that Santo Trafficante, Carlos Marcello, and Johnny Rosselli were involved, and simply let them go on living until called by Congress in 1976? The CIA supposedly had trained assassins (but they had lost six of those teams in Cuba, so maybe they were low on manpower), and they couldn't put any of them on the job of taking out the guys who killed the president?

I, for one, don't believe this narrative.

***

But in July 2022, the *Daily Mail* claimed they had the story which would finally reveal the truth about the Kennedy assassination in an article entitled "The Most Convincing Account Yet of How—and Why—the Mob Killed JFK: New Film by Relative of Mob Boss Sheds Fresh Light on the President's Assassination Nearly 60 Years on."

Aren't you trembling with anticipation that now, after all these years, you're finally going to get "the truth?" Get ready for that thrilling account!

> As the most notorious boss of the Chicago Mafia since Al Capone, Sam Giancana controlled a notorious criminal empire stretching across America.
>
> He had an army of thugs to call on, but for two days in November 1963, he asked for help from his little brother, Pepe.
>
> He was only a humble, illegal bookie in the Giancana empire, but Sam needed someone to chauffer him around while the mobsters who usually did so were out of town.
>
> As Pepe later confided to family, those men had gone to Dallas to do a job for Giancana—one that would become a seminal moment of the 20th century.[166]

You've got your exciting hook. Sam Giancana was the biggest, baddest Mafia chieftain since Al Capone, but this heartless villain had a soft spot for his little brother, Pepe, whom he brought in when his best evil henchmen had to go out of town on an important job. And it was the humble Pepe, who would finally give this truth to the world.

> Now, at long last, we may be coming close to the truth. Filmmaker Nicholas Celozzi—the great nephew of Sam Giancana—says his Great Uncle Pepe and other members of his family have finally confided to him exactly how the Mafia killed JFK—and just as importantly—allowed him to reveal it.
>
> He is working with the Pulitzer Prize-winning screenwriter and director David Mamet to produce a new—and what they believe could be definitive—version of the final 48 hours of President Kennedy's life.
>
> "The story I get from Pepe was the underbelly of what happened on those two days, from a man who was a fly on the wall listening to how this was coming together," Celozzi told the Mail this week. "Sam had a very tight circle of who he trusted. His brother, with whom he was very close, was one of them."[167]

Now, let me be clear about this. I can't tell you if everybody in this story is being honest or not. I wasn't chauffeuring Giancana around in 1963.

But as a former CIA investigator of some skill, when a crime family says they're finally going to "tell the truth," about an important historical event, I'm a little skeptical. But let's return to Pepe's story, as told by his great nephew.

> The 1964 Warren Commission into the killing decided that Oswald had acted alone, but 15 years later, the U.S. House Select Committee on Assassinations–set up to investigate the deaths of JFK and Martin Luther King–concluded that Kennedy was "probably assassinated as a result of a conspiracy."
>
> Oliver Stone's 1991 film "JFK" wove an elaborate web of conspiracy around the shooting, including the Mob, CIA, Army generals, FBI agents, Dallas police, Cuban dissidents, New Orleans gays, and pedophile ex-priests.
>
> But while it's hard to actually imagine any part of the U.S. establishment–even the spooks–executing a President, the Mafia sounds entirely feasible.[168]

And that, ladies and gentlemen, is the intelligence agency persuasion switch. They know the typical reader will be familiar with the Oliver Stone version of the Kennedy assassination, so they lightly mock it, then give you a simpler version, the Mob did it. They're hoping you've never really wanted to believe segments of our own government participated in this horrific crime, because you're a good person who doesn't want to believe our leaders could be so corrupt.

And so, they're giving you a psychological escape hatch.

It was the Mafia, and only the Mafia.

Now, that you're primed, they'll start picking away at the Warren Commission findings, but in a way that points not at our intelligence agencies or other branches of the government, but at the Mob.

> The Warren Commission accepted Ruby's claims that he acted impulsively, shooting Oswald outside Dallas police headquarters out of "insane grief" over JFK's killing.

According to Nicholas Celozzi, Ruby was one of three members of a crucial triangle in the Mafia's JFK operation that also included two Sam Giancana stooges and assassins–Johnny "Handsome John" Rosselli and Charles "Chucky The Typewriter" Nicoletti.

The suave, polished and perma-tanned Rosselli was the Mob's man out West, helping the Chicago Mafia (known as The Outfit) operate in Las Vegas and Hollywood. He was friends with Frank Sinatra and Marilyn Monroe and had even ventured into film producing.[169]

Can you understand how to the average mind, this is so much more psychologically compelling than believing in a government conspiracy? Those questions raised by generations of conspiracy theorists can be answered, but in a way that doesn't make you question the basic foundations upon which our current government is built.

Everybody's a winner, including the intelligence agencies! And since you're already on the hook, they'll feed you more details to seal the deal.

According to Pepe, Rosselli had become a "highly proficient" marksman while helping to organize the training of anti-Castro mercenaries at a secret camp in the Florida everglades.

Both Giancana and Rosselli had been deeply involved in running Mob-controlled casinos in Cuba and were furious when Castro took them over and closed them down.

According to CIA documents released in 2007, they were also furious when JFK closed down the U.S. operation to remove Castro. Nicoletti was a hulking, "stone-cold" hitman for Giancana. His very first "hit" had been his own father, whom he'd shot when he was 12, allegedly in self-defense after Nicoletti Sr. drunkenly pursued him with a knife.[170]

Do you see how you're being distracted from the question of CIA involvement in the Kennedy assassination? You're thinking about Rosselli becoming a good shot while working at the CIA's secret Cuban mercenary base in the Florida everglades. You're thinking about the Mob running casinos in Cuba and being angry when they get shut down. You're creating an image in your mind of Charles Nicoletti, the "hulking, stone-cold hitman" who killed his own father.

What you're not thinking about is whether those CIA elements, like Miami CIA station chief, Ted Shackley, were happy with Kennedy's shutting down of the Castro assassination plans.

And for one final detail about Charles "Chucky the Typewriter" Nicoletti there's this gem: "He was said to be so inured to violence that he calmly ate a plate of pasta while killing a man by squeezing his head in a vise."[171]

With that image in your brain, do you have any available space to question what the CIA was doing? And if you do, that available space will be taken up by throwing mud at the victim of the crime, President Kennedy.

> While other Mafia chiefs kept a low profile, Giancana reveled in the limelight, especially when he was out with one of his glamorous mistresses.
>
> Astonishingly, two of them—actress Marilyn Monroe and a beautiful woman named Judith Exner—were having affairs with him over the same period they were also seeing JFK.
>
> Rumor had it that Giancana helped get JFK elected by exploiting the Mafia's power over union votes, so he and his cronies were furious when Kennedy allowed brother Bobby, his Attorney General, to launch a crusade against organized crime.[172]

Every part of that passage may be correct.

But it may not be the entire story.

In some accounts of the story, it was JFK's father, Joseph Kennedy, who approached Giancana to help with the 1960 election, and JFK and Bobby were appalled when they found out, banishing their father from the White House.

And here's a news flash for you.

Accusations have been made that Nixon also made overtures to the Mafia during the 1960 election.

How else do you explain that in 1971, Nixon commuted the prison sentence of union boss, Jimmy Hoffa,[173] who was accused of investing union pension funds with the Mafia's Las Vegas operations?

Context is everything.

Otherwise, I think the account has a lot of truth behind it, as well as explaining some mysteries that have always puzzled me.

> According to Pepe, Rosselli was tasked with shooting Kennedy if Oswald missed–while Nicoletti's job was to dispose of Oswald afterwards.
>
> As noted by the House Select Committee on Assassinations, Oswald was connected to the Mafia through various people, notably an uncle, Charles Murrett, who was not only a father figure to him but a key lieutenant to the powerful New Orleans Mafia boss Carlos Marcello.
>
> Some have argued that Marcello was the real brains behind the Mafia plot to kill JFK. Celozzi, Giancana's great-nephew, accepts Marcello may well have been the one who suggested Oswald, whose admiration for Fidel Castro opened up the delicious possibility that the Cuban leader might be blamed for the president's murder.[174]

The dog which isn't barking (to steal an allusion to the famous Sherlock Homes detective story) is what the CIA or FBI were doing at this time? Or are we supposed to believe the Mob, on its own, was plotting the murder of the president?

To put it bluntly, the Mafia was the operational team for the CIA's campaign to kill Castro. Does it make sense that the Mafia would then freelance their own operation to take out Kennedy?

While the Mafia are outlaws, the FBI and CIA are even more powerful, having the force of law.

As I've said before, the best way to make people believe a lie is to tell as much of the truth as you can, then when you get to the critical part, you start to lie. Consider the possible different interpretations of the following passage.

> However, Pepe Giancana told his great nephew that Oswald, watching the Kennedy motorcade from an upper floor window of the Texas School Book Depository, was supposed to shoot him. But knowing he was 'unreliable,' Giancana sent down Roselli as backup.

According to Pepe, the plan did go wrong. Oswald fired at JFK but missed. When he heard a second shot go off–courtesy of the president's real killer, Roselli, who was lurking with a rifle near the infamous "grassy knoll" where a second gunman has long been alleged to have been waiting–he realized he'd been set up.

He fled the building, and on seeing Nicoletti and JD Tippit, a corrupt Dallas police officer, waiting in a car to pick him up, he took off. They followed and finally caught up with him an hour later in a residential neighborhood.[175]

I have to admit that the death of Dallas police officer, JD Tippit, has always been something of a mystery to me.

But here's an explanation.

Oswald knew the police officer with Nicoletti was there to kill him.

Celozzi wants us to believe Oswald was intended as the main shooter, but that makes no sense, given that Roselli, the clearly superior marksman, was supposedly insurance if Oswald missed.

I think it's just as plausible that Oswald was told (possibly by the CIA or FBI, who if he wasn't an asset before "defecting" to Russia, was most likely one afterwards), that he was part of a "fake" assassination of the president.

In other words, Oswald was a "patsy," just like he said he was. This is from the *Daily Mail* article:

> "There was a witness that saw it [Tippit and Oswald in their final encounter] and she said there were two guys in the car," said Celozzi. "Now, from what Pepe told me, Nicoletti was screaming at Oswald to get in and he said, excuse my French, 'F- you, you're trying to kill me.'"
>
> Tippit, the cop, then got out of the car and after a brief exchange, Oswald shot him, fatally. Pepe's account of Oswald then escaping with Nicoletti in hot pursuit certainly tallies with the statements of several witnesses who said they saw two men fleeing the scene.[176]

One of the skills you learn as an investigator and CIA analyst is you let the story unfold, keeping an open mind, because then you might begin to

Kevin with Robert Gates. *(photo courtesy of the author)*

Kevin as an antiterrorism instructor. *(photo courtesy of the author)*

Kevin on a counter assault team training exercise. *(photo courtesy of the author)*

Kevin on an antiterrorism assault team. *(photo courtesy of the author)*

Kevin on assignment. *(photo courtesy of the author)*

Certificate of Training – Managing and Leading in CIA.

Certificate of Graduate Study in Forensic Psychophysiological Detection of Deception.

Kevin next to armored limousines at William Casey's wake. *(photo courtesy of the author)*

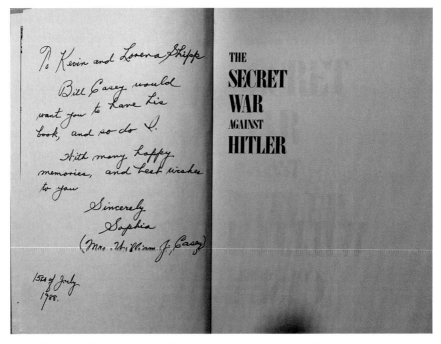

To Kevin and Lorena Shipp

Bill Casey would want you to have his book, and so do I.

With many happy memories, and best wishes to you

Sincerely
Sophia
(Mrs. William J. Casey)

15th of July
1988.

THE
**SECRET
WAR**
AGAINST
HITLER

Note from William Casey's wife, Sophia. *(photo courtesy of the author)*

Diabolical CIA Officials

Allen W. Dulles (*photo by Cecil W. Stoughton*)

William Casey (*photo by Michael Evans*)

Alvin "Buzzy" Krongard

Ted Shackley (left)

Kevin with George H. W. Bush. *(photo courtesy of the author)*

see the anomalies. We're supposed to disbelieve the Oliver Stone version of the JFK assassination because it has too many moving parts, the CIA, military intelligence, the Cubans, the Mafia, and of course, the Dallas police department.

But wait!

Pepe Giancana and his grandnephew, the filmmaker, Nicholas Celozzi, are telling us that the Dallas police were involved.

What does that mean for the other groups?

Six decades later, we still don't have all the facts about the JFK assassination.

But I'd hope the picture of what happened is clearing as you read. Like placing disjointed pieces of a large, complex puzzle, as you discover their linkages, they begin to click into place with a satisfying snap. And with the pieces falling into place, a clearer picture of events begins to emerge.

The only interpretation, which makes sense to me as to why our government didn't go after the Mafia for the JFK assassination, is that they were partners in the endeavor.

And they're managing still, to keep that final secret from all of us.

***

Shifting gears here, let's return to our examination of Ted Shackley, and what the CIA Miami station was doing just prior to and just after the Kennedy assassination. From the book, *Blond Ghost*:

> As Shackley-managed raids [into Cuba] continued and Castro's denunciations reverberated, far in the background Kennedy and Castro took slight moves towards accommodation. In early September, Carlos Lechunga, the Cuban ambassador to the United Nations, discreetly mentioned to William Atwood, the U.S. ambassador to Guinea, that Castro was interested in talks with his American enemy. The following month, Kennedy informed Jean Daniel, a French journalist on his way to see Castro, that he could live with a socialist Cuba, but not one ruled by a Soviet lackey. See me when you get back from Cuba, Kennedy told Daniel.[177]

Shackley's own book told us he didn't think Kennedy had sufficient enthusiasm for the Cuban operation. Kennedy had failed to provide air support to the Cuban rebels and as such, likely avoided their plans to be dragged into that conflict. Eighteen years after the end of World War II, Kennedy was looking for a way out of the Cold War. This was just another example of what some would call Kennedy's cowardice in confronting the communists, and others would call a bold move towards peace.

But even as Kennedy was trying to promote peace with Cuba, and by extension the Soviet Union, the CIA was meeting with one of its assets who was still inside Cuba, Rolando Cubela (code-named AMLASH.) Cubela was a hero of the fight against the previous Cuban dictator, Fulgencio Batista, a current government official in Castro's regime, and believed in the CIA goal of assassinating Castro. The effort with Cubela would also involve a CIA asset falsely posing as a representative of the attorney general of the United States, Robert Kennedy.

> Des FitzGerald, posing as a personal representative of Bobby Kennedy, saw Cubela in Paris on October 29. He promised Cubela that the United States would support a rebellion against Castro. On November 22, 1963, FitzGerald and case officer Nestor Sanchez again rendezvoused with Cubela in Paris. The CIA men pledged that Shackley's station would deliver Cubela weapons, including high-powered rifles that could be used to kill Castro. (Afterward, Langley cabled Shackley and told him to prepare a cache of hand grenades, guns, ammunition, and plastic explosives for AMLASH.) The two CIA men presented Cubela with a ballpoint pen rigged to contain poison. Surely, Cubela protested, the Agency could come up with something better. He refused to take the pen with him to Cuba.
>
> A CIA internal report, referring to the AMLASH case, later observed, "It is likely that at the very moment President Kennedy was shot, a CIA officer was meeting with a Cuban agent . . . and giving him an assassination device for use against Castro."[178]

When critics of the CIA suggest the Agency acts like a bunch of cowboys, the Cuban fiasco is often exhibit number one in their argument. What makes me exceedingly angry when I consider the Cuban operation is the question of whether this was an exception to how the CIA operates, or just business as usual. Much of this information was known when I was a young CIA officer. One of my jobs at CIA was onboarding new agents, standing in front of a bunch of new recruits in the auditorium known as "the bubble" and telling them the "truth" about the agency they had joined.

But instead of telling the truth, I'm now convinced I showered them with lies.

I said the Agency existed as a servant of our democracy and elected leaders, not the hidden hand. Of course, some would bring up the Cuban situation, Project Phoenix in Vietnam, perhaps even the recent Iran-Contra scandal, or any number of other instances, and maybe there would be some nervous laughter.

But I'd then gently guide them back to the Agency approved narrative.

What can I say?

I was a true believer.

Perhaps that's the path of all thinking people, we believe so fervently when we're young, and doubt so much when we're older.

Nothing makes me sadder than when I consider the following two paragraphs, realizing how Kennedy's attempt to broker a peace with Castro failed in the wake of his death, and how my Agency tried to use his death for their own ends, without even pausing for a moment to mourn his passing.

In Cuba, Castro on November 22 was lunching with Jean Daniel, the French journalist, when he learned Kennedy had been shot dead. "This is bad news," he responded. Later in the day, he asked Daniel, "What authority does [Lyndon Johnson] exercise over the CIA?"

The day after Kennedy's death, Langley ordered Shackley to activate JMWAVE's propaganda assets. The CIA wanted to make certain that media reports on the tragedy observed that Kennedy's "last major address to [a Latin America] audience concentrate[d] on Cuban freedom." Headquarters also cabled Shackley, "Postpone [sabotage] ops indefinitely. Rescheduling will depend upon consultations with appropriate officials"–the new President and his advisers.[179]

The mischief and sabotage operations against Cuba would continue for some time under the new president, Lyndon Johnson. But they would reach the same conclusion Kennedy had reached much earlier, namely that there was little we could do to dislodge Castro.

But there was a new war to be fought in Vietnam.

And Ted Shackley would be front and center in that effort as well. One might say he was at the peak of his powers, the ultimate arbiter of life and death for an entire nation.

***

CHAPTER SIX

TED SHACKLEY – FROM VIETNAM TO TUCKER CARLSON

Most Americans consider the Vietnam War to have begun in August of 1964 with the alleged attack by North Vietnamese patrol boats on the *USS Maddow* in what became known as the "Gulf of Tonkin" incident and ending with Nixon removing the last American troops in March of 1973. However, a more complete history is necessary to understanding the various players and interests involved.

> For over two decades, the CIA and its predecessor, had been on the prowl in Vietnam. In the latter years of World War II, OSS operatives forged an alliance with Vietnamese nationalists–particularly the League for the Independence of Vietnam, or Viet Minh–in the war against Japan, and cooperated closely with Ho Chi Minh, the Viet Minh leader, and a founder of the Indochinese Communist Party. But after the war, Washington's cold warriors supported France's bid to regain its colony–an effort that led to war between the Viet Minh and the French.[180]

That war would end with the French defeat at Dien Bien Phu in 1954, with the country divided into a northern and southern section, much as Korea had been after the end of the Second World War. For the president of South Vietnam, the Americans backed Ngo Dinh Diem, a Catholic bachelor living in Europe, which was probably not a good choice considering the country was overwhelmingly Buddhist. It also probably didn't help his popularity among average Vietnamese in that he had served under the French.

> Washington was not counting on Diem alone. There was also the CIA. In 1954, Edward Lansdale arrived in Vietnam on assignment for the Agency. His orders were straightforward: stop the communists. Lansdale pulled together a unit that waged paramilitary operations and political-psychological warfare against the Viet Minh. A Lansdale team based in the north, and run by Lou Conein, Shackley's former office mate in Nuremberg, sabotaged Hanoi's buses and railway equipment. In South Vietnam, Lansdale bribed religious and political sect leaders to support the aloof Diem.[181]

The effort in Vietnam mirrored much of the effort in the early 1960s in Cuba, with the exception, though, that American forces could openly operate in the country. If the Cold Warriors who'd lost the Cuba fight thought it was because Castro had thrown an iron curtain around their country, Vietnam would show what the American could do without such restraints.

But despite this covert war fought for more than a decade between the United States and the North Vietnamese, American forces were eventually needed, and the first combat troops arrived on March 8, 1965, 3,500 US Marines, joining 25,000 American military advisers already in the country.

But despite the presence of US combat forces in the country, the Viet Cong were winning, especially because they generally avoided large-scale battles, and instead focused on hit and run, guerilla tactics.

> In 1965 the CIA station helped create the South Vietnamese Census Grievance units that visited villages to elicit the residents' complaints and improve relations between villagers and Saigon. Another CIA program was less warm in intentions: the counter-terror (CT) teams. The CT squads were born out of frustration.

The regular army could not do much about VC guerillas who harassed, attacked, and killed Vietnamese civilians allied with Saigon. The CT units–funded, trained, and guided by CIA officers–were small paramilitary groups outside the normal military chain of command. Their goal, chief of station Peer DeSilva wrote in his memoirs, was "to bring danger and death to the Vietcong functionaries."[182]

The well-known intelligence agency expression, "plausible deniability," springs to mind when considering the Phoenix program.

Yeah, sure, the CIA "funded, trained and guided" the Phoenix effort.

But when things went badly, well, like killing the wrong person, or having suspects regularly die during interrogation, you couldn't really blame the CIA.

After all, it was supposed to be the South Vietnamese who were really in charge of the program. But even when the CIA stepped up its role, the results did not seem to improve.

In the name of efficiency, the Agency in 1967 established an outfit to coordinate all intelligence on the VC and gave birth to what would become the most notorious CIA venture of the war: the Phoenix program. Under Phoenix, field representatives of different U.S. and South Vietnamese agencies swapped intelligence and decided how to best "exploit" the material. Exploitation meant capturing or killing suspected VC leaders, ambushing Viet Cong couriers and suppliers, raiding VC strongholds. The intent of Phoenix was to develop lists of VC cadres and a solid picture of the VC network, so the CIA-backed PRUs and other forces knew where and whom to hit. The program, most CIA veterans have claimed, was not set up as an assassination unit. But deaths mounted, as suspected VC were killed by the PRUs and other units.[183]

That's the CIA's best defense? It was not "set up as an assassination unit," even though that's what it quickly became?

In December of 1968, Shackley took over as chief of the CIA station in Saigon, and it was under his tenure that the worst of the Phoenix program atrocities would take place. In *Blond Ghost*, this is how author David Corn describes Shackley during his Vietnam days:

> Befitting his position as the top U.S. spook in the hottest spot on the globe, Shackley struck an imperial manner. He drove through the crowded streets of Saigon in a large chauffeur-driven armor-plated American car. The floor was steel reinforced to protect against detonated mines. A security guard sat in the front seat with a shotgun. Bodyguards were always close by. He carried a .45 in his briefcase. There was talk among the junior officers that his briefcase contained steel plates. In the event of any trouble, he could flip it open and duck his head in.[184]

In the sixteen years since Shackley had first joined the Agency, from being humiliated by the Soviets with the fantasy of a rebel Polish army, losing to Castro while heading up the Miami station, two years heading up the Laos CIA mission and guiding American bombers to targets on the Ho Chi Minh trail, he was finally on top. Thousands of miles away from the politicians back at home, Shackley could exercise his will on the world's largest stage.

> Shackley desired complete control of the 600-person station. He insisted that base chiefs send reports to Washington through his office. He closely watched the finances. There was a constant stream of personnel problems: an alcoholic officer who wrapped his car around a tree, a pregnant secretary. On some days, Shackley had to race off to a meeting at the Presidential Palace. Once the Nixon administration settled in, Henry Kissinger was always on Shackley's back. Shackley briefed members of Congress, Vice President Spiro Agnew, and foreign dignitaries.[185]

Shackley was in charge of the largest US intelligence presence of any foreign country in the nation's largest battle. And like any good spook, he knew that part of the fight was the persuasion piece with the public back home, and Shackley knew how to play that game.

Shackley struck up friendships with a small number of journalists, the older Asian hands who were mostly sympathetic with Washington's aims in Indochina. The core group of those favored included Robert Shaplen of *The New Yorker,* Keyes Beech of *The Chicago Daily News* and later *The Los Angeles Times,* and Bud Merick of *U.S. News and World Report.* Shackley had little time for the young Turks of the press corps who reported the war with a mistrust previously unknown to mainstream American media.

The chief became a guardian source for the believers–but totally off the record. If one of the gang needed to file a story on the latest strategy indications out of Hanoi, Shackley graciously arranged for a briefing with a station officer.[186]

Once you realize that since their beginning, the CIA has always been focused on deceiving the American public in a manner consistent with their own aims, understanding our recent history becomes much simpler. And as much as that may be a sobering thought, it's also a sign of their fragility. The CIA needs the American public to believe their lies, or else it's game over. The people do hold the power, which is why the CIA has invested so much time in manipulating the perceptions of citizens and politicians.

Because as much as the CIA's version of truth may hold sway for a while, over time the ultimate truth does tend to appear.

Castro was more trusted by the Cuban people than the leaders who had come before him.

The Vietnamese were tired of being ruled by the French or the Americans and wanted all the foreigners gone.

And Project Phoenix was an assassination program. Much of the truth about it would eventually be reported in the pages of the *New York Times,* by a younger generation of reporters, who for a while, broke free of the confines of the national security state. This is how it was described in February of 1970, as the program grabbed the attention of the Senate Foreign Relations Committee:

Designed by the United States Central Intelligence Agency to weed out an estimated 75,000 Vietcong political leaders and agents from the civilian population, the program is not the sinister cloak-and-dagger, terror operation that some critics, including the Vietcong, have portrayed it to be, these officials insist.

"That's nonsense," one of them said, "Phoenix is just not a killing organization. The kind of things they (Foreign Relations Committee members] are probably looking for are not happening that much–which is not to say they are not happening at all."

Briefly, Phoenix works this way: When local officials feel they have enough evidence against a person suspected of being connected with the Vietcong, they arrest him. If he is not released quickly–suspects often vanish out the back doors of police stations within two hours of their arrests–he is taken to a province interrogation center.[187]

When I read this account, I'm amazed by the restraint of the reporter. He's clearly raising the suspicions felt by members of the Senate Foreign Relations committee, but he's also letting the CIA give their version of events. In some ways, this is a model of good investigative reporting, as it seeks to raise an important issue, lets both sides speak, then acquaints you with the important facts which will hopefully let you decide which side has the better argument.

In the course of normal military operations, some suspected Vietcong agents may defect, or be killed or captured. When reports of these operations filter back to the Phoenix district headquarters, officials simply call out the numbers and add them to their scores. This helps them meet quotas set by higher headquarters.

"One thing about the Vietnamese–they will meet every quota that's established for them," said one critic of the program. "That's what makes the head count so deceptive. How do you know they're not assigning names and titles to dead bodies?"

In 1969, according to official figures, 19,534 Vietcong were "neutralized." That number included 8,515 reportedly captured, 6,187 killed, and 4,832 who defected.[188]

Now we have an understanding about the size of the potential problem. According to the CIA's own numbers, in 1969, just a little under twenty thousand Vietnamese found themselves in the hands of the Phoenix program, and just a little over six thousand died as a result. (For a daily death rate of about seventeen people a day, a hundred and eighteen a week, or about five hundred and fifteen a month.) However, we also know these numbers aren't trustworthy. Is it likely the numbers of dead are over-inflated, or underinflated? On the one hand, the program is supposed to look successful, but on the other, there's a concern that if the number of dead is too high, it might look like a "killing organization." Let's just agree that it's an open question and look at other aspects of the program.

> Probably the most controversial arm of the Phoenix program in each province is a group called the Provisional Reconnaissance Unit. It consists of a dozen or more South Vietnamese mercenaries, originally recruited and paid handsomely by the C.I.A. to serve under the province chief as the major "action arm" of the program.
>
> According to Americans working at both the local and regional levels, these units are made up of local hoodlums, soldiers of fortune, draft-dodgers, defectors, and others who receive about 15,000 piasters a month–compared with 4,000 paid the common soldier–to conduct raids after Vietcong agents, ambush their trails and meeting places and simply arrest them under the direction of a South Vietnamese officer who takes orders from the province chief.[189]

Without even asking the question of the psychological makeup of the people involved in this program, there are significant problems involved in its very makeup. The relatively high salary means this would have been a coveted job to the South Vietnamese, and as a consequence, those involved would be highly motivated to please their superiors, namely the South Vietnamese government and the CIA.

Were there any incentives in this program to protect the rights of those who might have been falsely accused, protect the physical safety of those undergoing interrogation, or make sure any killings were justified?

Not that I can see.

As the hearings before the Senate Foreign Relations Committee into the Phoenix program continued, many Senators were confused by the testimony, as was the public. The *New York Times* published another story about the growing controversy.

> The Senate Foreign Relations Committee may have been confused by last week's testimony on Operation Phoenix. The committee had a report from the American military command in Saigon that seemed to give Phoenix the credit for hunting down and killing 6,187 Vietcong political cadres last year. Then it heard William E. Colby, the pacification chief in Vietnam, emphatically deny that Phoenix was an "assassination" program.[190]

The question might be, when is an assassination program not an assassination program? Do words change the reality of a situation? Or is the reality of a situation something solid, like the law of gravity, which may be denied, but continues to exist whether we acknowledge it or not? The *Times* tried to dance around the question as best they could.

> The information that may lead to the "neutralization" of these men— the official figures state that in addition to those killed, 8,505 were captured and 4,382 persuaded to defect in 1969–is then passed on to Vietnamese officials who can call any one of several shadowy specialist organizations for action.
>
> These include Provincial Reconnaissance Units, Armed Propaganda Teams, Kit Carson Scouts and Seal commando teams. Operating in small units, generally of six to twelve men, they quietly penetrate into contested or Vietcong-controlled territory to carry out their missions. And despite whatever denials are being made now in Washington and Saigon, their mission is to get their man, dead or alive.[191]

If you wanted somebody killed in Vietnam, or "neutralized" there were so many "shadowy" groups you could call on for assistance. Is it any surprise that a lot of bad things would happen?

By July of 1971, the Phoenix program had become such a subject of controversy that William Colby, the former head of the pacification program in Vietnam, appeared before the House Foreign Operations and Government Information Subcommittee to discuss the problems. As reported in the *New York Times*:

> In prepared testimony, Mr. Colby, who recently returned from his assignment in Saigon, gave the number of people killed under Operation Phoenix since 1968 at 20,587, of whom 3,560 were killed from January through May this year. For earlier periods the number of deaths were put at 2,559 for 1968, at 6,187 in 1969, and at 8,191 last year.
>
> Two Republican Representatives, Ogden R. Reid of Westchester and Paul N. McCloskey of California, charged that Operation Phoenix had been responsible for "indiscriminate killings" of civilians and the imprisonment of thousands of others in violation of international accords in legal actions in wartime.[192]

The CIA admitted that this program in Vietnam killed more than twenty thousand people, and there are strong indications that many of these victims may have had no role with the Vietcong. When three thousand of our citizens were killed on September 11, 2001, we initiated a wide-ranging global war which has now lasted more than twenty years.

Consider that for a twenty-three-year-old today, they have never known a time when their country was not at war somewhere in the world. (At this moment, we have admitted having special forces on the ground in Syria, and I'm convinced we also have similar forces, including CIA, on the ground in Ukraine.)

Even though congressional investigators were doing their best in 1970 and 1971, how does the Phoenix program appear to us many years later?

In 1990, the well-known political commentator, Morley Safer, wrote a review for a book about the Phoenix program by Douglas Valentine, which was published in the *New York Times*. After first describing the Phoenix program as "an unseemly liaison between impotent military tactics and money-logged technology," as well as a "monster child with its computer brain and assassin's instinct," Safer dug deep into what went wrong with the CIA's plan.

> So out into the countryside went teams of accountants and case offi-
> cers, Vietnamese assassins and their American counterparts, with
> bags and bags of money, the whole effort tethered to a computer in
> the United States Embassy in Saigon. And from the embassy came
> reports again and again that the program was working. Body count
> became our most important product . . .
>
> The Phoenix program became a playground for the demented
> fringes of both American and Vietnamese society. It was a brothel
> for both blood lust and printout lust, featuring a weird crew of
> characters: grizzled Army officers, bespectacled accountants and
> bloodless computer modelers. It had its own air force, training
> camps, and interrogation centers. Torture chambers, if you like.[193]

It's often the distance of years that gives one the best perspective on a situation. And as we've argued in this book, as human beings we want the truth to be revealed. Despite people's initial intentions, they want to tell others what they have done, even those who have participated in the most terrible of acts. If you don't understand that essential human need, you will forever be puzzled as to why most horrific acts eventually, and inevitably, come to light.

When during the Afghan war there was a suggestion made to create a Phoenix-type force in Afghanistan, a professor of history from Tulsa University and author of a book about drug use in Vietnam penned a remarkable opinion piece, recounting some of the history of the Phoenix program.

> The most disturbing aspect was its inordinately high human costs.
> A Phoenix advisor commented, "It was common knowledge that
> when someone was picked up their lives were about to end because the
> Americans most likely felt that, if they were to turn someone like that
> back into the countryside it would just be multiplying NLF follow-
> ers." In one publicized case, a detainee was kept in an air-conditioned
> room for four years to try and exploit his fear of the cold. His remains

were later dumped at sea. K. Barton Osbourne, a military intelligence specialist told Congress that he had witnessed acts of torture including the prodding of a person's brain with a six-inch dowel through his ear, and that in a year and a half with Phoenix, "not a single suspect survived interrogation." After being called before Congress to account for his actions, CIA Director William Colby conceded that Phoenix had led to the death of 20,000 civilians. The South Vietnamese government placed the total at over 40,000.[194]

However, after being briefly covered in the pages of the *New York Times* in 1970 and 1971, public discussion of the Phoenix program dwindled to almost nothing. As Americans we have a great historical memory for the 268 soldiers who died in Custer's Last Stand in 1876, for the 2,403 US personnel who died in the Japanese attack on Pearl Harbor in 1941, or the 2,996 people who died in the September 11, 2001, terror attacks on New York and Washington, DC.

But ask the average American about the twenty thousand to forty thousand Vietnamese killed by the CIA's Phoenix program and you're likely to get a blank stare.

Even in the book, *Legacy of Ashes*, by Tim Weiner, about the CIA, a National Book Award winner from 2007, a gargantuan read of 812 pages, there are only two mentions of the Phoenix program.

The first comes as the Vietnam War is winding down and there's the question of how to get some of the Vietnamese members of the Phoenix program out of Vietnam. The second is how much the Phoenix program was business as usual for the CIA.

The CIA had run secret interrogation centers before—beginning in 1950 in Germany, Japan, and Panama. It had participated in the torture of enemy combatants before—beginning in 1967, under the Phoenix program in Vietnam. It had kidnapped suspected terrorists and assassins before—most famously in 1997, in the case of Mir Amal Kansi, the killer of two CIA officers. But Bush gave the agency a new and extraordinary authority: to turn kidnapped suspects over to foreign security services for interrogation and torture, and to rely on the confessions they extracted.[195]

The Phoenix program is thus seen not as an aberration, but an example of how the CIA accomplishes its mission, in a way that would be shocking to the average American.

Shackley left Vietnam in early 1972, his tenure coinciding with the worst excesses of the Phoenix program, with which his name would be inexorably linked. As detailed in the book, *Blond Ghost*:

> Shackley returned to Washington from Saigon in February of 1972. He had not been stationed in headquarters since 1961. In the intervening years, secrets had been revealed, and the Agency's image had begun to tarnish. In 1964, Random House published the first significant expose of the Agency, *The Invisible Government*. Written by Washington journalists Thomas B. Ross and David Wise, the book spilled details of the botched Bay of Pigs invasion. It offered the first authoritative accounts of the CIA-backed coups in Iran and Guatemala. Ross and Wise suggested that the national security state had gone too far and that policymakers had become too reliant on the quick fixes of covert action.[196]

It's remarkable how contemporary 1964 seems in comparison to 2024. Sixty years later, we're still talking about how the CIA and the national security state has too much power. However, we're fortunate that we have more information, and can be a little more skeptical when we see situations which seemed to be guided by the hidden hand of the intelligence agencies. But do we genuinely consider how much they might be manipulating us?

> Three years later [in 1967], a series of articles in Ramparts magazine revealed the CIA's secret support of the National Student Association, proving that Shackley's colleagues were meddling in domestic affairs. Similar revelations followed in other media outlets, including The *New York Times*, which disclosed CIA connections with corporations, trusts, research centers, universities, and individuals. Some members of Congress grumbled that the CIA needed to be reined in.[197]

Shackley had once dreamed of becoming the director of the CIA, but as the Agency came under greater scrutiny, he would find his chances for advancement diminishing. Eventually, in 1979, he would be driven from the Agency.

However, Shackley always liked to be at the center of world events, and would eventually find his way back in a manner certain to cause enormous mayhem.

**

With the election of Jimmy Carter in 1976, America seemed to have chosen a different path from the darkness of the Johnson and Nixon years, as well as the caretaker presidency of Gerald Ford. While many were grateful for Ford's calm nature, others were suspicious because of his work on the Warren Commission, and many did not like the fact that he pardoned Nixon for his role in the Watergate scandal. Whatever one might think of the Georgia governor, Carter was not part of the Washington swamp.

Carter chose as his new director of the CIA, a Navy admiral, Stansfield Turner, with little experience in the shady world of intelligence. Shackley was quickly to find himself in Turner's crosshairs.

On the morning of April 12, 1977, Admiral Stansfield Turner sat at the breakfast table and stared at the banner headline on the front of *The Washington Post*. Turner, who had taken over as Director of Central Intelligence only five weeks earlier, could barely believe what he read. A story by Bob Woodward reported that a past CIA officer, Edwin Wilson, had procured the timing devices for the car-bomb murder of Orlando Letelier, a former Chilean ambassador to the United States. In September of 1976, the expatriate Letelier and an assistant had been killed while driving along Massachusetts Avenue in Washington. The ex-CIA man according to Woodward, also plotted with Agency-trained exiles–graduates of the Miami station [Shackley's former guys]–to assassinate an opponent of Libyan President Moammar Qadaffi. The DCI's exasperation heightened when he reached the following sentence: "There is some evidence that Wilson may have had contact with one or more current CIA employees."[198]

America was getting sick of its government, particularly the intelligence agencies, who in recent years, had been shown to be overthrowing foreign governments, engaging in war crimes like the Phoenix program, deceiving the public through its collusion with journalists in Project Mockingbird, as well as performing mind control and drug experiments on unwitting Americans with MK-Ultra.

Now the CIA apparently stood guilty of murdering foreign diplomats on Massachusetts Avenue in Washington, DC.

How dark were the secrets of the CIA?

Turner was going to get to the bottom of Woodward's allegations.

The information Turner received left him aghast. Two midlevel CIA men had worked with Wilson on deals that might be illegal. Worse, two senior officials had been associating with Wilson. The admiral sat at his desk stunned. How could anyone in the Agency hobnob with an assassin-for-hire? The senior officers were either crooked or dumb. They were the type who had brought disgrace onto the CIA, the ones who supplied ammunition to Agency critics. Had they learned nothing from the spasm of wrenching scrutiny the Company recently experienced? As long as Turner was at the helm, neither of the pair stood a fool's chance of promotion. One was Tom Clines, a senior officer in the training division; the other, Ted Shackley, the associate deputy director for operations.[199]

In 1977, Shackley had come to the attention of the new director of the CIA, and it wasn't for a positive reason. It might be shocking for the average person to realize that associating with a known assassin won't get you fired from the CIA. It will simply stop your upward career trajectory, which is exactly the position in which Shackley found himself in 1977.

But that didn't mean Shackley was without friends.

In fact, the previous CIA director had been a strong supporter of Shackley, and would eventually become vice president, and later president of the United States, George H. W. Bush, where he would bring Shackley in to troubleshoot tricky operations.

> When Shackley became ADDO [associate deputy director for operations] a year earlier in May of 1976–continuing his arc toward the Director's office–George Bush had been running the CIA for four months. Part cheerleader and part caretaker, Bush was no details man and assumed as his chief priority the soothing of the bruised egos of America's spies. Much of Bush's time was consumed by treks to Capitol Hill where he defended his new family.[200]

I need to take a brief detour here to talk about George H. W. Bush, Reagan's vice president from 1981 to 1989 and president from 1989 to 1993, and his association with the CIA. Bush was the director of the CIA from January 30, 1976 to January 10, 1977, the day of Carter's inauguration.

The question is whether Bush had a previous association with the Central Intelligence Agency, and perhaps more importantly, whether he was involved in the CIA campaign against Castro, and what role, if any, he may have had in the Kennedy assassination.

The evidence for such claims begins with an FBI memo released in 1988, dated November 22, 1963.

> At 1:45 p.m., Mr. George H.W. Bush, President of the Zapata Offshore Drilling Company, Houston, Texas, residence 5525 Briar, Houston, telephonically furnished the following information to writer by long distance telephone call from Tyler, Texas.
>
> BUSH stated that he wanted to be kept confidential but wanted to furnish hearsay that he recalled hearing in recent weeks, the day and source unknown. He stated that one JAMES PARROTT has been talking of killing the president when he comes to Houston.
>
> BUSH stated that PARROTT is possibly a student at the University of Houston and is active in political matters in this area. He stated that he felt MRS. FAWLEY, telephone number SU 2-5239, or ARLENE SMITH, telephone number JA-9194 of the Harris County republican headquarters would be able to furnish additional information regarding the identity of PARROTT.

BUSH stated that he was proceeding to Dallas, Texas, would remain in the Sheraton-Dallas Hotel and return to his residence on 11-23-63. His office telephone number is CA 2-0395.[201]

A couple things are notable about this FBI memo. Bush identifies his location at the time of the assassination as being in Tyler, Texas, rather than in Dallas. And what's remarkable is that in the immediate aftermath of the assassination he calls the FBI to provide them with the name of a suspect, but years later cannot recall anything about his whereabouts on that day.

Was he simply being a good American, trying to provide information which might be helpful to the authorities? Or was there possibly another agenda at play?

Another important FBI document (actually released in the 1970s, but not read until the late 1980s), from November 29, 1963, comes directly from the office of FBI Director J. Edgar Hoover and addresses Bush's role with the Agency. The revelation was covered in a July 11, 1998, article in the *New York Times*, just as the presidential race with Bush running as the Republican nominee, and Massachusetts governor, Michael Dukakis, running for the democrats, was entering its final stages before the November election.

> *The Nation* magazine, in its current issue, quotes a memo of Nov. 29, 1963, from J. Edgar Hoover, the Bureau's Director at the time, to the State Department about the assassination of President John F. Kennedy.
>
> In the memo, according to the magazine, Mr. Hoover stated that the bureau had briefed "Mr. George Bush of the Central Intelligence Agency" on the reaction of Cuban exiles in Miami to the assassination.
>
> The magazine article, written by Joseph McBride, also quoted an unidentified source "with close connections to the intelligence community" as saying Mr. Bush "started working for the agency in 1960 or 1961, using his oil business as a cover for clandestine activities."[202]

As you're probably not surprised to realize, the issue of Bush's possible CIA connections in the 1960s never became a significant part of the 1988 presidential race.

That's another way the Project Mockingbird media operates.

If by chance, the truth does find a way to get published by somebody who genuinely cares about informing the public, the Agency simply finds a way to deny the story its needed oxygen, and it gets tossed down the collective memory hole.

And of course, the *Times* printed the expected denials.

> Stephen Hart, a spokesman for the Vice President, said that he had talked to Mr. Bush about the story and that the Vice President denied any involvement with the Agency before President Ford named him its Director in 1975.
>
> "He was an oilman in the early 1960s, and in 1963 he was running for the Senate," Mr. Hart said.
>
> Bill Devine, a spokesman for the intelligence agency, declined to comment on the possibility that Mr. Bush, or someone else with that name, worked for the agency in the 1960s.[203]

Another article by Steven Hager, who has extensively researched the Kennedy assassination and the CIA's activities in the 1960s, wrote this on the 50th anniversary of the Kennedy assassination about the possible involvement of George Bush.

> I guess you know Dealey Plaza was flooded with spooks fifty years ago. One young spook at the scene may have been George H.W. Bush, who was working deep cover for the CIA through his fledgling oil company Zapata, building platforms in the Gulf of Mexico, some of which were designed as resupply depots for the anti-Castro network operating out of Miami. The Miami CIA office had become the biggest in the world outside Langley and they had been training an army of refugees to retake Cuba from the commies. Check out the picture of someone who looks just like Bush in front of the Texas School Book Depository. By the way, Bush says he "can't remember" where he was when JFK was murdered, despite several FBI memos relating his interest in the case. Also, if that isn't Bush standing on the steps of the Depository, whoever it is has never come forward to clear Bush from any involvement.[204]

Although one can't call these claims proof, they are consistent with the available evidence. A later article in *The Nation*, after the death of George H. W. Bush in 2018, suggested how Bush might have been recruited into the CIA as an undergraduate, in much the same way as Buzzy Krongard was in the 1950s.

> According to Phillips [the author of a book about Bush's family], "from Yale's class of 1943 alone, at least forty-two young men entered the intelligence services." (Bush attended from 1945 to 1948), and nearly every major player involved in the Bay of Pigs invasion had been in Yale's secret Skull and Bones society. By the time Bush became director of the CIA in 1976, Phillips writes, "three generations of the Bush and Walker families already had some six decades of intelligence-related activity and experience under their belts," which apparently also involved a Mexico-CIA "money line" that made its way into "the hands of the Watergate burglars."[205]

When you start to assemble the facts, as any good CIA analyst is trained to do, you start to get a better picture of the battlefield. There's what those in the shadows want you to believe, and there's what actually happened. And central to these efforts, from Cuba, to Vietnam, to the Iran-Contra scandal, was the pivotal role of Ted Shackley.

> Obituaries have transformed the terror that Bush inflicted—as head of the CIA, as Ronald Reagan's vice president, and as president, on poor countries—depicting it as heroism. The invasion of Panama is given scant notice, and the first Gulf War is judged "just." But Bush helmed the CIA when it was working closely with Latin American death squads grouped under Operation Condor, naming Ted Shackley, implicated in terror operations in Southeast Asia and Latin America—including Vietnam's Phoenix program and the 1973 coup against Chile's Salvador Allende—the Agency's powerful associate deputy director for operations. Bush gave the go-ahead to the neoconservative Team B project, founded on the idea that, after the U.S. debacle in Vietnam, the agency had become too

soft on Third World nationalism. Politicizing intelligence, Team B provided the justification for Reagan's escalation of the Cold War, including the various operations that made up Iran/Contra.[206]

Sometimes it's not just a case of learning new facts, but looking at the facts you already knew, in a different light. Consider for a moment how you might view the last several decades of American history if you put George H. W. Bush as working with the CIA from 1960 or 1961, becoming its director in 1975, then sliding onto the Reagan ticket in 1980 (nearly becoming president in March of 1981 when Reagan barely escaped the assassin's bullet of John Hinkley, the son of a good Bush family friend), serving as Reagan's loyal vice president, becoming president on his own in 1988, then having his son, George W. Bush, become president in 2000, nine months before the September 11 attacks would launch a revival of the CIA.

One might even see the fabrics of design in these developments.

In retrospect, it's interesting to go back to McBride's 1988 article in *The Nation* on the discovery of Bush's earlier alleged role at the CIA.

Vice President Bush's autobiography, *Looking Forward*, written with Victor Gold (Doubleday, 1987), is vague to the point of being cryptic about his activities in the early 1960s when he was running the Houston-based Zapata Off-Shore Company. ("Running an offshore oil company," he writes, "would mean days spent on or over water: not only the Gulf of Mexico but oceans and seas the world over.") But the 1972 profile of Bush in *Current Biography* provides more details of his itinerary in those years. And according to Nicholas King's *George Bush: A Biography*, Zapata was concentrating its business in the Caribbean and off South America in the early 1960s, a piece of information that meshes neatly with the available data on Bush's early CIA responsibilities.[207]

While Bush's earlier alleged ties to the CIA were undiscussed on the 1970s, there were many who questioned Ford's choice of Bush to head up the Agency, prime among them being Senator Frank Church, who'd been delving deeply into the misdeeds of the CIA.

The initial reaction of Senator Frank Church, chair of the Senate Select Committee on Intelligence, to the firing of William Colby and the naming of Bush as Director of Central Intelligence in 1975 was to complain that it was part of a pattern of attempts by President Gerald Ford (a former member of the Warren commission) to impede the Church committee's nearly concluded investigation into C.I.A. assassination plots, with which Colby was cooperating but which Ford was vainly trying to keep secret.[208]

If one is keeping track of a darker narrative of American history, it might look something like this: Kennedy wants to find a way to coexist with the Soviet Union and Cuba, and after some significant mistakes, finds his footing. He is also looking to keep the United States from getting more deeply involved in Vietnam. Kennedy gets assassinated and Johnson takes over, reversing Kennedy's policies.

Nixon gets into the presidency, appearing to be a hard-liner, but he's also interested in détente with the communist world. Close to his goal after meeting with Chairman Mao of China and Soviet leader, Leonid Brezhnev, Nixon was forced to resign because of the Watergate scandal, the burglary team lead by former CIA assets, and the prosecution led by the FBI.

Before he resigned, though, Nixon chose Gerald Ford, a congressman and former member of the Warren commission, to be his vice president.

It appears that little was being left to chance by the shadow government.

A former opponent of Bush in the 1964 election for the US Senate, Ralph Yarborough, was asked in 1988 about his thoughts on the allegations of Bush's earlier work with the CIA.

Yarborough said, "I never heard anything about it. It doesn't surprise me. What surprised me was they picked him for Director of Central Intelligence—how in hell was he appointed head of C.I.A. without any experience or knowledge?" Hoover's memo "explains something to me that I've always wondered about. It *does* make sense to have a trained C.I.A. man, with experience, appointed to the job."

Bush's appointment as the agency's director in 1975 was widely criticized because, as McBride writes, "Bill Colby, a professional in the intelligence field, was being replaced by a nonprofessional outsider—and a politician to boot." Senator Church commented: "It appears as though the White House may be using this important post merely as a grooming room before he is brought on stage next year as a vice-presidential running mate."[209]

If you're going to be an intelligence agency and try to control a country, this is how you do it.

By keeping things secret.

Even your own adversaries, like Bush's opponent in the 1964 US Senate race, didn't imagine Bush might be CIA.

The invisible hand can only exert its influence when it remains invisible. That's part of the reason why the wave of revelations in the 1970s was so important.

It brought back skepticism to the American people. Our Founding Fathers were remarkably skeptical about the use of power by any government.

Once people start talking about how we're being manipulated, as Tucker Carlson, Joe Rogan, and Robert Kennedy Jr., have been doing so bravely of late, people start to see it.

Look at how quickly former governor of South Carolina and US secretary of state, Nikki Haley, faded in her presidential run when accounts of her work for a defense contractor surfaced, as well as claims that she was nothing more than a tool of the military/industrial complex.

Before those revelations surfaced, I thought she was a remarkably attractive candidate, a conservative woman with a strong political resume, her Indian background showing that the Republican Party was open to all those of talent and accomplishment. And yet, when she was shown to be just another puppet for powerful interests, people turned away from her like sour milk.

When you have the truth on your side, it doesn't take much to show the true intentions of a person.

The public is beginning to have the instincts that Senator Frank Church showed in the 1970s by suggesting that George H. W. Bush was being put forward at CIA as part of an intelligence agency plan to take the White House.

In reviewing the intersection of Bush and Ted Shackley while Bush was head of the CIA in 1975–1976, we see the genesis of a later action of the Bush administration, namely the 1989 invasion of Panama, and the deposing of Panamanian leader, General Manuel Noriega.

> Bush won significant increases in the budget for spy satellites and signal intercepts. He tried to turn off the spigot of disclosures. When the Defense Intelligence Agency discovered that Manuel Noriega had purchased intelligence information from three U.S. Army noncoms in Panama, Bush elected not to prosecute the Americans. Doing so would expose sources and the embarrassing fact that a CIA asset was spying on his patrons. CIA people generally were glad to see Bush in charge. As Tom Clines put it, "Bush didn't say no to anything."[210]

Our Founding Fathers did not believe that humans had the capability to consistently make decisions in secret and have that turn out well. They understood all of us are flawed creatures, venial, likely to prefer our friends over our critics, and if left to our own devices, would make a mess of things.

We will never find our wise, philosopher king.

It will forever elude us, just as it eluded Plato when he first wrote about the idea in ancient Greece more than two thousand years ago. That's why our Founding Fathers encouraged a vigorous culture of debate and dissent and understood that while consensus might look like the answer to chaos, it is but a harbinger of inevitable disaster.

Keep in mind the CIA did not want people like Carter's pick for CIA director, Admiral Stansfield Turner, asking impertinent questions, and driving people from the Agency who were liabilities, like Ted Shackley and his friend, Tom Clines. By 1978, it was clear that Shackley was a marked man, as his friend and fellow CIA employee warned him:

> In early 1978, he resolved it was time to punch out. He thought Shackley had also overstayed his welcome. Clines sat down with his friend and put it to him bluntly: "Both of us—so long as Stansfield Turner and Jimmy Carter are alive—are dead meat. Let's get the hell

out of here." Shackley did not want to leave. He told Clines he still hoped he could get his CIA career on track. With twenty-seven years invested, Shackley was not ready to jump.[211]

But if Shackley would not jump, Turner might give him a push. In 1979, an opening came available in the National Intelligence Tasking Center, which might allow Shackley to build up the group into an influential part of the intelligence apparatus. As in much of government, you are not fired, you are simply ignored until you can take it no longer, then when you finally resign, they give you a medal as they kick you out the door.

> The promotion did not come. It was painfully obvious: Turner was not about to hand him Paris, London, Bonn, or Tokyo. Shackley had hung on for over a year since vacating the ADDO's [Assistant Director, Directorate of Operations] office. His patience was exhausted. He was going nowhere in Turner's service, and he was anxious about the direction in which Turner was leading the Agency. After twenty-eight years, Shackley decided it was time to exit the Central Intelligence Agency.
>
> There was a farewell ceremony at headquarters for Shackley. The man who once hoped to command the entire U.S. intelligence community was awarded his third Distinguished Intelligence Medal.[212]

While Admiral Stansfield Turner may not have had intelligence experience prior to assuming his role as director of the CIA, he seemed to have an appreciation for the immense burden the typical agent carried on his or her shoulders.

> Turner in his memoirs later mused on the impact of the clandestine life on CIA people: "Hiding your accomplishments, leading a double life, regularly facing difficult moral issues, and being subjected to criticism for doing what was acceptable at the time one did it can all take their toll. In many ways, a clandestine career can be said to deform the person involved."[213]

That might be said of Shackley, who was too young to fight in World War II, but often found himself outmaneuvered on the battlefields of the Cold War.

How did one face the evil of communism, without becoming a mirror image of the monster you were fighting?

Shackley had failed in Eastern Europe, in the Caribbean with the failure of the Cuban effort, perhaps assisted in the murder of a president, as well as the impeachment of another, and brought shame upon the Agency for what he'd done in Vietnam with the Phoenix program.

And of course, Shackley had a final act.

Nearly bringing down the Reagan administration in the Iran-Contra scandal.

***

The election of Ronald Reagan as president in 1980, as well as his vice president, George H. W. Bush, seemed to herald a rebirth for the recently retired Shackley.

> On December 5 and 6, 1980, a few dozen former spooks, journalists, Capitol Hill staffers, and foreign intelligence officers gathered in a Washington conference room. They had all been invited by the National Strategy Information Center, a conservative think tank, to participate in one of several conferences designed to shape the intelligence agenda of the 1980s. The mood at the gathering was hopeful. Jimmy Carter had been trounced by Ronald Reagan, who favored unleashing the U.S. intelligence community. George Bush, the former CIA Director, was about to become Vice President. The dark days of Turner were over.[214]

And Shackley was going to once again be at the tip of the spear in this new administration.

> Before his fellow ex-spies, Shackley read a paper on paramilitary covert actions in the 1980s. "As the decade of the 1980s opens," Shackley began, "Cuban mercenary armies sustain dictatorial

governments in two large African nations, Angola and Ethiopia. In the Western Hemisphere, Cuban and Soviet-trained revolutionaries rule in Nicaragua. Their comrades threaten to seize neighboring El Salvador. Guatemala is in turmoil for it knows it is next in line to receive priority attention from Havana's and Moscow's guerilla movements." The list went on: Soviet forces in the south of the Arabian Peninsula, threatening the West's supply of oil; a Soviet army in Afghanistan; the Moscow-backed forces of Vietnam fighting small armies in Cambodia and Thailand; Soviet-supported rebels in Honduras and Namibia. The real threat from the Soviets, Shackley declared, was not a nuclear one; it was conventional warfare and insurgency.[215]

Shackley was advocating much of the CIA's failed Phoenix strategy in Vietnam to be utilized around the world. While his observations of the success that communism was having around the world may have been accurate, he was not advocating a program which seemed to have any chance of success.

Shackley's program of the three "Ps", "propaganda," "political," and "paramilitary," didn't seem to work among regular human beings, especially once these efforts became visible to the general public.

They'd failed in Cuba, failed in Vietnam, and yet, were going to give it all one last try in Central America.

However, as much as Shackley was looking to work with the Reagan administration, a series of articles by journalist Seymour Hersh, regarding Shackley's previous work with Wilson, who participated in the assassination of the former Chilean ambassador to the United States, made that an impossibility. It looked like Shackley was on his own, using his intelligence connections and background to advise foreign clients, called Shackley's Research Associates International.

But in 1984, Shackley had found a scheme that might get him back into the Reagan administration's good graces.

In mid-1984, Shackley flew to Los Angeles to see a potentially valuable source. Manucher Hashemi was a brigadier general in Iran in the days of the Shah and headed the counterespionage section of the brutal SAVAK. He fled Tehran shortly before the revolution and now lived in London. Novzar Razmara, a Shackley employee who had worked with Hashemi in Iran, thought Shackley and the old general should meet.

According to Hashemi, Shackley poured it on thick when the two gathered in California. Shackley introduced himself as a former CIA official who was a businessman but also an intelligence adviser to Vice President George Bush. Shackley noted that his duties—perhaps those on behalf of Bush—included obtaining information about Iran, particularly what the Soviets were doing in that country.[216]

What are we to make of the tales told by spies? Maybe Shackley was working on behalf of Vice President Bush. Maybe he was lying. If so, the lies were about to get a lot larger, and would nearly drive a popular president from office. After some discussions between Shackley and Hashemi, an effort was made to bring other people into the discussion.

The next morning, Hashemi introduced Shackley to Manucher Ghorbanifar, an overweight, boisterous, goateed Iranian expatriate. Ghorbanifar, echoing Hashemi's account, later said that Shackley introduced himself as a "very close" associate of Bush and hinted he might be the next CIA Director. That day, Shackley and Ghorbanifar met three times. During the second session, the pair were joined by two other Iranian officials, including Ali Shahabadi, the chief Iranian purchasing officer in Hamburg and purportedly a friend of Adnan Khashoggi, the billionaire entrepreneur and arms dealer.

Shackley afterward told congressional investigators he had gone to Hamburg simply to get together with Iranians who could supply him inside information on the Iran-Iraq war. But Hashemi's recollection differed from Shackley's. He noted Shackley acted as if he still held an official brief and discussed with the Iranians renewing diplomatic relations between Washington and Tehran and ways to deliver to Iran weapons purchased by the Shah, but withheld by the United States.[217]

For many Americans, the Iran-Contra scandal is a mystery. There are a number of moving parts, many of which don't seem to naturally fit together, but the basic outline is fairly simple.

Iran and Iraq had been fighting a bloody war since 1980, losing millions on each side.

An Iranian-backed militia, Hezbollah, had taken three American hostages, including William Buckley, the CIA station chief in Lebanon.

Iran had some Soviet weaponry they thought the Americans might be interested in examining. In return, they wanted some newer American weapons, specifically TOW missiles, to help in their war against Iraq.

The Reagan administration was prohibited by a congressional resolution called the "Boland Amendment," which prohibited the US government from giving military aid to the Contra rebels fighting against the Nicaraguan government.

Israel, feeling isolated and surrounded in the Middle East by enemies, was anxious to do anything to lower tensions with Iran, as well as help their American allies.

To complete this picture, from 1979 to 1981, Iran had held fifty-two American diplomats hostage, humiliating the Carter administration, and allowing Ronald Reagan to win the presidency. And finally, the Democrats in America were reasonably concerned that Reagan's efforts to fight communism in Central America would lead to another debacle like the previous war in Vietnam.

Shackley's proposed deal, which might involve a transfer of weapons to the besieged Iranians in return for the release of the Hezbollah hostages as well as a possible cash payment, did not meet with enthusiasm at the State Department.

Ghorbanifar did not give up. He made contact with two Israelis, Al Schwimmer, an adviser to Prime Minister Shimon Peres, and Yaacov Nimrodi, an Israeli businessman. He proposed that the Israelis secretly sell him TOW missiles for Iran. In return, he said, he would arrange the release of William Buckley. About then, Michael Leeden, the onetime business associate of Shackley and

now an NSC [National Security Council] consultant, was trying to persuade Robert McFarlane, the national security adviser,
to consider a joint-U.S.-Israeli initiative regarding Iran. Ledeen's
effort coincided with a reevaluation being conducted by the U.S.
intelligence community of policy toward Iran. Government geo-
strategists were considering an opening to Iran, and a CIA memo
suggested that arms sales through an ally could kick off a dialogue
with Iran. Leeden met with Prime Minister Peres, who said that
Israel wanted U.S. approval to sell armaments to Iran.[218]

When the Iran-Contra scandal is viewed at a distance, much of it strikes
one as business as usual among the secretive part of governments. Are we
really surprised that even though crowds in the Tehran streets would march
daily and shout, "Death to America!" that the Iranian leaders would be
looking for ways to work with the Americans? And with Americans being
held hostage by Hezbollah, including a CIA station chief, is it unreasonable that the government wouldn't be considering every crazy idea to get
those people home?

Perhaps this would not have become such a scandal if not for the intervention of a Lieutenant Colonel Oliver North, who apparently came up
with a plan to divert some money from the sale of American arms to Iran
to the Nicaraguan contras, despite a congressional ban on such activities.
From *Blond Ghost: Ted Shackley and the Crusades of the CIA*:

> The Iran initiative quickly developed its own momentum. The
> arms sale to Iran, at first a one-shot deal, would snowball into an
> eighteen-month-long project. It would become intertwined with
> the White House's covert and arguably illegal campaign to arm
> the Contra rebels fighting the leftist Sandinista government in
> Nicaragua. It would fail. When revealed, it would spark public out-
> rage, congressional investigations, a grand jury probe, and several
> trials, and drag Shackley back to the public stage.[219]

One of the individuals most responsible for bringing to light the Iran-
Contra scandal, as well as dragging Shackley into the glare of the public
spotlight, was a lawyer named Danny Sheehan.

It was ironic in a way, as Sheehan started out his adult life wanting to become a Green Beret, taking ROTC classes at Northeastern University in 1964.

However, Sheehan became disgusted by his training, eventually leaving for Harvard, graduating from Harvard Law School, as well as attending their divinity school. He eventually served as general counsel to the Jesuit Office in Washington, DC, and spent much time considering becoming a Jesuit priest.

Sheehan often joked that in that role he was the beneficiary of the CIA, the "Catholic Intelligence Agency," as their clergy around the world often knew better what was actually happening than many intelligence agencies.

***

Danny Sheehan worked on many high-profile cases, including the Pentagon Papers case (detailing nearly forty years of government lying about Vietnam), and the Karen Silkwood case, the nuclear plant employee who was uncovering safety problems, and died in a mysterious car crash. Although Sheehan's role in these cases is a matter of public record, and to many, shining examples of the search for truth eventually being rewarded, Sheehan sees those cases differently.

While the Pentagon Papers case, in which the *New York Times* and *Washington Post* jointly published documents in 1971, showing the lies the government had told about Vietnam for decades (and claimed by many as one of the reasons the Vietnam War ended), Sheehan claims the intelligence agencies kept the most explosive information from those revelations, namely the CIA's participation in the Phoenix program.

And the Karen Silkwood case, turned into the Oscar-winning 1984 film, *Silkwood*, with Meryl Streep, Cher, and Kurt Russell, conceals a critical part of the story, according to Sheehan. The movie itself plays out as Streep trying to get to the truth of unsafe practices at a nuclear plant, and encountering corporate evil. While that part was true, according to Sheehan, there was another level to it, namely that nuclear material was secretly being diverted from the plant to help the Israeli nuclear program.

When Sheehan started to discover information about what the Reagan administration was doing in Central America, and it linked back to intelligence officials he'd been pursuing for decades, it seemed as if he'd found a way to go after what he perceived as America's greatest villains. Sheehan got most of his information from two controversial and colorful characters, Gene Wheaton and Carl Jenkins. As Wheaton explained to Sheehan:

> A whole crew was running amok, supporting Contras, conducting covert activity elsewhere. Drugs were involved. Some of this gang had engaged in corrupt government business in Iran and Southeast Asia. Now the same old boys were running weapons to Latin America. Central to the whole shebang was a former CIA officer named Ted Shackley. Sheehan was captivated. He had struck the mother lode.[220]

This became central to a cause Sheehan would pursue for several years, namely that Shackley was at the center of a "Secret Team" of former CIA assassins, available around the world for sale to the highest bidder. Sheehan would be unsuccessful in this effort, with his supporters claiming it was because the intelligence agencies didn't want to reveal their dirty laundry, while his critics said it was because Sheehan was deluded in his accusations. What cannot be denied is that Sheehan's investigations led directly to the revelation of the Iran-Contra scandal:

> Throughout the winter and spring, as Sheehan talked to Wheaton and Jenkins, he had something else on his mind: a two-year-old bombing in Nicaragua. On May 30, 1984, a bomb had exploded at a press conference in La Penca, Nicaragua, held by Eden Pastora, a maverick Contra leader who resisted cooperating with the CIA and the main Contra force. Several people were killed, but not Pastora. Afterward, Tony Avirgan, an American journalist who suffered shrapnel wounds at La Penca, and his wife, Martha Honey, set out to uncover who plotted the attack. A year later they produced a book that charged a small group of Americans and Cuban exiles—some with ties to the CIA and the Contras—with planning the murderous assault. One of the persons fingered was John Hull, a Contra supporter with a spread in northern Costa Rica and a

relationship with North and the CIA. Their report noted that some
Contra supporters were moonlighting in the drug trade.[221]

Sheehan's investigation of the La Penca bombing would lead him into a
dark world of intelligence operatives, fueling a lurid story, which I find has
echoes of what I read in the news every day. I understand that in the eyes
of many, Sheehan's claims have been dismissed. But for me, I still consider
the accusations to be an open question.

> In Sheehan's secret history, Shackley and his comrades had con-
> spired with the Mafia in Miami and then transferred to Laos where
> they allied themselves with a drug-dealing Ving Pao and used his
> dirty profits to fund a clandestine operation that assassinated over
> 100,000 civilians in Laos, Cambodia, and Thailand. Next Shackley
> and company directed the overthrow of Allende in Chile. Once
> that was accomplished, Shackley, as Saigon station chief, ran the
> Phoenix program and financed it with drug money from Vang Pao.
> Then in 1973, Shackley and Clines created their own "private com-
> munist assassination and unconventional warfare program." They
> set up base in Tehran and retained Wilson to head an assassina-
> tion program. The Secret Team banked its drug money in Nugan
> Hand in Australia. It offered "assassination services" to Somoza
> in Nicaragua. The Shackley cabal formed EATSCO [Egyptian-
> American Air Transport and Services Corporation] and supplied
> weapons to the Contras. When the Reagan administration decided
> to sell arms secretly to Iran, the White House turned to the profes-
> sionals: Shackley's Secret Team.[222]

While the allegations by Sheehan were detailed, they were never proven.
Whether one thinks Sheehan did a bad job, making wild accusations, or
whether he was prevented from getting the needed information by the
intelligence community, depends on whom you ask. Sheehan's accusations
have strong partisans and equally strong detractors.

We interviewed Sheehan for this book in 2024 and this is what he had
to say of Shackley: "He was the most malignant individual, perhaps in the
history of the United States, who was put into a position of authority by

a president. He supported the malignant activities of massive drug smuggling, political assassinations, and ultimately supervised the team of people who assassinated the President of the United States, John Kennedy."[223]

Sheehan also asserted that Shackley was the protégé of Nazi Major General Reinhard Gehlen, who had been head of the Waffen-SS intelligence services for the Eastern bloc, who was recruited by Western intelligence after the Second World War and served NATO for twenty-six years.[224]

But even the author of the most detailed account of Shackley's life admits that there are mysteries about Shackley that we may never know. In the epilogue for *Blond Ghost: Ted Shackley and the Crusades of the CIA*, there is this passage:

> Theodore G. Shackley lived the Cold War. In the name of America, he sent foreign intelligence agents to their doom in Germany. He managed a small secret war against Cuba, then oversaw a larger one in Laos. He directed intelligence in Vietnam during a war of profound intelligence failures. In Washington, Shackley signed the orders for scores of espionage and covert action operations around the globe. He was responsible for ugly things: political payoffs, the suborning of journalists, the enlistment of spies, the misleading of Congress. His flight toward the Director's chair stalled. After he left the Agency he was ensnared in scandals that bared the seamier side of the clandestine struggle between the United States and the Soviet Union. The Iran-Contra affair was propelled by the calculations of geo-strategists obsessed with achieving an edge over Moscow, even if that meant selling arms to a country they derided as a terrorist state or promoting a war in the jungles of Central America.[225]

What is left unsaid is that while Shackley's life did encompass a great deal of the Cold War, the American people paid for that work. And yet, we do not have an accounting of it. Because so much of it still remains classified, it is left to people like me and Danny Sheehan to try and uncover that truth.

In early 2002, after I'd rescued my family from the secret base that had poisoned us, I was walking in the atrium with my attorney, Clint Blackman, as we were on our way to see the CIA's Office of General

Counsel, when Ted Shackley, the Blond Ghost, just a few months away from death, walked past me.

I recalled the brief, weird meeting in his office in 1998, and couldn't help but recall that one of the things I'd stumbled across at the secret base where I'd been sent, were buried weapons and munitions from the Phoenix program, which Shackley had run in Vietnam.

Had it been a coincidence that Shackley had sent me and my family to that facility where we'd become so sick and nearly died?

Did he consider me a colleague, a fellow patriot?

Or because of what I uncovered, was I an enemy to be put down, like he had done to so many before?

***

When Shackley died in December 2002, his career received glowing coverage in the *New York Times* and the *Washington Post*, almost as if the Agency itself were honoring him. This is from the *New York Times*:

> Mr. Shackley was a three-time recipient of the Distinguished Intelligence Medal, the C.I.A.'s highest honor. In nearly three decades of service with the agency, he was on the front lines, though surreptitiously, in the cold war against Communism.
>
> Mr. Shackley was the subject of the book, "Blond Ghost: Ted Shackley and C.I.A.'s Crusades," published by Simon and Shuster in 1994.
>
> The author, David Corn, described Mr. Shackley as one of the C.I.A.'s best and brightest, a good bet to become director of central intelligence, until his career ran off the tracks.[226]

Well, that's a nice little opening, right? But they needed to deal with a couple of unpleasant allegations that are in the public record, so they didn't waste any time dispelling those rumors.

> He served in the hot spots of West Berlin, Saigon and Vientiane, Laos, and other places in a career that lasted from 1951 to 1979.

Along the way, he was involved in some of the spy agency's most famous and controversial undertakings.

But not as many as his biographers have written, his daughter said today. She said that her father was not involved in Operation Mongoose, an intelligence operation said to have been ordered by Attorney General Robert F. Kennedy to assassinate Fidel Castro.

Nor, despite rumors to the contrary, was he involved, after leaving the C.I.A., in the Iran-Contra-arms-for-hostages scandal that rocked the administration of President Ronald Reagan, Ms. Shackley said.[227]

Okay, here's what they want you to believe. Shackley was this amazing spy, and while he did a lot of secret things, and a number of bad things are attributed to him, he didn't do those bad things, like Operation Mongoose, assassinating Kennedy, running the Phoenix program that killed somewhere between twenty thousand to forty thousand people, or initiating the Iran-Contra scandal.

And if you go to Shackley's obituary in the *Washington Post*, I'm sure you'll get the exact same story you got from the *Times*.

In 1951, he was recruited into the CIA from the Army. His first foreign assignment was West Berlin, then the espionage capital of the world. In 1962, he was named CIA station chief in Miami with responsibility for assisting Cuban exiles bent on overthrowing Fidel Castro. He held the post during the Cuban missile crisis, when the Kennedy administration forced the Soviet Union to withdraw missiles from the island nation.

He also ran Operation Mongoose, an anti-Castro intelligence campaign that had been ordered by Attorney General Robert F. Kennedy, President John F. Kennedy's brother.[228]

Wait a minute.

The *New York Times* said Shackley *did not* run Operation Mongoose, the assassination plan ordered by Attorney General Robert F. Kennedy.

The *Washington Post* says Shackley *did* run Operation Mongoose, the anti-Castro intelligence campaign ordered by Attorney General Robert F. Kennedy.

First of all, did Shackley run Operation Mongoose or not?

And second, was it an assassination plan of Castro, or was it an "anti-Castro intelligence campaign?"

And finally, which program did Attorney General Robert F. Kennedy, think he was approving?

***

It occurs to me that the fight over the past is really a fight about the future.

This was never so clear to me as when I was finishing up this chapter on May 6, 2024, and happened to hear an interview by Tucker Carlson, with longtime CIA figure, Felix Rodriguez.

Rodriguez was a young Cuban at the time Fidel Castro took over in Cuba, was part of the Bay of Pigs invasion (but eluded capture by Castro's forces), was present at the execution of Cuban revolutionary, Che Guevara, served in Operation Phoenix in Vietnam, later in Central America on behalf of the Contra rebels, and was questioned in the Iran-Contra scandal. In other words, he was one of Shackley's guys. And in the interview, he seemed interested in rehabilitating Shackley's reputation, as well as pointing blame away from the CIA about the Kennedy assassination, and onto Cuban leader Fidel Castro.

> Tucker Carlson: What was Ted Shackley like?
> Felix Rodriguez: Oh, he was the most intelligent man that I have ever met in my life. He was the one responsible for the Berlin tunnel. He was chief of station in Miami, and we became close friends until the day he died. And we were close. We used to meet. He was the head of station in Saigon, and we developed a personal friendship.[229]

In the interview, Rodriguez attempted to portray himself as an old man, only interested in the truth, and somebody who was a genuine patriot. And yet, he came across to me as a company man, pushing the same company propaganda, throwing in a few facts one might not have known, but only as a way to distract you from the obvious contradictions.

I consider this next answer to Tucker Carlson to be a master class in CIA lying. If you want to get people to believe your lie, you stick to the truth as closely as you can, then when it gets to the important part, you lie. Watch how Rodriguez pulls the listener in, then pulls a fast one. Tucker asked Rodriguez about whether he believed Cuban exiles or the CIA were involved in the Kennedy assassination. This was the response:

> Felix Rodriguez: I'll tell you, most of the brigade members believed Kennedy was a traitor. He was the one who definitely had the responsibility, and he was responsible for the failure. Looking from another point, I believe that he was a young president, ill-advised, and we paid the price. And I believe that actually he was killed because he tried to amend that.
>
> After, he was able to pull the brigade out of prison, he opened the Air Force of the United States for the brigade members. I became a second lieutenant in the U.S. Army in 1963 and then he promised also Special Operations, which was started in Central America, in three different bases, and not many people know about that.
>
> But then he was assassinated.
>
> A lot of people believed that it was only one shooter. I believe there were two shooters. We have information that there was a Cuban, who is now a retired general, Fabian Escalantes, who was a captain at that time, who was in Dallas, and he was the second shooter in the assassination of the President . . .
>
> And he was in Dallas that day, and then he left. It was something that, and Castro said he knew the United States was trying to kill him. But be very careful because the Cubans also had a very long hand.[230]

And that, ladies and gentlemen, is how you tell a really big lie.

It is as absurd to believe Cuban intelligence assassinated Kennedy and got away without the CIA going after them with their trained killers, as it is to believe that the Mafia killed Kennedy on their own, without the assistance of the CIA.

Rodriguez makes the further claim that the reason there was no attempt at a second invasion of Cuba, was because after the Cuban missile crisis of 1962, the Soviets left four operational nuclear missiles as a deterrent force.[231]

That may be true, and even seems likely to me.

But if the CIA believed Cuban Captain Fabian Escalantes was the second shooter in the Kennedy assassination, the CIA would never have let him live long enough to become a general in Castro's army.

Just as if they genuinely believed Johnny Roselli was acting on behalf of Chicago mob boss, Sam Giancana, the CIA would not have let Roselli live thirteen more years, until called to testify before Congress in 1976 on the JFK assassination.

The past still matters.

If they can lie about what happened in the past and make you believe it, they'll have little hesitation to do the same thing in the future.

CHAPTER SEVEN

THE ORIGINAL SIN OF ALLEN DULLES: SELLING DRUGS IN THE INNER CITY TO FIGHT THE COMMUNISTS

Many Americans are aware of the fact that our intelligence agencies have had alliances in the past with organized crime, as they did in the CIA's campaign against Fidel Castro.

But even for those who are well-informed, there's a question of how such an alliance was first formed.

The answer seems to be, at least in the beginning, that the Mob tricked our intelligence agencies into such an alliance. Whether our intelligence agencies later learned of this deception, and took action, or perhaps marveled at the skill of the Mob's false flag, is unknown.

It's a well-established fact that by the 1940s, the Mafia had infiltrated the labor unions, and controlled many of the major ports. Chief among the effort to control the New York docks was Charles "Lucky" Luciano, and his longtime friend and accomplice, Meyer Lansky. One of the best books on how this collaboration began, and was sustained over decades, is *Operation Gladio*, by Paul L. Williams, for which I was glad to write one of the endorsements on the back cover.

During Prohibition, Luciano and Lansky gained control of the New York docks and longshoreman's union by means of muscle and blood in order to supply speakeasies within Manhattan with scotch from Scotland, rum from the Caribbean, and whiskey from Canada. When a bloody war broke out between the families of Giuseppe "The Boss" Masseria and Salvatore Maranzano from 1927 to 1929, Luciano put an end to it by arranging the elimination of both Mafia chiefs and laying down the law to survivors. "I explained to 'em that all the war horseshit was out," he later explained. "I told 'em we was in a business that hadda keep movin' without explosions every two minutes; knockin' guys off because they came from a different part of Sicily; that kind of crap was givin' us a bad name, and we couldn't operate until it stopped."[232]

What is less well-known is that in Italy, Mussolini had nearly eliminated the power of the Sicilian mafia, starting with his rule in that country in 1922.

Though failing in Italy, the Mafia was a powerful entity in the United States. However, by 1936, it seemed that Luciano's fabled luck had run out.

On February 2, 1936, US Attorney Thomas E. Dewey launched a raid of brothels in Manhattan and Brooklyn, which netted arrests of ten pimps and one hundred prostitutes. Unable to come up with the cash for the stiff bonds of $10,000 imposed by the presiding judge, several of the prostitutes bartered with Dewey for their release by fingering Luciano as the ringleader. On June 7, Lucky was convicted on sixty-two counts of compulsory prostitution and sentenced to thirty to fifty years of hard time at the Clinton Correctional Facility in Upstate New York.[233]

As it turned out, World War II presented an amazing opportunity for the Mafia.

With the attack by the Japanese on Pearl Harbor in the Pacific on December 7, 1941, and Nazi U-boats prowling the North Atlantic, many in intelligence feared it was only a matter of time before important US ports, like New York, were attacked.

Some of Luciano's crew, Frank Costello, Albert Anastasi, and Tony Anastasio believed this fear of sabotage might be the perfect vehicle to spring their boss from prison, as well as make an alliance with the United States government against the Nazi threat. As Luciano later told the story to his biographers:

> Costello got in touch with me right away. Albert had worked this idea out with his brother, Tough Tony. Albert said the guys from Navy Intelligence had been all over the docks talkin' to em' about security; they was scared to death that all the stuff along the Hudson, the docks and boats and the rest, was in very great danger. It took a guy like Albert to figure out somethn' really crazy; his idea was to give the Navy a real big hunk of sabotage, somethin' so big that it would scare the shit out of the whole fuckin' Navy."[234]

The target was the *S.S. Normandie*, a French ship that had been docked in New York when the French surrendered to the Germans in June of 1940. It was more than a thousand feet long, and with its four-bladed propellors, it could cross the Atlantic in less than four days.[235] The plan was for the United States to turn it into an aircraft carrier. But before that could happen, on February 9, 1942, it caught fire and capsized, later being cut up for scrap.

The destruction of the *S.S. Normandie* had the desired effect:

> Lt. Commander Charles Radcliffe Haffenden of the ONI [Office of Naval Intelligence] paid a visit to the Clinton Correctional Facility, where he offered Lucky the promise of pardon and deportation to his native Sicily in exchange for his help in securing the harbor and preventing strikes by the Manhattan longshoremen. "As far as Haffenden was concerned, he didn't know nothin' that was goin' on except that he was sittin' there with his mouth open, prayin' I would say yes and help his whole department," Luciano later said. Thus, Operation Underworld got underway, with Lucky transforming from a mob thug to an agent of the ONI.[236]

The operation to secure the nation's ports and keep the unions quiet was such a success, that when it came time for the military to plan the invasion of Sicily, they called again on Luciano. Specifically, they needed help with making an introduction to Don Calo Vizzini, the boss of all bosses in Sicily, who'd been imprisoned for several years by Mussolini. (Vizzini had been recommended by Monsignor Giovanni Montini, the Vatican under-secretary of state, who would later become Pope Paul VI.[237]) It's always a good thing when you get your gangsters referred to you by a Catholic priest, especially one who would later become pope!

> At Donovan's [William Donovan, head of the Office of Strategic Services] request, Commander Haffenden again appeared at Lucky's cell with a request for help. Luciano complied by drafting a communique that was airdropped near Don Calo's farmhouse. Two days later, American tanks rolled into Villalba after driving fifty-five miles from the beachhead of General Patton's Seventh Army in Palermo. Don Calo and his men climbed into the tanks and spent the next six days guiding the division through western Sicily and organizing support among the local populace for the advancing US troops.
>
> Thanks to the success of Operation Husky (the code name for the Allied invasion of Sicily), Don Calo was appointed Mayor of Villalba. As soon as he assumed public office, Don Calo murdered the local police chief, whom he found "too inquisitive."[238]

And thus, was the future outline for the CIA and Mafia relationship established. The Mob was a good partner to the intelligence agencies, whether that be the Office of Naval Intelligence (ONI), or the Office of Strategic Services (OSS), and both sides would profit. The intelligence agencies would come up with the objective, but it was the Mob who would do the dirty work.

During World War II, the Mafia would work through military intelligence, and lay the groundwork for a Europe free from communism.

> The ascendancy of the Mafia also became apparent with the appointment of Vito Genovese, Luciano's right-hand man, as chief translator for the U.S. Army headquarters in Naples. New York's former lieutenant-governor, Charles Poletti, who Lucky described as "one of our good friends," was also appointed as military

governor in Italy. Thanks to Poletti, Genovese's men controlled the major Italian ports, and thereby most of the black market in American and Sicilian goods, such as flour, oil, sugar, beans, salt, and cigarettes . . .

Thanks to the success of the invasion, Lucky Luciano became the subject of massive media hype, which culminated in radio broadcaster Walter Winchell proclaiming that the mobster should receive the Congressional Medal of Honor.[239]

Once you start making deals with gangsters, it's difficult to extricate yourself from the relationship. Especially since the criminals are so good at illegal and violent activities, an off-the-shelf, ready-to-go army, that never asks any questions.

And the US government lived up to its word with Luciano, who would be deported to Sicily. But his right-hand man, Vito Genovese, would be the government's go-to guy in the next phase of the relationship.

In the summer of 1946, Luciano arrived in his hometown of Lecara Friddi in Sicily, where he received a hero's welcome. Hundreds of people lined the streets waving small American flags. A four-piece band played "The Stars and Stripes Forever" as the mayor, draped in a red sash, ushered the American mobster out of a police car. "Half the people I met in Sicily was in the Mafia," Lucky later reflected, "and by half the people, I mean half the cops, too. Because in Sicily, it goes like this: the Mafia is first, then your own family, then your business, and then the Mafia again."[240]

Luciano and the United States government had learned that they could do business together. It was an understanding shared by both sides of the relationship, the government and the Mob.

And while the Mafia had assisted in the defeat of the Axis powers, another threat loomed in Europe, Stalin and the communists.

But a plan had already been developed, by a man named Colonel Paul E. Helliwell, who was serving in China during and after the Second World War, as chief of Special Operations for the Office of Strategic Services (OSS). From *Operation Gladio*:

Within Kunming, a town within the South China province of Yunnan, Helliwell observed that General Chiang Kai-Shek, leader of the Kuomintang (KMT–the Chinese National Army), sold opium to Chinese addicts in order to raise funds for the army's planned war against the Communist forces of Mao Zedong. Since Helliwell's task was to provide covert assistance to the KMT, what better help could he provide than steady shipments of opiates for the good general?

Helliwell presented this idea to his boss, General William "Wild Bill" Donovan. Donovan shared it with James Jesus Angleton, Allen Dulles (the OSS Swiss Director), and William "Little Bill" Stephenson, master spy of the British Security Coordination. Delighted with the concept, the officials arranged to funnel money to Helliwell, who now "became the man who controlled the pipeline of covert funds for secret operations throughout Asia." The money for the opiates would eventually come from Nazi gold that had been laundered and manipulated through the World Commerce Corporation, a financial firm established by Wild Bill.[241]

One of the misconceptions held by many people is to believe that the CIA's creation in 1947 is the date to which we should look for when things started to diverge from American ideals.

However, doing that is a significant mistake.

One must look back further, to the actions of the men who ran the Office of Strategic Services in World War II, men like Allen Dulles, and what they did in the war (such as the alliance with the Mafia), as well as the development of a drugs for weapons program, to understand the CIA was the vehicle for which these programs would be implemented.

In other words, the Office of Strategic Services had come up with the plan, and the CIA would be how they got those things done.

For the conflict in China between the Nationalists and the Communists, the drugs for weapons program needed a delivery system, and some soon-to-be-infamous names, would be in charge of setting all that up. From the book, *Operation Gladio: The Unholy Alliance between the Vatican, the CIA, and the Mafia*:

By the close of World War II, Helliwell and a number of fellow Army intelligence officers–E. Howard Hunt, of Watergate fame; Lucien Conein, a former member of the French Foreign Legion with strong ties to the Corsican Mafia; Tommy "the Cork" Corcoran, a lawyer serving the Strategic Service unit; and Lt. General Claire L. Chennault, the military advisor to Chiang Kai-Shek and the founder of the Flying Tigers–had created the Civil Air Transport (CAT) from surplus aircraft, including C-47 Dakotas and C-46 Commandos. The CAT fleet transported weapons to a contingency force of the KMT in Burma. The planes were then loaded with drugs for their return trip to China. The pilots who flew these bush-type aircraft were a motley group of men, often serving as agents or go-betweens with the Chinese National guerillas and the opium buyers. Some were former Nazis, others part of the band of expatriates that emerges in countries following any war. Helliwell and his compatriots had created a model for trafficking in drugs that would result in the formation of Air America–the CIA fleet of planes that transported opiates and cocaine during and after the Vietnam Conflict.[242]

Once you begin to see the pattern, you can't unsee it.

How does one fight Mao's Communist forces in China? Sell opium to addicts in China in order to get money to buy guns and ammunition for the Nationalists.

How do you raise extra money to support the CIA in Vietnam? Sell opiates from Burma's Shan Plateau, part of the so-called "Golden Triangle."

How do you raise extra money for the Contras in Nicaragua? Pull this plan off the shelf, figure out who your new drug suppliers are, and how to get the drugs transported, and you're in business.

It's important to realize that the CIA did not "become corrupt." It was corrupt from birth, made that way by the men who founded the Agency. It was the Frankenstein monster into which Allen Dulles and his collaborators implanted a diseased brain.

In October [1946], at the request of US intelligence agents, Lucky traveled to Cuba where he met with Frank Costello, Vito Genovese, Albert Anastasia, and Meyer Lansky to discuss the

Helliwell plan. Also in attendance were Mike Miranda, Joseph Magliocco, Joe Adonis, Tommy Luchese, Joe Profaci, Willie Moretti, the Fischetti brothers (heirs to Al Capone), and Santo Trafficante–all important members of the American Mafia. The conference was held at the Hotel Nacional, where Frank Sinatra made his Havana singing debut in honor of Luciano. Several of the Mafiosi voiced their opposition to Lucky's plan by maintaining that dealing in junk was beneath them. But, at the end of the conference, all became convinced that providing heroin to blacks was simply giving them what they wanted and who cared what happened to "niggers."[243]

But using Asian grown drugs, Italian gangsters, and customers in America's inner cities was only part of the plan to fight communism.

They only needed two more elements to complete the picture, Nazis and Ivy Leaguers. Both would be delivered by Allen Dulles.

***

Allen Dulles might be one of the greatest unindicted traitors in the history of the United States. One of the most authoritative books on Dulles is *The Devil's Chessboard: Allen Dulles, the CIA, and the Rise of America's Secret Government*, by David Talbott, published in 2015.

It's worth noting that Allen Dulles and his brother, John Foster Dulles, were the elite of the New York financial world, and yet managed to worm their way into the administration of Franklin Delano Roosevelt, even though they considered him a "traitor to his class." John Foster Dulles would be Eisenhower's secretary of state. But it was in World War II, with Allen serving as the Office of Strategic Services (OSS) in Switzerland, that he entered the spy game.

But in Switzerland, Dulles wasn't serving his president, Franklin Roosevelt, who demanded unconditional surrender of the Nazi regime, but pursuing his own foreign policy. A negotiated peace with Germany, with Hitler gone, of course, but with somebody easier to manage at the top, like maybe Heinrich Himmler, head of the German SS.

As recounted in *The Devil's Chessboard*:

There was nothing undercover about Allen Dulles's wartime exploits in Switzerland. Afterwards, he made much of his espionage adventures with a sympathetic press and then equally credulous biographers dutifully repeating his beguiling tales. But, in truth, there was little daring involved—for a very simple reason. Dulles was more in step with many Nazi leaders than he was with President Roosevelt. Dulles not only enjoyed a professional and social familiarity with many members of the Third Reich's elite that predated the war; he shared many of these men's postwar goals. While serving in his Swiss outpost, Dulles might have been encircled by Nazi forces, but he was also surrounded by old friends.[244]

While Dulles had originally been slated to go to London on behalf of the OSS, he argued with Wild Bill Donovan, the head of the intelligence agency, that he should go to Bern, Switzerland, as it was the financial capital of the war. The small mountain nation promised neutrality to both sides, but actively profited from both the Axis and Allies.

Dulles knew many of the central players in the secretive Swiss financial milieu because he and his brother had worked with them as clients or business partners before the war. Sullivan and Cromwell, the Dulles brothers' Wall Street law firm, was at the center of an intricate international network of banks, investment firms, and industrial conglomerates that rebuilt Germany after World War I. Foster, the law firm's top executive, grew skilled at structuring the complex merry-go-round of transactions that funneled massive U.S. investment into German industrial giants like the IG Farben conglomerate and Krupp Steel. The profits generated by these investments then flowed to France and Britain in the form of war reparations, and then back to the United States to pay off war loans.[245]

The view of Dulles seems to have been that Nazism and the destruction of World War II shouldn't come between good friends, especially when the business prospects were so good. Conflicts come and go, but commerce is eternal. Perhaps it's unfair in retrospect to say, but Foster Dulles couldn't seem to separate himself from his old German law partner, Gerhardt Westrick, and when Westrick tastelessly threw a party at the Waldorf-Astoria on June 26, 1940, to celebrate Germany's defeat of France, Foster defended Westrick, saying he "had a high regard for his integrity."[246]

But even three years into the war, Allen Dulles was looking for a way to close out the war on terms favorable to the Germans. After the Casablanca Conference of July 12–13, 1943, and Roosevelt's declaration that Germany must surrender unconditionally, Dulles met with two friends, Prince Maximilian Egon von Hohenlohe, often called the "Nazi prince," and Royall Tyler, a wealthy Bostonian globe-trotter.

> Now Dulles and Hohenlohe, and their mutual friend Royall Tyler, were gathered amiably around the OSS man's fireplace at 23 Herrengasse. Dulles broke the ice by recalling old times with Prince Max in Vienna and New York. Then the men got quickly down to business—trying to determine whether a realpolitik deal could be struck between Germany and the United States that would take Hitler out of the equation but leave the Reich largely intact. As they spun out their visions for a postwar Europe, there was much common ground. Dulles and Hohenlohe clearly saw the Soviet Union as the enemy, with a strong Germany as a bastion against the Bolshevik and Slavic menace. The two old friends also agreed that there was probably no room for the Jewish people in postwar Europe, and certainly should not return to positions of power.[247]

This was not how the American people, who were fighting and dying on battlefields around the world, or were enduring wartime deprivation, expected our intelligence services to be conducting this war. The common people understood this was a war against German, Italian, and Japanese fanaticism, and there could be no negotiation with such evil.

But Dulles was more than happy to entertain an alliance with the worst of Hitler's Nazi hierarchy, SS leader Heinrich Himmler.

> The fireplace meeting was, in fact, a double betrayal—Dulles of President Roosevelt, and the Nazi prince's of Adolf Hitler. Hovering

over the tete-a-tete at 23 Herrengasse was the presence of Heinrich Himmler. He was the Reich's second most powerful man, and he dared to think he could become number one. With his weak chin, caterpillar mustache, and beady eyes gazing out from behind wire-rimmed glasses, Himmler looked less like an icon of the master race than an officious bank clerk . . .

It was Himmler whom the Fuhrer had entrusted with the Final Solution, their breathtaking plan to wipe the Jewish people from the face of the earth. It was Himmler who had the nerve to justify this plan, standing before his SS generals in October of 1943 and assuring them that they had "the moral right to destroy this people which wanted to destroy us," to pile up their "corpses side by side" in monument to the Reich's power.[248]

During the war, even despite warnings from Washington, Dulles kept trying to find a way to conclude a separate peace with the worst of the Nazi regime. But at this time Dulles did not have the power to defy a president.

In the end, Dulles's machinations with Hohenlohe went nowhere. President Roosevelt was very much in control of the U.S. government, and his uncompromising position on Nazi capitulation was still firmly in place. When OSS chief Wild Bill Donovan informed the president about the Himmler peace initiatives, FDR made it clear that he remained adamantly opposed to cutting any deals with the Nazi high command.[249]

Dulles would seem to learn the lesson that politics was too important to leave to the politicians, even ones like Roosevelt, who would seek to thwart his own plans for shaping the world to his liking. And as much as Dulles held out hope for an alliance with Himmler, the SS chief seemed to do the same for Dulles until the end as well.

Despite Heinrich Himmler's elusive quest to cut a deal with the Allies, he never lost faith in Dulles. On May 10, 1945, just days after the war ended, Himmler set out from northern Germany with an entourage of SS faithful, heading south toward Switzerland– and the protection of the American agent. He was disguised in a threadbare blue raincoat and wore a patch over one eye, with his trademark wire-rims stashed in his pocket. But Himmler never made it to his rendezvous with Dulles. The SS chief and his retinue were captured by British soldiers as they prepared to cross the Oste River. While in custody, Himmler cheated the hangman by biting down on a glass capsule of cyanide.[250]

But even with Hitler and Himmler dead, Dulles would make sure that some of the worst of the Nazi regime found a home in American intelligence, business, or engineering, as the global race with the Soviets was heating up.

However, Dulles first had to create the Agency he needed to make all his dreams come true.

***

In September 1945, President Truman abolished the OSS as a separate spy agency, and placed what remained under the war department, first calling it the Strategic Services Unit (SSU). After a few months, it was designated the National Intelligence Authority, and finally the Central Intelligence Unit, (CIU), which would remain until the Central Intelligence Agency (CIA) was founded in September of 1947.[251]

The Central Intelligence Agency (CIA) was created in 1947, under the National Security Act, to carry out covert operations "against hostile foreign states or groups or in support of friendly foreign states or groups but which are so planned and conducted that any US government responsibility for them is not evident to unauthorized persons." True to Wild Bill's vision, the new agency was exempt from disclosure of its "organization, functions, officials, titles, salaries, or numbers of personnel employed." Even its solicitation and distribution of funds was to be concealed from Congressional and judicial scrutiny."[252]

The CIA was definitely not set up by anybody with the slightest under-standing of how completely screwed up and twisted people can get in the absence of any oversight.

In our adolescent fantasies we may dream of James Bond's "license to kill," but we understand that's a fiction that can be sustained for only a few hours on a movie screen. Wild Bill Donovan and his gang had just pulled off one of the greatest heists in history, that of our American government. "Never let a crisis go to waste," is an expression common to our politics today, but it might have been said in 1947.

But not to worry, Mr. and Mrs. America, this power would only be wielded by our very best! (With the exception of the gangsters and Nazis, of course.)

> President Truman authorized Dulles to supervise the organization of the new agency. In keeping with OSS protocol, Dulles recruited almost exclusively the nation's elite millionaire businessmen, Wall Street bankers and lawyers, members of the national news media, and Ivy League scholars. The new recruits included Desmond Fitzgerald, Tracy Barnes, and Tommy "the Cork" Corcoran, three Harvard-trained Wall Street lawyers; Richard Bissell, a Yale eco-nomics professor; William F. Buckley, Jr., a Yale graduate and son of a prominent oil baron [founder of *National Review*, good friend of Ronald Reagan, and one of the most influential conservatives of the 1980s]; Phillip Graham, a Harvard graduate and future owner of *The Washington Post*,; William Colby, a graduate of Princeton and the Columbia Law School; and Richard Mellon Sciafe, the principal heir to the Mellon banking, oil, and aluminum fortune.[253]

The names of many on this list may be unfamiliar to readers today, but during their time, many of them were leading figures in the public spot-light. When one considers that William F. Buckley Jr., who to many on the Right was the epitome of a polished intellectual conservative with his many books and prominent magazine, *National Review*, as well as Phillip Graham, who would become the owner of the *Washington Post*, occupying a similar position on the Left, one can see how the CIA quickly gained its influence over American political debate.

The illusion of conflict would be generated between Left and Right to prevent the public from seeing who was holding the puppet strings behind these establishment figures.

***

You'll forgive me, but I have to spend a little time on William F. Buckley Jr., as for decades he was portrayed as the preeminent independent conservative voice, the founder of the magazine *National Review*, and the erudite host of the long-running political show, *Firing Line*, which ran from 1966 to 1999.

As much as I rarely trust a CIA employee to tell you the entire truth, I'll quote from one of Buckley's own articles, published in March of 2007, in the *Los Angeles Times*, entitled, "My Friend, E. Howard Hunt." I'll let you judge whether he's telling you, "the truth, the whole truth, and nothing but the truth."

> I met E. Howard Hunt soon after arriving in Mexico City in 1951. I was a deep cover agent for the CIA–deep-cover describing, I was given to understand, a category whose members were told to take extreme care not to permit any grounds for suspicion that one was in service to the CIA.
>
> The rule was (perhaps it is different now) that on arriving at one's targeted post, one was informed which single human being in the city knew that you were in the CIA. That person would tell you what to do for the duration of your service in that city; he would answer such questions as you wished to put to him and would concern himself with all aspects of your life.
>
> The man I was told to report to (by someone whose real name I did not know) was E. Howard Hunt. He ostensibly was working in the U.S. Embassy as a cultural affairs advisor, if I remember correctly.[254]

I think that part of Buckley's article is true, but from that point he starts to tell lies, or engage in misdirection. He says he never did much for Hunt, aside from translating a book by a defector from the Communist Party in Peru, and that he "quit" the Agency in 1952. Then he starts laying what I believe to be a false trail, such as this paragraph:

Our friendship was firm, and Howard came several times to Stamford, Conn., where my wife and I camped down, and visited. I never knew—he was very discreet—what he was up to, but assumed correctly, that he was continuing his work for the CIA. I was greatly moved by Dorothy's message to me that she and Howard were joining the Catholic communion, and they asked me to serve as godfather for their children.

Years passed without my seeing Howard. But then came the Watergate scandal—in which Howard was accused of masterminding the break-in at the Democratic Party headquarters, among other things, and was ultimately convicted of burglary, conspiracy, and wiretapping—and the dreadful accident over Midway Airport in Chicago that killed Dorothy in December of 1972. I learned of this while watching television with my wife, and it was through the television that I also learned that she had named me as personal representative of her estate in the event of her demise.[255]

Buckley wants us to believe he "left" the Agency in 1952, but decades later he's still so close to Hunt that he ends up as godfather to Howard and Dorothy's children, as well as the estate representative for Dorothy?

That strains my credulity.

And what about that "dreadful accident" over Midway Airport in Chicago on December 8, 1972, which also took the lives of forty-two other passengers? (Testifying about the activities of the CIA does seem to have "dreadful" consequences, like dying in a plane crash, being shot in your home by a "burglar" like Sam Giancana, or being found floating in a fifty-five-gallon drum, sawed in half, like Johnny Roselli.) It seems to have happened at the worst possible time in Hunt's life, as his wife was carrying "hush money" for the Watergate burglars. From an article in the *Washington Post*, commemorating the fiftieth anniversary of the fateful crash:

Dorothy Hunt was the spouse of one of the Watergate ringleaders, former CIA operative E. Howard Hunt. Hunt was under indictment in Washington, D.C., facing a trial with his co-defendants that was scheduled to begin the second week of January 1973.

Dorothy was later identified as the "paymistress" of hush money to the Watergate defendants and their families to keep the burglars from cooperating with authorities and testifying at the trial.

Investigators combed through the wreckage and found a packet of $100 bills totaling $10,000 in a purse belonging to Dorothy Hunt. It was also discovered that she had taken out a $225,000 flight insurance policy at Washington National Airport before departing.[256]

I suspect if you were E. Howard Hunt, the death of your wife in a suspicious plane crash, as she's carrying hush money to pay off your fellow conspirators in one conspiracy, is almost enough to make one suspect another conspiracy, of which Hunt was completely in the dark. Especially when there were certain statements made after the crash, which have still not been answered after all these years, as the *Washington Post* article explained:

> Fifty years later, it is still unclear whether there was "foul play," as the National Transportation Safety Board characterized the speculation, in the downing of United 553. The NTSB ruled the crash an accident due to pilot error. The Cook County coroner's office, which initially described one of the first-class passenger fatalities as resulting from "apparently some explosive force" and another in the coach section as "blast injuries and severe burns," later confessed to "a bad choice of adjectives" and clarified that the victims died from "injuries from high energy impact."[257]

We have an "official" report that the plane crashed because of pilot error, but we also have those statements from the coroner's office. Was the "high energy impact" a bomb, or is it meant to refer to the plane hitting the ground at high speed?

I guess it could cover both, so that one might say it's both a truth and a lie.

However, I read Buckley's 2007 confession as coming down in the idea it was a planned attack.

That terrible event came at a high point in the Watergate affair. Then I had a phone call from Howard, with whom I hadn't been in touch for several years.

He startled me by telling me that he intended to disclose to me everything he knew about the Watergate affair, including much that (he said) had not yet been revealed to congressional investigators.

What especially arrested me was his saying that his dedication to the project had included a hypothetical agreement to contrive the assassination of syndicated muckraker Jack Anderson if the high command at the Nixon White House thought this necessary. I also remember his keen surprise that the White House hadn't exercised itself to protect and free him and his collaborators arrested in connection with the Watergate enterprise. He simply could not understand this moral default.[258]

Near the end of his life (Buckley would die less than a year later in February of 2008), was Buckley trying to get some measure of justice for Dorothy Hunt? As I've said before, I've always believed people *want* to tell the truth, no matter how horrible that truth might be.

We are not designed to keep secrets.

While Buckley seemed to still be withholding some facts (such as his claim to have "left" the Agency in 1951), he still reveals some remarkable information. It's almost in passing that he lets slip the "hypothetical agreement" to kill columnist Jack Anderson, if his articles came too close to the truth.

And why might the White House not protect Hunt, if he was "their guy"?

Perhaps Nixon worried that even though Hunt was working for the reelection campaign, the fact that he was also CIA, meant he was far from being on the team.

In the end, perhaps neither Hunt, nor Buckley, understood for whom they were truly working, and what agendas were being pursued.

***

I think it's important for readers to understand that examples like William F. Buckley Jr., are emblematic of the idea that media disinformation efforts, such as Project Mockingbird, were part of how the Agency operated from the very beginning.

However, aside from media relations, the Agency had an initial, much more pressing problem. Money.

> The first concern of the newly created Central Intelligence Agency was funding (since it had received no allocation in the federal budget), which would be solved with the implementation of the brilliant idea of Col. Paul E. Helliwell.
>
> During the summer of 1947, the terms of the working relationship between the CIA and the Mafia were ironed out by Frank Wisner and Angleton. Meyer Lansky and Helliwell would work in tandem to handle the financial aspect of the narcotics venture through General Development Corporation, a shell company in Miami. Angleton would handle any legal disputes between the mob and the CIA through New York lawyer Mario Brod. The two hundred kilos of heroin for the test run would come from Schiaparelli, one of Italy's most respected pharmaceutical companies. The product would be shipped by the Sicilian mob in crates of oranges . . . The drugs would then be shipped to New York for distribution in the jazz clubs of New York.[259]

It's a mistake in understanding to think the CIA was founded with noble intentions, but there were "rogue elements" over time who have sullied its good name.

The truth is the CIA was founded as a criminal enterprise, with some of the worst of the world's criminals. The CIA was selling drugs in the inner city to finance its anti-communism crusade in Europe, particularly Italy, where the communist party was showing remarkable popularity.

And the CIA, along with its organized crime partners, would infiltrate urban police departments as well to keep things under control on the local level.

Col. Albert Carone, a New York City policeman, served the new drug network as a "bagman for the CIA," paying law enforcement officials to "look the other way" when drugs were being distributed in Harlem and other black communities. A made man within the Genovese crime family, Carone also collected money for drug payments, and later, for money to be laundered by the Vatican from Mafia families in New York, New Jersey, and Pennsylvania. In recognition of his service, the cop/bagman became a Grand Knight of the Sovereign Military of Malta, which has been described as "the military arm of the Holy See." Protection of the drug trade would become reflected in the fact that not one major drug bust was conducted by US officials from 1947 to 1967, despite the rise in heroin addicts from 20,000 to 150,000.[260]

When one understands the system that's in place, a lot of history makes more sense.

Many have questioned why the FBI, under its legendary founder, J. Edgar Hoover, never went after the Mafia. Some claim it was because the Mob had a compromising picture of Hoover in a dress or possessed blackmail information about Hoover's rumored homosexual life with longtime aide and housemate, Clyde Tolson.

Personally, I think those stories are a distraction, meant to make you laugh for a moment, then not consider the darker, more likely explanation.

Hoover couldn't move against organized crime because the CIA was in business with them.

***

The CIA's funding mechanism was in place, now, what was the goal?

It was to fund an effort called, Operation Gladio, a stay-behind network of personnel and ammunition in Western Europe, designed to conduct a guerilla war against an expected Soviet invasion, or communist takeover by elements supported and directed by Moscow.

Probably the most authoritative book on the subject is *NATO's Secret Armies: Operation Gladio and Terrorism in Western Europe*, by Daniele

Ganser, a senior researcher at the Center for Security Studies at the Federal Institute of Technology in Zurich, Switzerland. The book was published in 2005, and the author freely acknowledges that many documents were still classified and unavailable for her to review. But that there was already abundant information released to make some preliminary assumptions. From the Foreword to the book:

> The executive agents in the creation of the stay-behind networks were the Central Intelligence Agency (CIA) of the United States and the Secret Intelligence Services (SIS or MI6) of the United Kingdom. Other major actors included security services in a number of European countries. In all cases identical techniques were used. The intelligence services made an effort to establish distinct networks for spying on the occupiers, that is for espionage, and for sabotage, or subverting an enemy occupation. To establish the networks the CIA and others recruited individuals willing to participate in these dangerous activities, often allowing such initial, or chief, agents to recruit additional sub-agents. Intelligence services provided some training, placed caches of arms, ammunition, radio equipment, and other items for their networks, and set up regular channels for contact. The degree of cooperation in some cases ranged up to the conduct of exercises with military units or paramilitary forces. The number of recruits for the secret armies ranged from dozens in some nations to hundreds or even thousands in others.[261]

That's what drug sales in Harlem and other black communities by the CIA and the Mob were purchasing in Western Europe, a stay-behind secret army to be used in case the Soviets invaded. However, since the Soviet invasion never materialized, these secret armies got themselves involved in local and national politics of their host countries.

The existence of these secret "Operation Gladio" armies was one of the most closely guarded secrets of the Cold War, the information about some parts of it coming to light only in 1990, after the fall of the Berlin Wall.

Retired CIA officer Thomas Polgar confirmed after the discovery of the secret armies in Western Europe that they were coordinated by "a sort of unconventional warfare planning group" linked to NATO. This was also confirmed by the German press, which highlighted that this secretive department of NATO had during the entire Cold War remained under the dominance of the United States. "The mission of the secret armies are coordinated by the 'Special Forces Section' in a strictly secured wing of NATO headquarters in Casteau," the German press related. "A grey steel door, which opens as a bank vault only through a specific number combination, prohibits trespassing to the unauthorized."[262]

This sounds like some paranoid left-wing fantasy from the 1970s, and yet you can read scholarly accounts of the program. They just won't get much coverage in the mainstream media, well, because so much of what they print is approved by the intelligence agencies.

I'm not saying the occasional truth might not sneak through (and with the passage of time, that becomes even more likely), but by the time the intelligence agencies admit to their past crimes, they're already well on their way to committing the next one.

While original copies of the secret anti-Communist NATO protocols remain classified, speculations concerning their content have continued to increase after the discoveries of the secret anti-Communist stay behind armies. US journalist Arther Rowse in his Gladio article claims that "A secret clause in the initial NATO agreement in 1949 required that before a nation could join, it must have already established a national security authority to fight Communism through clandestine citizen cadres." Italian expert on secret services and covert action, Giuseppe de Lutiis, found that when becoming a NATO member in 1949, Italy signed not lonely the Atlantic Pact, but also secret protocols which provided for the creation of an unofficial organization "charged with guaranteeing Italy's internal alignment with the Western Block by any means, even if the electorate were to show a different inclination."[263]

The CIA was setting itself up as an institution which was higher than the democracy it was supposed to serve.

The people of Europe were not to be trusted.

Is it any wonder that if this was the underlying philosophy of the CIA regarding Europe, it was only a matter of time before the same logic was applied to the United States?

The CIA may have believed it was setting up these protocols as a measure of last resort, but it was a step that could only lead to tyranny. Once you cross that line and take away the freedom of an individual, you have made them a slave.

All the pretty words in the world will not conceal this ugly fact.

> While the debate concerning the existence or non-existence of a "secret government" in the United States continues, the Gladio evidence shows that the CIA and the Pentagon have repeatedly operated outside democratic control during the Cold War, and also after the end of the Cold War remained unaccountable for their actions. Admiral Stansfield Turner, Director of the CIA from 1977-1981, strictly refused to answer questions about Gladio in a television interview in Italy in December 1990. When the journalists insisted with respect for the victims of the numerous massacres in Italy, the former CIA Director angrily ripped off his microphone and shouted: "I said, no questions about Gladio!" whereupon the interview was over.[264]

Sometimes it's instructive to have incidents, which may, for a moment, reveal the true architecture of the world. In the West we've been led to believe in the freedom of conscience, the freedom of speech, the freedom to pursue happiness in ways that make the most sense to us, provided we do not harm others in the process. We do this because we believe that we are the sovereign rulers in our system of government, constrained by laws of course, but otherwise free men and women, able to make our way in the world.

However, when one considers that powerful agencies like the CIA seek to control the way we think, take actions in the political realm to achieve their desired outcomes even though they may conflict with popular sentiment, and are even willing to go so far as to stage what Ted Shackley called "paramilitary" action, which may require the use of phony political groups and the use of political violence, we begin to see the invisible chains that have been placed around our necks.

> Retired middle ranking CIA officers were more outspoken about the secrets of the Cold War and illegal operations of the CIA. Among them Thomas Polgar, who had retired in 1981 after a 30-year-long career in the CIA and in 1991 had testified against the nomination of Robert Gates as Director of the CIA because the latter had covered up the Iran Contra scandal. When questioned about the secret Gladio armies in Europe, Polgar explained with an implicit reference to CPC and ACC that the stay-behind programs were coordinated by a "sort of unconventional warfare planning group linked to NATO." In the secret headquarters the chiefs of the national secret armies "would meet every couple of months in different capitals."[265]

It's well-known by experts in the addiction field that the only way to break negative behavior is by making a radical commitment to truth, as well as surrendering your will to a higher power. I'm sure there are many who may think such an approach need not be so extreme. But the evidence strongly suggests otherwise. Consider Admiral Stansfield Turner, whom most would consider the most honest man to ever head the CIA.

It should be noted, though, in that 1990 interview, Turner was still protecting the dark secrets of the CIA, and in doing so, forever tarnished his legacy.

It's a simple, binary choice.

You either tell the truth or support the lie.

There is no needle to thread.

> Journalist Arthur Rowse, formerly on the staff of the *Washington Post*, thereafter in an essay on Gladio in Italy drew "The lessons of Gladio": "As long as the US public remains ignorant of this dark chapter in US foreign relations, the agencies responsible for it will face little pressure to correct their ways. The US . . . still awaits a real national debate on the means and the ends and the costs of our national security policies."[266]

This book has been an attempt to create just such a national debate on the actions and the continued existence of the CIA, if we are to have any chance of remaining a system of representative government.

***

I'm going to give the final words in this chapter to Allen Dulles, who wrote about his time in the OSS and CIA in a book entitled *The Craft of Intelligence: America's Legendary Spymaster on the Fundamentals of Intelligence Gathering for a Free World*, published in 1963, shortly before he served as head of the Warren Commission, which would determine that President Kennedy was killed by a lone gunman, and not the result of any conspiracy.

As I've mentioned before, I believe in reading books written by those you seek to understand. Because despite our best efforts, we cannot help but reveal ourselves, even those among us who might be a "legendary spymaster." Let's first turn to what Dulles thought of "agents."

> In a chapter of the *Art of War* called "Employment of Secret Agents," Sun Tzu gives the basics of espionage as it was practiced in 400 B.C. by the Chinese–much as it is practiced today. He says there are five kinds of agents: native, inside, double, expendable, and living. "Native" and "inside" agents are similar to what we shall later call "agents in place." "Double," a term still used today, is an enemy agent who has been captured, turned around and sent back where he came from as an agent of his captors. "Expendable agents" are a Chinese subtlety which we later touch upon in considering deception techniques. They are agents through which false information is leaked to the enemy. To Sun Tzu they are expendable because the enemy will probably kill them when he finds out their information was faulty. "Living" agents to Sun Tzu are later day "penetration agents." They reach the enemy, get information and manage to get back alive.[267]

As I read Dulles, it becomes clear to me that he simply can't get enough of the "dark arts" of the intelligence field. In the section which follows this passage, he delights in telling the reader that the Chinese communists under Mao Tse-tung, follow the teachings of Sun Tzu, as if that's a reason for us to adopt it as well.

As I read through *The Craft of Intelligence*, I kept looking for any section in which Dulles might show a similar reverence for the principles of Christianity, or the beliefs of the Enlightenment in the ability of humans to discern the truth through study and reflection, or the ideals of our Founding Fathers that governments will inevitably seek to acquire more power to themselves, and the only remedy for that is the oversight of the citizenry.

Alas, this search was in vain.

Dulles could easily be mistaken for Sun Tzu or Nicolo Machiavelli in his outlook, but never for Thomas Jefferson.

But he did want to explain exactly how the CIA had been set up, and why its unique structure made it superior to all the intelligence agencies that had come before it.

> The CIA was not patterned wholly either on the OSS or on the structural plan of earlier or contemporary intelligence organizations of other countries. Its broad scheme was in a sense unique in that it combined under one leadership the overt task of intelligence analysis and coordination with the work of secret intelligence operations of the various types I shall describe. Also, the new organization was intended to fill in the gaps in our existing intelligence structure without displacing or interfering with other existing intelligence units in the Departments of State and Defense. At the same time, it was recognized that the State Department, heretofore largely dependent for its information on the reports from diplomatic establishments abroad, and the components of the Defense Department, relying mainly on attaches and other military personnel abroad, could not be expected to collect intelligence on all those parts of the world that were becoming increasingly difficult of access nor to groom a standing force of trained intelligence officers.[268]

In this section I believe Dulles puts his finger on the fundamental flaw of the CIA, and it explains exactly why it's caused so much mayhem around the world.

The CIA was unique in that it "combined under one leadership the overt task of intelligence analysis **and** coordination with the work of secret intelligence operation."

In both theory and practice this meant that those engaged in gathering and analyzing the intelligence on an enemy, could at the very same time be planning a covert action against that same group. This gave the CIA complete authority, making it both prosecutor and defense, the trial court, the appeals court, and if necessary, executioner.

No tyrant in history had ever given such broad power to an intelligence agency. They understood the risks inherent in such an organization.

And if one wanted to cause mischief, abroad or at home, Dulles lets the reader know how such things might be accomplished. I encourage you to consider recent events in our own country, and question whether our intelligence agencies might be engaged in such activities within our own borders.

> For quick and effective placement of plausible deception directly into the hands of the enemy's high command, few methods beat the "accident," so long as it seems logical and has all the appearances of being a wonderfully lucky break for the enemy. Such an accident was cleverly staged by the British in 1943 before the invasion of Sicily, and it was accepted by the Germans at the time as completely genuine. Early in May of that year the corpse of a British major was found washed up on the southwest coast of Spain near the town of Huelva, between the Portuguese border and Gibraltar. A courier briefcase was still strapped to his wrist containing copies of correspondence to General Alexander in Tunisia from the Imperial General Staff. These papers clearly hinted at an Allied plan to invade southern Europe via Sardinia and Greece. Hitler sent an armored division to Greece, and the Italian garrison on Sicily was not reinforced.[269]

Feel free to choose your own particular example of disinformation over the past couple years.

Russian collusion?

The COVID lockdowns, being forced to stay inside away from vitamin D, social distancing, masks, dancing doctors and nurses in TikTok videos, those "warp speed" vaccines?

Maybe not being able to do anything about the cartels at the border bringing in fentanyl and killing more than a hundred thousand Americans last year?

Not letting Robert F. Kennedy Jr. actually run in a Democratic primary and denying his Secret Service protection because after all, he's only lost two family members to suspicious deaths?

Are all these things just "accidents"?

How many more are likely to happen in the next year?

Maybe a bird flu virus that "accidentally" makes the jump to humans, just at the same time a nearby "Bird Flu" lab was doing "gain of function" research on it?

A Hamas terrorist attack on a local shopping mall?

A bunch of suspiciously well-dressed "white supremacists" wearing masks, which confuse facial recognition devices, that might show them to be George Soros–funded political operatives, or even, horror of horrors, federal agents!

And even in 1963, the CIA was dealing with charges of elitism, and all that has come to mean in today's America.

> The charge has been leveled against CIA that it recruits almost exclusively from the so-called Ivy League colleges in the East with an overtone that possibly we have too many "softies" and possibly too many "liberals" for the tough job that the CIA has to do. It is quite true that we have a considerable number of graduates from Eastern colleges. It is also true that in numbers of degrees (many of the CIA personnel have more than one degree) Harvard, Yale, Columbia, and Princeton lead the list, but they are closely followed by Chicago, Illinois, Michigan, University of California, Stanford, and MIT.[270]

I don't know how anybody can make the claim that the CIA is elitist, especially when they're scraping the bottom of the academic barrel by hiring graduates from Stanford and MIT. The problem that many people, especially liberal supporters of Israel, are discovering today, especially in the wake of the terrible Hamas attacks of October 7, 2023, is that students are celebrating the killers of women and children, while condemning the Israeli soldiers responding to these monstrous attacks. The colleges today are intent on promoting propaganda, usually accompanied by fiery denunciations, rather than reasoned debate backed up with facts.

As if to prove my assertion that Dulles does not genuinely appreciate free speech in America, I offer this curious paragraph near the end of his book.

> Our Founding Fathers put the guarantee of freedom of the press in our Bill of Rights, and it became the First Amendment to the Constitution: "Congress shall make no law . . . abridging the freedoms of the speech or of the press." As a result of this and other constitutional safeguards, it has generally been judged that although we have several espionage laws, we could not enact federal legislation comparable to that in effect in another great democracy, Great Britain. The British Official Secrets Act provides penalties for the unauthorized disclosure of certain specified and classified information, and British legal procedures permit prosecutions without publicly disclosing classified information.[271]

What can I say in response to that, except for the fact Dulles got his wish after the September 11 attacks of 2001, and the promulgation of the "State Secrets Privilege" under which my family had to suffer for years?

I ask you to consider the possibility that what Dulles hoped to bring about in 1963, has been achieved in our current system, through a program of government infiltration of the media and coercion of our social media platforms.

> Here is a possible order of procedure: (1) the executive branch of government, particularly the Departments of State and Defense and the intelligence community, should do what they can to prevent the unnecessary publication of information that is valuable to our enemies and to deal more effectively with the leaks from the executive branch; (2) in conference with Congressional leaders and in agreement with them, steps should be taken to restrict the publication of sensitive hearings in the field of our national

security, particularly in the military field. After some progress has been made in (1) and (2), there should be quiet (hopefully) discussions between selected government officials most immediately concerned and the leaders of the press and other news media, radio, technical, and service journals, to determine to what extent there can be mutual agreement for setting up machinery to keep the press confidentially advised as to the matters in which secrecy is essential to our security, particularly to those pertaining to military hardware and sensitive intelligence operations.[272]

It is through such machinations that a democracy dies in darkness and shadows.

This approach, getting all the "important" people together for a "sit-down" is a strategy which would likely meet with approval from Mafia crime-lords "Lucky" Luciano, Sam Giancana, and Santo Trafficante.

It is sobering to realize that all the things wrong with the CIA, the secrecy, associations with criminals and the worst of humanity, as well as the drug trade, were present from the very beginning.

It did not have to be this way, and the truth is that over the years many have fought this monster.

President Harry Truman, who created the CIA, came to regret his decision, even publishing a famous op-ed a month after the Kennedy assassination, accusing the CIA of meddling in domestic affairs.

President Dwight D. Eisenhower seemed to have lost control over the CIA during his term, but tried to redeem himself by giving his famous "Military-Industrial Complex" speech for his farewell address in 1961.

President John F. Kennedy kept the peace during his brief administration, and likely paid the ultimate price for his courage.

President Lyndon Johnson led us into the madness of the Vietnam War and did not choose to run for a second term.

Although a deeply strange individual, it seems that President Richard M. Nixon had a strategy to free us from the grip of the secret government. But they brought him down with a joint CIA-FBI operation, popularly known as the Watergate scandal.

President James Earl Carter tried to end much of the secrecy, but he fell victim to the Deep State as well.

President Ronald Reagan, a much sunnier character than Nixon, seemed to have a similar plan, dramatically increasing the military budget to bring the Soviets to the negotiating table, which actually seemed to work.

However, the next president, George H. W. Bush, former director of the CIA, and likely longtime CIA asset, wanted to keep tensions high, and with Iraq's invasion of Kuwait, had an opportunity to let loose the dogs of war.

President Bill Clinton, who followed Bush, seemed to be a brilliant, slick character, and he may have outwitted the CIA's plans for further conflict, as his term was relatively quiet, and we actually balanced the budget, a longtime Republican objective.

With the election of President George W. Bush, and the September 11, 2001, attacks, the reins were off of the CIA. I'll let others speculate what secrets may yet lay undiscovered behind that attack. But suffice to say that Bush and his powerful vice president, Dick Cheney, launched us into decades of war, and the erosion of American freedom.

President Barack Obama was supposed to bring "hope and change," but brought more of the same, keeping Guantanamo Bay open, letting the CIA continue to run wild, and letting the cancer of ISIS grow in the Middle East.

Then there was President Donald Trump, who promised to drain the swamp, and while his intentions seemed genuine, he placed swamp creatures to run important agencies, collaborated with people like Anthony Fauci to close down the country, and delivered untested vaccines to the general public. (Perhaps he has learned the lesson of how duplicitous our own government can be and might do better in a second term. But I'm not hopeful. If there is to be genuine change, it must come because we the people, demand it.)

And now we have President Joseph Biden, who campaigned on the "fine people hoax," and never met a lobbyist or war he didn't like. I understand that for many reading this book, they will believe our recent history offers little reason for optimism.

However, I'm filled with hope because I've seen empires fall.

I was at CIA when the Berlin Wall came down, and I recall the shock and disbelief of those times.

I had joined the CIA to fight a war I expected to last decades more, but they were already living on borrowed time.

While many credited Ronald Reagan's bold and challenging words to the Soviet Union as the catalyst for the fall of communism in Russia and the Eastern Bloc, I think it was an earlier event, which few have commented upon.

I believe it was the Reverend Billy Graham's visit to the Soviet Union in 1982, which began the fall of that despotic regime. Hundreds of thousands of Russians turned out to listen to him speak, showing that even after nearly seven decades of communism, the spiritual yearnings of human beings could not be repressed. They saw a genuine man of God, speaking His truth in a way their leaders never had, and it touched their souls, in a way that arrogant displays of tanks and nuclear missiles never could.

And while petty tyrants like Allen Dulles will continue to worship the writings of Sun Tzu, the rest of the world is more interested in the art of peace, raising their kids in a world of safety and abundance, and living in friendly communities.

The practitioners of the dark arts of persuasion can lead people to fear and suspicion, and even keep them there for long periods of time.

Because that is not who we are as human beings.

We long to tell the truth and live in the beautiful sunlight, not hidden in the shadows.

Even my brothers and sisters still working in the CIA.

I think often of the Iranian assassin with whom I spent so much time in the hills of that unnamed country, and how he must have weighed in his mind the question of whether or not to kill me.

But something convinced him to let me live, and every day after that, even during the toughest of times, I've been thankful for that decision.

I'd like to think it was because seeing me up close he realized I was not the monster his agency had painted me out to be. Perhaps our common humanity, our love for our families and children, changed his mind about this supposed enemy. In my travels and the operations in which I've been involved, I've learned that people are more alike than different. We all share a basic need for meaning in our lives and desire to find someone we can trust.

We must all make that decision to stand proud in the light, showing our true selves, and fighting the battles we face. In doing that, our collective acts of courage can turn the tide, and banish the shadow government forever.

CHAPTER EIGHT

PROJECT MOCKINGBIRD IS ALIVE AND WELL

My disturbing experience with journalist Bob Woodward clearly revealed to me that the CIA's Operation Mockingbird was still in operation today, just in a modified form. The Church Committee in the Senate revealed much of what the "secret government" had been up to from World War II until 1976.

But most people today probably don't know much about Senator Frank Church, who might have ended up as president if he hadn't gone after the CIA and the intelligence agencies. He expected the investigation would propel him into the presidency from a populace tired of war and corruption.

But the fortuitous murder of a CIA station chief, thousands of miles away from Washington, DC, would blunt the most explosive findings of the Church Committee and derail Church's presidential ambitions.

However, before we get to that story, I'll start off by quoting from the US Senate website on the "Senate Select Committee to Study Governmental Operations with Respect to Intelligence,"[273] which became popularly known as the "Church Committee."

In 1973 the Senate Watergate Committee investigation revealed that the executive branch had directed national intelligence agencies to carry out constitutionally questionable domestic security operations.In 1974 Pulitzer Prize-winning journalist Seymour

Hersh published a front-page *New York Times* article claiming that the CIA had been spying on anti-war activists for more than a decade, violating the agency's charter. Former CIA officials and some lawmakers, including Senators William Proxmire and Stuart Symington, called for a congressional inquiry.[274]

When people say to me that secrets can't be kept, part of me agrees, and then the other part says, well, sometimes they can be kept for a while. From the start of the Vietnam War in 1964 until 1974, the CIA was breaking the rules on domestic spying, and nobody talked about it. (Many suspected, but nobody knew for sure.) It's important to realize that when things are secret, that's both a strength and a weakness for the agencies. Nobody will know if they're lying when they deny having engaged in some activity, but it looks suspicious when they resist even a cursory investigation or submitting to questioning under oath.

After a meeting with President Gerald Ford and his top national security advisors, Church and Vice-Chairman Tower secured from the president a pledge that the White House would cooperate with Senate investigators. Staff identified potential programs for study and began requesting documents from intelligence agencies. Though staff did not always receive documents in a timely fashion, they enjoyed unprecedented access to materials that had never before been made public. Perhaps the most well-known of these internal reports, the CIA's so-called "Family Jewels," outlined the agency's misdeeds dating back to President Eisenhower's administration.[275]

In truth, the corruption would go back as far as World War II. When one asks the question, have the intelligence agencies violated the rights of Americans, the answer, as provided by the Church Committee, is a clear "yes."

Despite these numerous challenges, the Church Committee investigated and identified a wide range of intelligence abuses by federal agencies, including the CIA, FBI, Internal revenue Service, and National Security Agency. In the course of their work, investigators identified programs that had never before been known to the American public, including NSA's Projects SHAMROCK and MINARET, programs which monitored wire communications to and from the United States and shared some of that data with other intelligence agencies. Committee staff researched the FBI's long-running program of "covert action designed to disrupt and discredit the activities of groups and individuals deemed a threat to the social order," known as COINTELPRO. The FBI included among the program's many target organizations such as the Southern Christian Leadership Conference, the Vietnam War movement, and individuals such as Martin Luther King, Jr., as well as local, state, and federal elected officials.[276]

One of my favorite expressions is, "You can trust your government, or you can know your history. But you can't do both." When one reads a news story today suggesting some dark agenda being put forth by the intelligence agencies to go after whistleblowers, or those calling for greater transparency, all you have to do is look at their historic playbook, as revealed by the Church Committee. And despite all the roadblocks that were thrown in their way, the Church Committee uncovered a great deal.

After holding 126 full committee meetings, 40 subcommittee hearings, interviewing some 800 witnesses in public and closed sessions, and combing through 110,000 documents, the committee published its final report on April 29, 1976. Investigators determined that, beginning with President Franklin Roosevelt's administration, and continuing through the early 1970s, "intelligence excesses, at home and abroad" were not the "product of any single party, administration, or man," but had developed as America rose to become a superpower during a global Cold War.

"Intelligence agencies have undermined the constitutional rights of citizens," the final report concluded, "primarily because checks and balances designed by the framers of the Constitution to assure accountability have not been applied."[277]

If you know your history, you don't trust your government. At least not without a healthy system of checks and balances, and journalists who aren't on the payroll of the CIA.

I just wish that CIA leadership actually wanted to protect the government the Founders bequeathed to us.

***

In 2023, two-time Pulitzer Prize–winning author James Risen published a long overdue biography on Senator Frank Church, called *The Last Honest Man: The CIA, the FBI, and the Kennedys–And One Senator's Fight to Save Democracy*. It was a *New York Times* bestseller and details an overlooked part of our history.

The book opens with what might have been the most dramatic moment of the hearings, the production of a "heart-attack" gun by CIA Director William Colby, which he handed over to the Senator.

> "Have you brought with you some of those devices which would have enabled the CIA to use this poison for killing people?" Senator Frank Church, dressed in a dark brown suit with a color-splashed designer tie, stares out at the Senate Caucus Room and employing the precise diction that is his trademark, questions William Colby, the director of the Central Intelligence Agency . . .
>
> The subject of the hearings is an investigation into why the CIA secretly stored a cache of lethal shellfish toxin for use in assassinations despite a presidential order to destroy it. Church has just asked Colby to show him what kind of weapon a CIA assassin would use to fire the toxin at a victim.
>
> "We have indeed," replies Colby, staring unsmilingly right back at Church from behind his glasses, carefully combed hair, and light tailored suit.[278]

All the trademark qualities of the CIA were on display in that hearing, from the crazy idea of a poison dart gun to the defiance of presidential power. The account of the September 1975 hearing continued:

Mitchell Rogovin, a dark-haired, left-leaning civil liberties lawyer hired by Colby to be special counsel to the CIA specifically to deal with the Democratic-controlled Church Committee, takes out a strangely designed, battery-operated pistol, shaped like a .45 handgun with a large sight attached across its barrel. He walks up to the dais and lays the gun down in front of Church . . .

Church holds up the gun in his left hand, pointing it toward the ceiling, his finger off the trigger. John Tower, the committee's ranking Republican, sitting on Church's left, stares at the gun as Church holds it aloft. News photographers, kneeling in front of the committee dais, quickly go to work, taking shot after shot of Church holding up the dart gun.[279]

The image of Church holding the gun, and John Tower (who years later would head up the Tower Commission, which essentially absolved President Reagan of criminal wrongdoing in the Iran-Contra scandal) becomes the symbol of the Church Committee hearings.

Although Risen paints a picture of the Church Committee hearings as a righteous cause, he is evenhanded in his assessment of Frank Church, making sure to quote the man's supporters, as well as his critics.

The hearings showcased the two sides of Frank Church, the ambitious, publicity-seeking politician yearning for acceptance in Washington—the Frank Church who knew that holding up the dart gun would generate buzz and headlines—and the radicalized outsider who hated the Washington establishment, the Frank Church who despised the American imperialism represented by a spy agency prepared to kill foreign leaders with toxin filled darts . . .

"I think perhaps our addiction to war in the last thirty years has had something to do with [CIA] abuses," Church said in an appearance before the Women's National Democratic Club on September 8, 1975. "We've engaged in more active warfare than any other nation in the world, and that has a certain brutalizing effect."[280]

For many of us the 1970s doesn't seem so distant, and yet for some it will appear as almost ancient history. But the concerns of Frank Church, as the country was emerging from the shadow of Vietnam, do not seem so different from our time as we emerge from the shadows of Iraq, Afghanistan, and wonder what might await us in Ukraine, the Middle East, or Taiwan.

With the relatively antiquated technology of the 1970s, the intelligence agencies were attempting surveillance on a massive scale. The march of technology has only fed the appetite of the intelligence agencies to know everything about us, and yet for us, the public, to know so very little about them. They treat us as the children, and when we question their actions and edicts, they slander us by asking "Are you a Putin apologist?" or "Don't you believe in science?" When you can't answer the questions, you attack the questioner. I doubt that anything in our latest headlines would have surprised Frank Church.

> By 1975, Frank Church had come to believe that the future of
> American democracy was threatened by the rise of a permanent
> and largely unaccountable national security state, and he sensed
> that at the heart of that secret government was a lawless intelligence
> community. In order to save the nation, Church was convinced,
> America's spy agencies would have to be reined in.[281]

But the Church Committee's hearings have direct relevance to events decades after their conclusion. They were having a devastating effect on the country's perception of itself as a champion of freedom and democracy. Our methods "seemed" little different than the communists we were fighting.

In fact, they WERE little different.

Then came the murder in December 1975 of the CIA station chief in Greece and blame quickly began to attach itself to Senator Church's hearings.

> On the night of December 23, 1975, Ron Estes, the CIA's deputy
> station chief in Athens, was lounging on the couch in his girlfriend's
> apartment when the Greek driver for Richard Welch, the CIA's sta-
> tion chief, burst in the front door. He yelled, "A shooting, and Mr.
> Welch is down!" Estes grabbed his coat and ran out with the driver,
> while his girlfriend yelled at him not to go.

When he got to Welch's house, Estes found the 46-year-old station chief lying on the sidewalk on his back, with his wife, Kika, kneeling beside him. Blood covered Welch's face, and Estes could see immediately that his boss was dead. "I didn't need to feel for a pulse," recalled Estes.[282]

A year later, as reported by the *New York Times*, there had been no progress on the case. But immense damage had been done to both the Church Committee, as well as his presidential ambitions, courtesy of a few names that may be familiar to contemporary readers.

> Mr. Welch was returning from a party given by the United States Ambassador, Jack B. Kubisch, on December 23 when three gunmen shot him in the street outside his home in a wealthy suburb of Paleo Psychio. Some weeks earlier Greek and American journals had identified him as the head of the C.I.A. operation here, and supporters of the agency accused its critics of "fingering" agents and endangering their lives.
>
> The outcry that followed the Welch murder helped sidetrack investigations of the Central Intelligence Agency then taking place in Congress: Some critics accuse the agency of having distorted and exploited the Welch case to quash those Congressional inquiries.[283]

Who would be leading the charge on behalf of the CIA against the Church Committee's questions, blaming Church personally for the Welch murder? That would be none other than George H. W. Bush, the then director of the CIA, whom Church had vehemently opposed.

> Frank Church was stunned by the sudden reversal of the political climate in the wake of Richard Welch's murder. In early 1976, Church had to navigate through the Pike Committee's [an inquiry in the House] epic flameout and also deal with a more confrontational CIA under the leadership of its newly confirmed director, George Bush.
>
> During one closed hearing of the Church Committee, "Bush blurted out, 'you were responsible for Welch's assassination,'"

recalled Fred Schwartz. "It pissed off everybody. We forced Bush to apologize during the hearing."[284]

One gets the sense that if the CIA wants to assassinate you, they might very well use a poison dart gun, or if that might attract too much attention, there's always the casual character assassination they can pull off in a closed-door Senate hearing. It's probably a good way to get those other independent-minded Senators singing from the same sheet of music.

And who might have been at Bush's side in that meeting, whispering in his ear? Some evidence suggests it was none other than William Barr, the two-time attorney general under George H. W. Bush, then for President Donald Trump.

When Barr was nominated in 2019 to be Trump's attorney general, CNN did a piece on Barr with the title, "What Barr's Work Under Bush 41 Tells Us about How He'll Handle His New Job." In a surprising move, Barr was quite open about his CIA background.

Barr first met Bush in the 1970s when both men worked for the CIA–Barr beginning his career in Washington as a junior officer at the agency, Bush as its director.

In the 2001 interview with the Miller Center, Barr described one of their first interactions–as Bush was quizzed at a congressional oversight hearing.

"He leaned back and said, 'How the hell do I answer this one?'" Barr recalled. "I whispered the answer in his ear, and he gave it, and I thought, 'Who is this guy? He listens to legal advice when it's given.'"

In a statement to CNN, Barr called Bush "a great man by every measure and a gentleman of the old school–kind, considerate, decent."[285]

I think it's important for the reader to put themselves in the shoes of a CIA director, and ask yourself the question, "If I was going to secretly run a country, how would I do it?" My answer is to have somebody on my side that nobody would expect, like maybe a two-time attorney general, who with his roly poly, rumpled, grumpy academic, fat cat face appearance, looks about as far removed from being a secret agent as humanly possible.

And if you know where to look, such as a *Vanity Fair* profile on Bill Barr from 2019, you can find support for the idea that Barr might be part of just such an effort.

> At one point, the young Barr even declared to his Horace Mann adviser that when he grew up, he wanted to become head of the CIA . . .
>
> Soon after graduation, Barr joined the CIA as a China analyst while attending George Washington University law at night and married Christine Monihan, a librarian . . .
>
> According to James Zirin, the legal commentator and former federal prosecutor, "Barr is from the school of *L'etat, c'est moi*–I am the state."[286]

In his mind, Barr may have considered himself the state. Within a few years of joining the Agency, to be able to whisper answers into the ear of the director of the CIA, and have the director repeat his words verbatim to an inquisitive congressional investigation, he would have had an excellent reason to believe just such a thing.

With Barr on the attack, Church's situation continued to worsen.

> Johnny Roselli's grisly murder was the horrific postscript to the Church Committee. And coming on the heels of the shocking deaths of Sam Giancana and Orlando Letelier [a Cuban exile leader], it sparked an immediate response from members of the Church Committee. The coincidences of the murders were piling up–and it was no longer possible to ignore the connections to the committee's investigation.
>
> Two days after Roselli's body was found, Senator Howard Baker called for both the FBI and CIA to provide any information they had about Roselli's murder. "There appears to be a connection" between the Roselli and Giancana murders," Baker told reporters. "Both agreed to testify on the same subject. Both were involved in the same assassination operation."[287]

That's not even throwing in the death of Dorothy Hunt, the wife of Watergate ringleader, E. Howard Hunt, or the killing of CIA station chief, Richard Welch.

That's five deaths of people connected to the CIA's dirty tricks, and not a single person was ever convicted in any of the cases.

One person who found these events highly disturbing was Senator Gary Hart, from Colorado, who himself would run for president in 1984, only to find himself the center of a sex scandal, which forced him to drop out of the race.

> Gary Hart took the murder of Johnny Roselli harder than any other member of the Church Committee. He believed that it was crucial to find out whether Roselli had been murdered because of the Church Committee testimony, especially after Sam Giancana had also been murdered right before he was scheduled to testify. Hart was shocked that "no federal agency seemed interested in the Roselli murder," he recalled. "Not the FBI, not the CIA—no one wanted to look into it."
>
> "It seemed pretty obvious to me that [Roselli] was killed because of his testimony before the committee," Hart added. "Same with Giancana. To me it set off all kinds of warning signals and red lights. I just assumed that people would jump all over it, and the FBI and CIA would send in their top people to find out who killed these guys."[288]

But of course, this would not happen, especially with George H. W. Bush in charge at the CIA. Bill Barr would have us believe George H. W. Bush was a "gentleman." That's how he wants the history to be written. However, it's difficult to reconcile Barr's picture with the same man who, in private session, accuses a United States Senator of culpability in the death of a CIA station chief.

For me, the picture painted is that of a tyrant, hiding behind the country club façade of being a gentleman.

Church's presidential campaign suffered from two defects. First, his tenure on the Church Committee after the killing of CIA station chief

Richard Welch made him a pariah, and second, he entered the race too late. But even with these two problems, there were significant betrayals.

> Even Senator Joe Biden, who Frank Church had helped by lending him staff during his 1972 campaign, and then helped again after his wife and daughter were killed in a car crash just after his election to the Senate, snubbed Church and went with Carter. Biden became chairman of Jimmy Carter's national steering committee during the Democratic primary season; Biden's move to Carter was just one of many signs that influential Democrats were not waiting around for Frank Church to finally get into the race. "I think that hurt Church," when Biden endorsed Carter, recalled Susan Hunter, who worked on the Church campaign, and later in his Senate office. Biden told reporters that Carter appealed to him because he was running a campaign based on his personal integrity, rather than on political issues. That was a pointed rebuke to the party's liberals, including Frank Church.[289]

You always kind of had to suspect that Joe Biden would be somewhere in the picture, didn't you, the hale and hearty joking guy, ready to stab you in the back, right? Don't vote for Carter, Biden seemed to be saying in 1976, because he's got the right policies.

Vote for him because he's not the other guy.

It's the same strategy Biden would use to ride his way into the White House in 2020. I challenge you to name a single Biden policy with wide support in 2024.

You can't.

But he makes you think, at least he's an honest gentleman, not like that other guy.

It's a trick that worked a couple times for George H. W. Bush, and one that Biden apparently hopes will work again for him.

***

Senator Frank Church lost his Senate election in 1980 to Republican Steve Symms. Many of his fellow liberals also lost their races in the Reagan landslide. The CIA seemed to take note.

Frank Church exited politics quietly, and with relatively little apparent rancor. But Church's defeat was cause for celebration in CIA circles.

"After I won the Senate race, I was invited to a party at someone's house, and I was about the only person there who was not former intelligence," recalled Symms. "It was quite impressive to meet all these people–and see how deeply they all despised Church."[290]

Winston Churchill once said that a man is known by his enemies. If we judge Church by his enemies in the CIA, we see that he's somebody who wanted to end the secrecy they so deeply cherished. If you are somebody who values openness, Church should be on your shortlist of American patriots, regardless of party affiliation.

In 1984, Church was diagnosed with pancreatic cancer, and though he would die within the year, went out swinging against the shadow government.

But even as he was facing death, Church continued to sound the same alarms that had become his hallmark. In one of his last interviews in January 1984, Church warned once again about the threat of American imperialism, now embodied by Ronald Reagan's hawkish foreign policies. "We seem unable to learn from the failure of our Vietnam policy, or the equally evident failure of our hardline policy toward Castro in Cuba," Church told David Broder of the *Washington Post*. "It is this idea that the communist threat is everywhere that has made our government its captive and its victim."

"This country has become so conservative–so fearful–that we have come to see revolution anywhere in the world as a threat to the United States. It's nonsense. And yet, the policy we have followed has cost so many lives, so much treasure, such setbacks to our vital interests, as a great power ought not to endure."[291]

The players may change, but the game remains the same—fool the public. When the intelligence and defense agencies play their secrecy games, they keep us in a perpetual state of fear. The public doesn't share their bloodlust or greed, it's just that they're confused about the proper course of action.

Confusion serves the purposes of the Deep State because it allows them to continue operating in the shadows.

We need to get better at watching their hands, and not the shiny objects they use to distract us from what they're doing.

***

How does one get better at seeing the propaganda games?

Well, usually there comes a time when the Deep State has failed so miserably at their plans that they have to admit some of what they've done, just to remain credible with the public.

That's the situation that took place in 2008, after years of having the Pentagon try to spin the Iraq War as being won, and Guantanamo Bay as a place you'd want to be held if you were a terrorist. And while I'm generally not a fan of the *New York Times*, the 2008 Pulitzer Prize–winning article by David Barstow entitled, "Behind TV Analysts, Pentagon's Hidden Hand," was an excellent expose of a modern-day Project Mockingbird operation. From the opening of the article:

> In the summer of 2005, the Bush administration confronted a fresh wave of criticism over Guantanamo Bay. The detention center had been branded "the gulag of our times" by Amnesty International, there were new allegations of abuse from United Nations human rights experts and calls were mounting for its closure.
>
> The administration's communication experts responded swiftly. Early one Friday morning, they put a group of retired military officers on one of the jets normally used by Vice President Dick Cheney and flew them to Cuba for a carefully orchestrated tour of Guantanamo.
>
> To the public, these men are members of a familiar fraternity, presented tens of thousands of times on television and radio as "military analysts" whose long service has equipped them to give authoritative and unfettered judgments about the most pressing issues of the post-Sept. 11 world.[292]

This is how they deceive the public. They knew people were scared about terrorism, worried that the wars in Iraq and Afghanistan weren't going well and had heard concerns about abuses at Guantanamo Bay.

How do you calm those fears?

Get some of those "authoritative and unfettered judgments" in front of the viewers.

The only problem is those views were far from "authoritative" and they'd certainly been "fettered" by the shackles of Pentagon spin. The article continued:

> The effort, which began with the buildup to the Iraq War and continues to this day, has sought to exploit ideological and military allegiances, and also a powerful financial dynamic: Most of the analysts have ties to military contractors vested in the very war policies they are asked to assess on air.
>
> Those business relationships are hardly ever disclosed to the viewers, and sometimes not even to the networks themselves. But collectively, the men on the plane represent more than 150 military contractors either as lobbyists, senior executives, board members or consultants. The companies include defense heavyweights, but also scores of smaller companies, all part of a vast assemblage of contractors scrambling for hundreds of billions in military business generated by the administration's war on terror.[293]

You can't exactly call it "bribery," and you can always make the excuse that you're just providing "access" to the news media or seeking to "educate" them so they can provide a more informed opinion to the public.

But sometimes the stench gets so bad, you have to say something, or else you'll never get anybody to believe you in the future.

> Analysts have been wooed in hundreds of private briefings with senior military leaders, including officials with significant influence over contracting and budget matters, records show. They have been taken on tours of Iraq and given access to classified intelligence. They have been briefed by officials from the White House,

State Department and Justice Department, including Mr. Cheney, Alberto R. Gonzales and Stephen Hadley.

In turn, members of this group have echoed administration talking points, sometimes even when they suspected the information was false or inflated. Some analysts acknowledge they suppressed doubts because they feared jeopardizing their access.[294]

It's quite a challenge to do your job as an analyst for some network TV shows, at the same time you're working as a lobbyist for a defense contractor, trying to land that fat government contract. It's in both your financial interests, as well as the company you represent, that you provide analysis favorable to the government.

Kenneth Allard, a former NBC military analyst who has taught information warfare at the National Defense University, said the campaign amounted to a sophisticated information operation. "This was a coherent, active policy," he said.

As conditions in Iraq deteriorated, Mr. Allard recalled, he saw a yawning gap between what analysts were told in private briefings and what subsequent inquiries and books later revealed.

"Night and day," Mr. Allard said, "I felt we'd been hosed."[295]

The next time you see James Clapper, former director of National Intelligence from 2010 to 2017, or John Brennan, former head of the CIA from 2013 to 2017, on a news program giving their opinion about a topic, realize they're just the tip of the media disinformation iceberg.

Trailing in their wake are hundreds of military and defense "analysts," likely moonlighting for the defense contractors as well, who want to give you their independent opinion.

Don't fall for it.

***

And if you think the intelligence agencies aren't trying to reach you through social media, all you need to do is read their own words, such as this September 8, 2021, article from *Politico*:

In the bowels of its Langley headquarters, a fluorescent-lit, mundane office space houses a team of about a dozen people engaged in what is perhaps the Central Intelligence Agency's least covert mission: to make American citizens "like" the agency on social media.

An edict is posted to the wall: "Every time you make a typo . . . the errorists win."

The United State's premier intelligence agency has slowly ramped up its social media presence since joining Facebook and Twitter in 2014, creating one of the federal government's quirkiest, creative, and controversial PR campaigns.

The aim: to dispel some of the negative press and conspiracy theories that have dogged the agency over the years by showing the CIA staffers are just like us.[296]

The CIA is supposed to be a secret agency, but they want you to "like" them on social media? Isn't this an influence campaign against the American public, something which is supposed to be forbidden?

And yet they act like it's normal.

Does anybody see a problem with the most feared intelligence agency posting on social media platforms? Does anybody else see a potential power imbalance between the two entities?

If you're Facebook, and the CIA calls you up expressing displeasure about how much engagement a certain post is receiving do you tell them, "Sorry, there's nothing I can do about it?"

Or do you tweak the algorithm a little to make the post go more viral? The article continued:

The agency now boasts robust followings on Instagram (398,000 followers), YouTube (60,000 subscribers), Facebook (993,000 likes), and Twitter (3.2 million followers) . . .

The team has harnessed social media tropes and hashtags including Girl Boss-y posts touting "Women Crush Wednesday," #KnowYourValue, pumpkin spice lattes, #TuesdayTrivia, and a recurring "Humans of CIA" series modeled on the popular "Humans of New York" photography project that went viral just over a decade ago.

They argue that the CIA is just adapting to a media environment where every person and corporation is a potential publisher that can put forward a brand. "One of the reasons that we're on social media is if we're not talking about ourselves, other people still will be and then there's a vacuum," explained Sara Lichterman, a CIA spokesperson and liaison to the entertainment industry who joined the conversation at Langley. "So we have to come and tell our own story.[297]

Is the CIA simply "adapting" to the media environment, or is it trying to control the narrative? How do you think a spy agency would play that game?

Lay all their cards out on the table?

Or figure out how to lie and get away with it?

If you were in Hollywood and the CIA liaison to the entertainment industry approached you with a request, what do you think you would do?

Perhaps in addition to a little lying, a good helping of bullying?

An answer to the question of whether the CIA is simply using the platforms, or attempting to control them, may have recently been answered by the journalists Michael Shallenberger, Matt Taibbi, and Alex Gutentag. As reported by *ZeroHedge* on May 26, 2024:

> While the CIA is strictly prohibited from spying on or running clandestine operations against American citizens on US soil, a bombshell new "Twitter Files" report reveals that a member of the Board of Trustees on InQtel–the CIA's mission-driving venture capital firm, along with "former" intelligence community (IC) and CIA analysts, were involved in a massive effort on 2021-2022 to take over Twitter's content management system, as Michael Shallenberger, Matt Taibbi and Alex Gutentag report over at Shallenberger's *Public*.
>
> According to "thousands of pages of Twitter Files and documents," these efforts were part of a broader strategy to manage how information is disseminated and consumed on social media under the guise of combatting "misinformation" and foreign propaganda efforts–as this complex of government-linked individuals

and organizations has gone to great lengths to suggest that narrative control is a national security issue.[298]

One can see the same pattern we've consistently documented through this book, namely that security services try to co-opt corporations and media in order to deceive the public by seizing control of the narrative.

For many people, the crimes of the CIA, such as drug running since the late 1940s, political intrigue, assassinations, and regime changes, are simply facts which won't move them to action if they believe that overall, the CIA has done a good job of protecting us.

The public needs to realize that the evidence is overwhelming that the CIA worries about its public image, as much as it worries about anything.

It is their weakness and our strength.

Consider this section of the *ZeroHedge* article dealing with Nina Jankowicz, who for a short period of time was poised to become our national "Minister of Truth," before a bizarre video of her singing about the perils of misinformation made her slink from public view.

Jankowicz (aka "Scary Poppins"), previously tipped to lead the DHS's now-aborted Disinformation Governance Board, has been a vocal advocate for more stringent regulation of online speech to counteract "rampant disinformation." Jim Baker, in his previous capacity as FBI General Counsel and later as Twitter's Deputy General Counsel, advocated for and implemented policies that would restrict certain types of speech on the platform, including decisions that affected the visibility of politically sensitive content.

Furthermore, companies like PayPal, Amazon Web Services, and Go-Daddy were mentioned as part of a concerted effort to de-platform and financially de-incentivize individuals and organizations deemed threats by the IC [Intelligence Community]. This approach represents a significant escalation in the use of corporate cooperation to achieve what might essentially be considered censorship under the guise of national security.[299]

As an old CIA guy who bought the line that the CIA's job was to collect intelligence and present that information to the representatives of our civilian government, who would then make informed decisions on how to proceed, I can only view such developments with the greatest of alarm. If I have not been clear enough before, let me state that I am a rock-solid believer in our Constitution. Our Founding Fathers understood the nature of man, our tendency towards corruption and darkness, and created a system in which sunlight and transparency were constant correctives so that such infections could not spread.

My experiences and the writing of this book have convinced me that we likely lost our democracy sometime in the 1950s during the Eisenhower Administration, because of the actions of men like Allen Dulles and Ted Shackley, who believed they knew better than you. Kennedy discovered this coup and tried to take our country back, but was killed for it, laying down a marker for all other presidents who came after him.

Did they love their country enough to die for it?

Would they take the necessary risks for such a bold effort, knowing that a family member's plane might mysteriously crash, as happened to Dorothy Hunt, the wife of Watergate ringleader, E. Howard Hunt, and good friend of conservative icon, William F. Buckley Jr.?

The shadow government plays for keeps.

But they are strong only as long as they remain in the shadows. That's a little more difficult when they're searching for "likes" on Facebook, Twitter, and Instagram. Even more than our Constitution, I believe God leads evil people to their own destruction. And I see evidence of this plan unfolding with every news story I read.

As much as I mock Nina Jankowicz, I believe she has also placed herself at significant risk from the intelligence agencies. In attempting to become a beloved media celebrity and arbiter of truth, she has made an embarrassment of herself, and the Agency doesn't like such loose ends. Consider this section of the *ZeroHedge* article:

> Remember Nina? A huge fan of Christopher Steele–the architect of the infamous Clinton-funded Dossier which underpinned the Trump-Russia hoax, and who joined the chorus of disinformation

agents that downplayed the Hunter Biden laptop bombshell, Jankowicz previously served as a disinformation fellow at the Wilson Center and advised the Ukrainian Foreign Ministry as part of the Fulbright-Clinton Public Policy Fellowship. She also oversaw the Russia and Belarus programs at the National Democratic Institute.

Jankowicz compares the lack of regulation of speech on social media to the lack of government regulation of automobiles in the 1960s. She calls for a "cross-platform" and public-private approach, so whatever actions are taken are taken by Google, Facebook, and Twitter, simultaneously.[300]

Maybe it's just me, but whenever I hear somebody advocating some form of "public-private" partnership, I think to myself, "Yeah, that's what Mussolini had in Italy, and Hitler had in Germany." I wonder how that will work out.

It's my sincere hope that Nina Jankowicz lives long enough to see the error of her ways.

But I'm not optimistic about her chances.

***

It's important to realize that part of being effective with the soft power of propaganda is that you need to know what the citizenry is thinking, which is why the surveillance technologies are so important to the Deep State.

While the public may have some concern over the government being able to blackmail future political leaders (although that's normally done more in the Jeffrey Epstein style), the real value to your data is predicting what the public is going to do.

I understand why pundits may talk about your "privacy." But in my opinion, that's really not the long-term play. Governments aren't concerned about individuals threatening their power. They're concerned about what groups of individuals are likely to do.

In 2013, National Security Agency (NSA) contractor Edward Snowden released a large cache of data revealing the misbehavior of the NSA. He was initially celebrated in the media, but they quickly turned against him, almost like they had against Senator Frank Church. Remarkably, in

2014, the editorial board of the *New York Times* supported Snowden. They recounted Snowden's actions and the response:

> Seven months ago, the world began to learn the vast scope of the National Security Agency's reach into the lives of hundreds of millions of people in the United States and around the globe, as it collects information about their phone calls, their email messages, their friends and contacts, how they spend their days and where they spend their nights. The public learned in great detail how the agency had exceeded its mandate and abused its authority, prompting outrage at kitchen tables and at the desks of Congress, which may finally begin to limit these practices.
>
> The revelations have already prompted two federal judges to accuse the N.S.A. of violating the Constitution (although a third, unfortunately, found the dragnet surveillance to be legal.) A panel appointed by President Obama issued a powerful indictment of the agency's invasion of privacy and called for a major overhaul of its operations.[301]

Although I understand Snowden's actions, I can't help but notice that what the *New York Times* says, makes little sense.

In other words, there's the big idea that nobody's talking about.

Does anybody believe the NSA was monitoring millions of Americans in the hopes of catching a terrorist?

I don't.

So, what's the play?

Federal agents knocking at your door to ask questions about your browsing history, or a text message you sent a friend?

Maybe if you're a public figure, but not for the vast majority of the citizens.

No, what they want is what's called "big data," the information that can serve as an early-warning system to the establishment that the people have had enough of their antics.

The surveillance shows their lack of faith. If you knew what they were doing, you wouldn't like it. The surveillance doesn't show their strength, it shows their weakness. Let's look at the list of violations that Snowden's leaks revealed:

The N.S.A. broke federal privacy laws, or exceeded its authority, thousands of times per year, according to the agency's own
internal auditor.

The agency broke into the communication links of major data
centers around the world, allowing it to spy on hundreds of millions of user accounts and infuriating the Internet companies that
own the centers. Many of those companies are now scrambling to
install systems that the N.S.A. cannot yet penetrate.

The N.S.A. systematically undermined the basic encryption
systems of the Internet, making it impossible to know if sensitive
banking or medical data is truly private, damaging businesses that
depended on this trust.[302]

While I agree with much of what the *New York Times* said in the editorial,
there's one glaring lie I just have to call out.

I don't believe for a minute that internet companies were caught off-
guard by this snooping. And I don't even fault them for it.

Imagine you're an executive at one of these companies, and somebody
from the NSA comes knocking at your door and says, "We'd like to be
able to tap into your system because we think terrorists may be using it to
plan an attack on the United States."

What executive says "no" to that?

And they shouldn't.

However, it's clear the NSA and other intelligence agencies aren't
looking for a terrorist, they're trying to determine whether the public has caught onto their manipulation. The article continued with the
Snowden revelations:

His leaks revealed that James Clapper Jr., the director of national
intelligence lied to Congress when testifying in March that the
N.S.A. was not collecting data on millions of Americans. (There
has been no discussion of punishment for that lie.)

The Foreign Intelligence Surveillance Court rebuked the N.S.A.
for repeatedly providing misleading information about its surveillance practices, according to a ruling made public because of the
Snowden documents.

A federal district judge ruled earlier this month that the phone-records collection program violates the Fourth Amendment of the Constitution. He called the program "almost Orwellian" and said there was no evidence that it stopped any imminent act of terror.[303]

The comparison by the federal district judge of the surveillance program to something out of a George Orwell novel (I'm assuming the judge means Orwell's classic work, *1984*) raises some interesting questions.

The surveillance state in that dystopian world exists not simply to punish those who question Big Brother, as Winston Smith does, but to create the understanding in those who might seek to rebel, that such hopes are foolish.

In other words, the surveillance is not just to catch crimes against the state and punish them, but to destroy the slightest shred of optimism in the citizens that such an effort might be successful.

But in what the Deep States does, they show us what genuinely terrifies them.

They fear that you will lose your fear of them.

If you believe they exist in the shadows where you cannot find them, you will live in terror of what they might do to you.

If you know they live down the street, and his name is Bob, and hers is Alice, and their daughter has purple hair, or the police are always checking on the son because they suspect he's a drug dealer, you're going to mock them.

That's what happened in East Germany before the fall of the Berlin Wall.

There were so many "informants" that everybody knew who they were. They could not hide from the public when they were so large, and it was their fatal flaw.

It was not violence that brought about the fall of communism in Eastern Europe.

It was ridicule of the idiocy of their system.

You cannot rule over a people who do not fear you.

A long opinion piece from the Brookings Institute by Stuart Taylor Jr. in 2014, entitled "The Big Snoop: Life, Liberty, and the Pursuit of Terrorists," examined the legacy of Edward Snowden.

With the approach of the first anniversary of the most copious and sensational leakage of intelligence secrets in history, the consequences of his actions continue to reverberate. In addition to evidence that the NSA had been collecting and storing some of the phone records of most Americans as well as the emails and other private Internet correspondence of many citizens, Snowden revealed the agency had the ability—and indeed the practice—of listening in on phone conversations of foreign officials, most notoriously (but no longer) Angela Merkel, the chancellor of Germany.[304]

One subject I haven't covered (because I don't think genuinely strong information has yet been revealed) is what was really going on during the presidency of Barack Obama.

But let me share my suspicions with you.

Obama avoided trouble with the intelligence agencies in a way that escapes our attention until we compare it with what happened to President Donald Trump. The difference was striking. But I feel people on the Right saw it, while people on the Left simply chalked it up to the inevitable result of Trump's many personal failings.

I believe much remains to be revealed about Obama's relationship with the intelligence agencies and leave it at that.

What is in evidence is that the NSA was monitoring the private conversations of arguably our most reliable ally in Europe, Germany, and that information was going directly to President Obama. In other words, this wasn't a secret to Obama.

But somehow Obama was able to float above it all, as if it was simply an "embarrassment" rather than a "scandal" that demanded the appointment of a special prosecutor and congressional hearings.

With the fall of Soviet communism, the security state needed a new enemy, and just before America got that supposed "peace dividend," a new enemy appeared, Osama Bin Laden.

With the cold war over, the new, increasingly preoccupying threat to America was personified by Osama bin Laden. Believed to have connections to the bombers of the World Trade Center in New York in 1993, he was indicted for the destruction of two U.S. embassies

in Africa in 1998 and his organization, al Qaeda, claimed responsibility for the deadly attack on the USS Cole at harbor in Yemen
in October 2000. The emergence of this new menace to America
and its allies brought an upsurge in political and public support for
aggressive surveillance of potential terrorists, and a muting of the
concerns that had arisen in the 1970s about the past sins and excessive zeal of U.S. intelligence agencies.[305]

And with the attacks of September 11, 2001, the concern of most Americans
was not with a threat from their government, but from terrorists. The
public has always had a divided mind about the need for "security" and
"liberty," and with little genuine information from the intelligence agencies being covered in the news, most people operated under the default
assumption that they were simply trying to protect the country. While the
Patriot Act passed Congress with near unanimous support in 2001, critics
soon emerged—Senator Ron Wyden of Oregon, among the most prominent. From the Brookings Institution article on Snowden's revelations:

> Ron Wyden also joined the nearly unanimous vote for the Patriot
> Act shortly after the 9/11 attacks. But before long he came to a
> conclusion that was nearly the opposite of Feinstein's and Brenner's.
> He worried that the pendulum was swinging too far away from a
> proper regard for the Constitution and would inevitably lead to
> abuses by the intelligence community. In 2003, he led the battle
> in the Senate that defunded the Total Information Awareness pro-
> gram, a Pentagon unit established to hunt down terrorists by scour-
> ing mountains of data to reconstruct the electronic footprints of
> millions of people.
>
> However, just as Wyden feared, the prevailing sentiment on
> Capitol Hill was that the reforms of the 1970s had impeded the
> NSA from uncovering the 9/11 plot in time to prevent the attacks.
> It was in that atmosphere that two new programs were put in place
> during George W. Bush's presidency.[306]

It's in the discussion of the 9/11 attacks that I perceive the greatest peril is
that some readers of this book may tune out what I have to say, claiming

I'm being too conspiratorial, while others will claim I'm being too conservative in my assumptions.

I consider there to be three strong pieces of evidence that some part of the intelligence agencies had a hand in the 9/11 attacks.

First, the suspicious airline stock market activity of Buzzy Krongard.

Second, the unexplained fall of Building 7 at the World Trade Center.

And finally, the concealment of information that Saudi diplomats had contact and gave support to some of the 9/11 attackers.

All of this information has been publicly reported, and anybody who cares to research these issues will see that they can be confirmed as facts.

One of the challenges of being an analyst is to make the jump from confirming facts, to tell you what they mean.

I will tell you that for me, personally, the idea that intelligence agencies had a hand in the 9/11 attacks, either encouraging or allowing them to go further, is as likely that the intelligence agencies were responsible for the assassination of President Kennedy.

But if I were in a court of law, or had the ear of the president, I probably wouldn't make my argument to rein in the intelligence agencies on that basis.

Instead, I would make my argument based on stronger ground, that whatever the truth of the initiating event, the intelligence agencies are fixated on increasing their power and never returning the power they seized to the American people. Consider the two programs that George W. Bush, the son of the former director of the Central Intelligence Agency, imposed on the American people while he was president.

In 2006, the FISA [Foreign Intelligence Surveillance Act] Court secretly authorized the NSA to collect from phone companies the records of trillions of phone calls made within, to, or from the United States for analysis and storage. The purpose of this gigantic undertaking was to identify foreign terrorists' actual, possible, or potential collaborators who were on American soil. It came to be known as the "bulk phone records program," or the "Section 215 program," after a provision in the Patriot Act that allowed the government to demand access to "any tangible things," so long as the government specified that they were "relevant to an authorized investigation . . . to protect against international terrorism or clandestine intelligence activities."[307]

It's genuinely breathtaking when one looks back at our recent history to understand how the intelligence agencies have manipulated the government to make their blatantly unconstitutional actions have the cover of law. The Fourth Amendment to our Constitution does protect against "unreasonable search and seizure."

But the slippery legal slope being used here is that "you" are not being targeted.

It's "bulk" collection of information.

However, if you present a possible challenge to the government, such as running for president on a platform of taking out the Deep State, all the intelligence agencies have to do is say there's a fear that foreign intelligence agencies want to influence your campaign (which probably happens with any major political campaign in the United States) and they're free to go digging through all that information they've collected on everybody involved in your campaign, and it's all legal.

In order to complete the picture of this overwhelming architecture of information control, some of their final moves would wait until near the end of the Bush presidency.

Two years later, near the end of the Bush presidency, Congress passed Section 702, an amendment to the Foreign Intelligence Surveillance Act, authorizing the targeting of communications of "foreign persons who are located abroad." This provision became the basis for sweeping, clandestine NSA programs including one called PRISM, an acronym for "Planning Tool for Resource Integration, Synchronization, and Management." It was actually a gargantuan collection tool that enabled the NSA to gather from U.S. based Internet companies hundreds of millions of emails, Internet voice calls, videos, photos, chat services, stored data, and other private Internet communications, if the targets were "reasonably believed" to be non-U.S. persons overseas who possessed "foreign intelligence information."

Unlike the phone-records program, PRISM made available to the NSA the contents of the communications that were collected.

At least nine U.S.-based companies were compelled by the surveillance court to cooperate with the NSA in facilitating access to
PRISM data: Google, Facebook, Microsoft, Apple, Yahoo!, Paltalk,
AOL, YouTube, and Skype. The companies rarely appealed court
orders and complied with alacrity.[308]

I'm aware that many readers will want me to go further, and address accusations that many of these internet companies were intelligence agency
collection creations from their inception.

I acknowledge the validity of such accusations, and also agree there is
some strong evidence to support such claims. However, I will let others
seek to uncover the validity of those truths, although I suspect such claims
are well-founded.

However, what is undisputed is that the internet companies most people rely on are regularly handing your data over to the intelligence agencies, who are sifting through it to figure out how you think. And once they
know how you think, they know what arguments they need to make to
convince you to agree to their plans.

It's like the devil's old trick to corrupt your soul. Satan never forces you
to do something he wants you to do. He simply sells you tempting lies,
and then sits back, and watches you willingly take the steps toward your
own demise, and perhaps even of your entire world.

In that vein, what I have described in this chapter is nothing more than
Project Mockingbird, updated for the twenty-first century.

CHAPTER NINE

REFORMING THE CIA

How do we reform a dark, global juggernaut, hidden in secrecy and funded by billions of tax dollars in secret budgets that cannot be audited?

How do we oppose the massive US corporations like Lockheed Martin that perform most of the CIA's surveillance and technical work?

How do we motivate elected members of Congress to risk losing their next election, through blackmail or a smear campaign?

How do we overcome members of the Congress and the Senate who do not have the CIA clearances to know what different directorates of the CIA are doing?

How do we insulate and protect the congressional intelligence oversight committee members, who are also dependent on their reelections, financial support, and the financial backing of Secret Intelligence Industrial Complex (SIIC) corporate lobbyists and Political Action Committees (PACs)?

We begin by telling the truth, as I've attempted to do in this book. How large is the shadow government? These are the latest numbers (estimated) from 2023:

The US budgeted just shy of $100 billion for intelligence-gathering in fiscal 2023, a nearly $10 billion jump over FY 22, according to newly released figures from the Director or National Intelligence and the Pentagon.

In separate announcements today, the ODNA revealed Congress had provided $71.7 billion for the National Intelligence Program (NIP), and the Defense Department said $27.9 billion had been appropriated for the Military Intelligence Program (MIP), totaling $99.6 billion. For FY22, the combined total was $89.8 billion.

The FY23 NIP was over $3 billion more than the ODNI had requested, and the MIP came in $1 billion more than the DoD ask. For FY24, ODNI wants $72.4 billion for the NIP, and DOD wants $29.3 billion for the MIP. [$101.7 billion][309]

In 2024, the United States, that means you and me, is spending more than a hundred billion dollars a year for the shadow government. Like an alcoholic struggling with recovery, we cannot find salvation without honesty. And once we tell the truth, the imperative to act will become clear.

And what might the American public be purchasing for that $100 billion dollar price tag?

A January 9, 2023, report by the Congressional Research Services entitled "Intelligence Community Spending Trends," sketched out the structure of our shadow government:

Department of Defense Components:

1. Defense Intelligence Agency (DIA)
2. National Geospatial Intelligence Agency (NGA)
3. National Reconnaissance Office (NRO)
4. National Security Agency (NSA)
   Intelligence services of the military services:
5. U.S. Air Force Intelligence (USAF A2/6)
6. U.S. Army Intelligence (USA G2)
7. U.S. Marine Corps Intelligence (USMC/MCISR-E)
8. U.S. Navy Intelligence (OPNAV N2/N6)
9. U.S. Space Force Intelligence (S-2)

Non-DoD Components:

1. Office of the Director of National Intelligence (ODNI)
2. Central Intelligence Agency (CIA)
   Department of Energy (DOE) intelligence element:
3. Office of Intelligence and Counterintelligence (I&CI)

Department of Homeland Security (DHS) intelligence elements:
4. Office of Intelligence and Analysis (I&A)
5. U.S. Coast Guard Intelligence (USCG/GG-2)
    Department of Justice (DOJ) intelligence elements:
6. Drug Enforcement Administration's Office of National Security Intelligence (DEA/ONSI)
7. Federal Bureau of Investigation's Intelligence Branch (FBI/IB)
    Department of State (DOS) intelligence element:
8. Bureau of Intelligence and Research (INR)
    Department of Treasury (Treasury) intelligence element:
9. Office of Intelligence and Analysis (OIA)[310]

Every book has its limitations, and this one has been concentrated on my work with the CIA, as well as historical events well-documented by others. I cannot give you a truly informed opinion about the workings of the other seventeen intelligence agencies of our government, other than to give you some tentative conclusions and thoughts.

My general impression, though, is that the other intelligence agencies are generally staying in their lane of simply providing good intelligence to the president of either party and his administration. That may be a function of the fact these agencies are filled with individuals of a different profile than that of a typical CIA person.

But in all honesty, I have to say that most of the CIA people I worked with were fantastic professionals, and patriotic citizens you would be proud to call a friend.

My concern throughout this book has been that the very structure of the CIA itself promotes and encourages the worst instincts of very bad people.

The vast majority of the problems are caused by a relatively small number of powerful people, convinced they can bend the world to their will. Add to that the compromised structure of the CIA, which acts almost like a gravitational force to those in positions of power, encouraging them to take shortcuts in the pursuit of what they may believe to be noble goals.

And what do we know of the role of the CIA among those seventeen other intelligence agencies and a hundred-billion-dollar annual pie to split between them?

It was only in 2012, with the revelations of Edward Snowden, that we got a glimpse at a possible answer. A BBC article stated that the CIA's budget was $14.7 billion out of a then total US intelligence agency budget of $52.6 billion dollars,[311] or a little more than a quarter (27.9 percent).

If this percentage is accurate as a rough measure of what the CIA gets relative to the other intelligence agencies, that means the current yearly budget for the CIA is just a little under $28 billion dollars a year, making it a leviathan among the other seventeen intelligence agencies.

The CIA is unique in that it combines an intelligence gathering function with an active operations program. In other words, it is the only intelligence agency that can take action in furtherance of what it believes to be the best interests of the United States. As I have shown through several historical examples, they have often taken these actions without the approval of the chief executive, and in many instances, seem to regard the president of any party as simply a nuisance that must be handled, like an annoying child.

The CIA monster has infected every sector of America, and in coordination with other elements of the intelligence agencies, compromises independent journalism and classic American business by engaging in crony capitalism as exemplified by people like Buzzy Krongard.

Even President Truman, who created the CIA in 1947, saw by December 1963, a span of a mere sixteen years, how far the Agency had shifted from its original intended mission. In a letter to the *Washington Post*, he wrote:

> For some time I have been disturbed by the way the CIA has been diverted from its original assignment. It has become an operational and at times policy-making arm of the Government. This has led to trouble and may have compounded our difficulties in several explosive areas.
>
> I never had any thought when I set up the CIA that it would be injected into peacetime cloak and dagger operations. Some of the complications and embarrassment I think we have experienced are in part attributable to the fact that this quiet intelligence arm of the President has been so far removed from its intended role that it is

being interpreted as a symbol of sinister and mysterious intrigue—and a subject for cold war enemy propaganda . . .

But there are now some searching questions that need to be answered. I, therefore, would like to see the CIA be restored to its original assignment as the intelligence arm of the President, and that whatever else it can properly perform in that special field—and that its operational duties be terminated or properly used elsewhere.[312]

I consider Truman's 1963 op-ed on the CIA to be at least as important, if not more critical to our survival as a constitutional Republic, as Eisenhower's famous 1961 "Military-Industrial Complex" farewell address. Both men, each heroes in their own right, even though their ideologies and political passions were far apart, saw the same danger.

The intelligence gathering arm of the CIA should have NO connection with the operational arm, which has the potential of getting bloody. The president, regardless of party, should sit between those two groups, keeping them forever separate, so that we as a people may control the CIA and be free of its clandestine controls.

After all, the CIA got this powerful by keeping the American public and government in the dark. Hell, they even lie to the other members of the CIA and the broader intelligence community. And how are we kept in chains of ignorance?

The intelligence community lets insiders know hidden truths, but not the American taxpayer. Because if you know things the public does not, you have an advantage over them.

An article from CNN in 2022, regarding former President Trump's alleged retention of secret documents, contained this alarming statistic:

The Director of National Intelligence publishes what is described as an annual report, "Security Clearances Determination," although the most recent one I could find was from 2017.

In it, more than 2.8 million people are described as having security clearance as of October 2017—more than 1.6 million have access to either Confidential or Secret information and nearly 1.2 million are described as having access to Top Secret information.

There are additional people who have security clearances, but don't currently have access to information. This includes civilian employees, contractors, and members of the military.[313]

As the comedian George Carlin once observed, "It's a big club, and you ain't in it." I've heard reasonable estimates that up to four million eight hundred thousand Americans have security clearances, and that sounds about right to me.

Do I believe that all of them are using such knowledge in the selfless service of the United States?

I do not.

From personal knowledge, I'm also aware of thousands of affiliated CIA sites and corporate locations across America. The authors of the 2011 book, *Top Secret America: The Rise of the New American Security State*,[314] Dana Priest and William Arkin, made the following statements in an article in the *Washington Post*:

> The top-secret world the government created in response to the terrorist attacks of Sept. 11, 2001, has become so large, so unwieldy and so secretive that no one knows how much money it costs, how many people it employs, how many programs exist within it or exactly how many agencies do the same work.
>
> These are some of the findings of a two-year investigation by the *Washington Post* that discovered what amounts to an alternative geography of the United States, a Top-Secret America hidden from public view and lacking in thorough oversight.[315]

The authors were able to put some flesh on the bones that to many had been an invisible beast stalking our body politic. Consider whether the following is a reasonable response to nineteen hijackers, as found in 2011 by the authors of *Top-Secret America*:

> Some 1,271 governmental organizations and 1,931 private companies work on programs related to counterterrorism, homeland security and intelligence in about 10,000 locations across the United States.

An estimated 854,000 people, nearly 1½ times as many people as live in Washington, D.C., hold top-secret security clearances.

In Washington and the surrounding area, 33 building complexes for intelligence work are under construction or have been built since September 2001. Together they occupy the equivalent of almost three Pentagons or 22 U.S. Capitol buildings–about 17 million square feet of space.[316]

If you wonder where the National Security State is, the answer is, especially if you're anywhere near our nation's Capital, all around you.

***

In the excellent book, *The CIA and the Politics of US Intelligence Reform*, Brent Durbin wrote,

> Despite these challenges, elected representatives must develop tools to monitor intelligence agencies effectively; anything less risks subverting the democratic values these agencies are tasked to defend. During the earliest debates over establishing a central intelligence organization, numerous commentators–including members of Congress, Eleanor Roosevelt, and even President Truman–expressed fears that such a body might become an "American Gestapo." At times, the CIA and other members of the intelligence community have shown tendencies in that direction. Investigations launched by both media outlets and government representatives have uncovered illegal programs to spy on Americans, assassinate foreign leaders, and to defy explicit statutory limits imposed by Congress. To maintain domestic and international legitimacy, US leaders must convincingly demonstrate that they control the agents of the secret state.[317]

In this book, we have devoted considerable time to detailing the historic crimes of the CIA, their successful attempts at avoiding reform, and how they have in many ways taken control of our media and business community. These are twelve concrete steps, which if taken by an administration, will break the power of the shadow government:

294 TWILIGHT OF THE SHADOW GOVERNMENT

1. Intelligence Oversight committees, especially the HPSCI and the SSCI, must be given access to information regarding CIA activities, with very rare exceptions, and Congress must gain complete authority over the CIA budget. Penetrating the CIA's unconstitutional shield of secrecy and taking charge of the Agency's dark budget are two of the most powerful tools in reforming the CIA, and especially covert operations.

2. The White House must issue an executive order stipulating that specific US congressional representatives and senators, who can pass a rigorous national security clearance process, have access to CIA information.

3. Congress can use its new power over the CIA budget to promote or dismantle specific programs.

4. Legislation must be passed ensuring that information is properly shared among intelligence agencies. Counterproductive security procedures and excessive secrecy must be reduced as much as possible. Whistleblowers must be protected, not persecuted.

5. Congressmen/women who occupy positions of CIA oversight must be given significant incentives and career protection.

6. Legislation should be passed requiring that the executive branch and Congress agree on foreign policy regarding CIA programs.

7. Congress must be held accountable for placing career promotion before genuine national security. Incentives must be put in place for congressional members who place national security before their own interests.

8. When the CIA resists congressional reform, special oversight committees must use the investigatory and budget sanctioning authority they possess. Additional legislation is needed to force the CIA to grant cleared congressional committees access to CIA information.

9. If the CIA refuses to cooperate with oversight committees, Congress must issue budgetary sanctions against the Agency and demand compliance.

10. The CIA must be reorganized by issuing a new National Security Act. This act must remove covert operations from the

CIA and move its funding to a new Pentagon office in charge of US covert operations.

11. The state secrets privilege must be repealed, and a new, constitutional version protecting individual civil liberties should be put into place in the new National Security Act. This new National Security Act should specifically designate what information is to be protected for legitimate national security and important provisions for civil liberties must be added to prevent use of the privilege to conceal illegal, negligent, or embarrassing activity.

12. Citizens who have filed legitimate cases against the CIA should, under the new legislation, have the right to a jury trial, which can be done while still protecting legitimate classified information and operations. Misuse of this rare privilege must be met with criminal penalties.

In the past, the CIA has held all the cards regarding what information gets to Congress using their power to classify the information. Congress has learned from experience that requesting the information they need for proper oversight, from the CIA, is little more than a pipe dream.

If there are no consequences for intelligence agency abuses, they will continue.

If the renegade members of the CIA do not comply with these remedial measures, the patriots at the CIA, the larger intelligence community, as well as the rest of the government, and the citizenry, must be prepared to stand against them.

What do I mean by this?

If the CIA does not willingly submit to civilian oversight, the other members of the intelligence community, the military, and our justice system, must be prepared to arrest and prosecute the renegades.

One way or another, this shadow government must end.

***

I understand that, for many, this effort to take on the CIA will remind them of a barbarian in the provinces attempting to take on the power of Imperial Rome.

It seems a fool's errand, something that only a crazy person would attempt.

The doubters can recite the roll call of those who attempted to take on the power of Rome: Hannibal and his elephants crossing the Alps; Viriathus, the barbarian leader who resisted the Romans coming into western Spain and Portugal; the slave leader, Spartacus; and Arminius, given as a hostage by his father to Rome, who eventually turned against Rome, leading the Germanic tribes to slaughter three Roman legions at the Battle of the Teutoberg Forest, and successfully resisting Roman rule during his life.

In England there was the bloody queen Boudicca, who while she lost her battle against the Romans, in death became a symbol of British resistance. The Balkan leader, Alaric, had been an ally of Rome in their wars against the French, but after being betrayed, turned against the Romans, and sacked Rome, permanently hobbling the Roman Empire. From that point, the Romans were in trouble, battling against Atilla the Hun, and finally meeting their end under the might of the Vandal king, Geiseric.

In the traditional telling of the Roman Empire, it's simply one victory after another over the barbarians.

But a 2016 Netflix series I watched, called *Barbarians Rising*, took a different approach to this history.

The claim of the series is that far from the barbarian uprisings always ending in defeat, they were each, in their own way, an inevitable step in the victory of the various European people over the Roman Empire. Hannibal's march from North Africa, across the Alps, and to the very gates of Rome convinced other leaders, like Virathus, that victory was possible. Rome responded to these barbarian uprisings by bringing back the defeated barbarians in chains.

This led directly to the slave revolt of Spartacus, which shook the Roman Empire to its core. As a response to the Spartacus revolt, slavery was greatly diminished, with Rome attempting to convert the barbarians with the promise of Roman citizenship.

However, despite the fighting prowess and dedication of many barbarians, the Romans didn't want these foreigners in their empire. This led many to abandon Rome, like Alaric, who eventually sacked Rome.

The war with Britain, although technically a victory, was in many ways a disaster.

Near the end, many Roman citizens didn't even want to defend the empire, requiring the political leaders to enlist barbarian armies, who thought they would receive the benefits of Rome but were often disappointed. This led directly to the struggle with Attila, and the eventual end of the Roman Empire under the Vandal king, Geiseric.

But the centuries-long wars with the Roman Empire had created new countries in their wake: Spain, Portugal, England, France, Poland, Germany, all the tribes that had united against the Roman Empire. If you claim Spanish, Portuguese, English, French, Polish, German, or any other myriad European heritages, other than Italian, you are descended from the barbarians who opposed the empire.

And if you are of Italian heritage, you may very well be descended from those brave Romans who realized their empire was not worth defending. As I realized all too well, the American empire will even try to kill its own, if it's believed their loyalty is suspect.

The Roman Empire collapsed because even its own citizens did not want to defend it.

It is also the same way that the communist nations of Eastern Europe collapsed.

I like to view the long battle against the CIA in a similar way.

Each battle they have fought has cost them precious resources, nothing more important than the faith of the American people.

In the 1950s, there were few people who stood up to the CIA.

However, at the dawn of the 1960s, voices began to rise, starting with President Eisenhower in his Farewell Address, warning of the dangers of the military-industrial complex. That was followed by Kennedy's disdain of the Agency, his suspicious death, and the curious December 1963 op-ed of former President Truman.

More Americans began to understand.

Nixon seemed to understand the power of the shadow government, and tried to negotiate around it, using similarly underhanded tactics, and was in the end, "politically" assassinated by his own intelligence agencies. However, that led to the Church Committee, and still more people were awakened.

In the 1980s, there was the Iran-Contra scandal, and we got to learn more about shady characters like Ted Shackley.

More came out in the 1990s, and although there were bad decisions, like the "Torricelli Rule" (not to associate with known bad actors) once can understand why some thought it a good idea. The CIA hadn't exactly covered itself in glory with its associations.

The September 11, 2001, attacks united America for a time, but the response of the Bush administration, specifically the Patriot Act, rendition, and torture at CIA black sites around the world, as well as the disastrous 2003 invasion of Iraq, woke up even more people.

The 2013 revelations of Edward Snowden shocked America, revealing that the bargain the intelligence agencies had struck with the American people is that they'd be put in the same box as foreign terrorists.

The machinations of the intelligence community in the Russia-gate charges against President Trump in 2016, the prosecution of Michael Flynn, and other assorted mischief made many think no American president was genuinely in charge of the government.

For many, the last straw was COVID-19. The mysterious appearance of a virus with no known predecessor, escaping from a US-funded lab in Wuhan, China, the unnecessary lockdowns, and the draconian social shaming of those who asked questions, made many wonder what had happened to their previously free country.

In 2024, is there anybody who will stand in front of the public and defend the intelligence agencies, aside from former CIA director, John Brennan, and former director on National Intelligence, James Clapper?

All the smart people are on the other side.

The avalanche against the security state has already begun and is unstoppable. Once trust has been broken, it is difficult to repair, especially if the guilty party does not confess and show a determination to change its ways.

I am not an advocate of eliminating the CIA, just reforming it, eliminating its unconstitutional power of secrecy, removing its control over elected officials, and preventing it from conducting illegal covert operations and human rights violations.

Because of the sacrifice of so many, the truth is clear for all to see.

I was in the CIA for seventeen years and believed the lies.

Most of the people I worked with did as well.

And yet that simple fact shows me that the lies of the CIA cannot continue.

The Agency attracts people because they believe it is working for the good of America.

As more and more see that is not true, they will simply ignore its call, as the citizens did of the Roman Empire, as the citizens of Eastern Europe did under communism.

People want the truth.

They hunger for it.

They will dedicate their lives to finding it.

The Soviets realized that the greatest threat to their system was not our bombs and missiles, but the simple power of a man like Billy Graham, talking to the Russian populace about the power of faith to change lives. The truth has a certain ring to it, a spiritual vibration, and regardless of the years of propaganda to which people have been exposed, they recognize it.

I was trained at CIA that the most powerful piece of intelligence I could ever uncover was the question of how a person thought. If I knew that, everything else would fall into place.

And that's how I know I'm different from people like Allen Dulles, Ted Shackley, Buzzy Krongard, George Tenet, or even the man I once protected, William Casey.

I believe that given all the information, people will choose to love, rather than hate each other. They will choose to live for their families and friends, rather than die in useless wars that serve the military-industrial complex.

I believe humanity is reaching an inflection point in its spiritual evolution.

Do we live in truth, or will we support the lies?

I cannot tell you how it will happen, but having lived so many years, having had so many experiences, both good and bad, I've come to believe the good people far outnumber the bad.

The end of the shadow government is already upon us.

The light from so many of you is making sure of that, exposing the details and the secret alliances that have kept us in chains, and leading us into a bright future of genuine freedom.

It's up to all of us to start the avalanche.

THE TRUMP ASSASSINATION ATTEMPT: ARE THEY VILLAINS OR FOOLS AND DOES IT MATTER?

On July 13, 2024, an attempted assassination was made targeting former President Donald Trump while he spoke at a rally in Butler, Pennsylvania. The gunman was twenty-year-old Thomas Matthew Crooks.

The incident shocked the American public, drawing condemnation from both sides of the political aisle.

In this account, I will follow the facts and evidence where they lead and provide my conclusions regarding what occurred on that horrible day.

As the facts unfolded, it was clear that the attempt was either gross malpractice by the Secret Service and others, or an inside job. Huge gaps in Secret Service protection protocols caused Americans to demand answers as to how this could happen. Security lapses of this magnitude have never been seen in nearly a hundred and sixty years of Secret Service history.

Many internet personalities and at least one congressman immediately jumped to the conclusion that the attempt was an inside job conducted by the Biden administration, which was believed to be in danger of losing the 2024 election.

In my years of analysis, I have learned to wait a minimum of three days to a week before discussing even my initial conclusions of breaking events.

That is what I have done here.

That being said, there remain several significant unanswered questions that must be addressed in the weeks, months, and years ahead.

***

I worked as a protective agent on the detail of CIA Director William Casey during the Iran-Contra scandal, was a team leader for high-risk defector protection, and acted as chief of training for the CIA's federal police Security Protective Service (where I started my career). In the CIA Counter Terrorism Center, I trained protective details for several foreign presidential and prime minister details. I supervised the protective detail for Afghanistan President Mohammad Karzai, worked as detail leader and protective agent for an internationally known celebrity, and was a counter terrorism driving instructor and advanced weapons training instructor.

I was assistant team leader on a Counter Assault Team (CAT), worked with retired Navy Seals, Delta Force Team members, Secret Service agents and, of course CIA operators. I have done executive protection at all levels, including performing security advances.

I am not an armchair analyst.

I know this world well, having placed my life on the line countless times, having often observed inexcusable lapses in security, but never having lost a client.

I must tell you though, that doing this kind of work in the real world is very humbling. It's one thing to do this sort of training and another to do it when your life or the life of others are at stake and bullets are coming in your direction. Some of the most humble, likable, and capable men I know are former Navy Seals and Delta Force operators.

They are the real heroes.

If there are villains, or fools, to be found in this story, it is likely we must look to the leadership of the Secret Service.

***

The following information has been obtained by multiple, vetted news reports, eyewitness accounts at the event, and expert testimony from former Secret Service agents, FBI agents, and retired government snipers. This is my own assembled account, and I would not be surprised if some facts undergo additional revisions or additions as more facts emerge.

July 13, 2024:

5:45 p.m. EST

- The police command center is alerted with two photos of Crooks sent by police officers.

6:02 p.m.

- Trump takes the stage to the strains of "God Bless the U.S.A."
  Around 6:10 p.m.
- Outer ring police are alerted by witnesses of a man who was acting suspiciously, pacing near metal detectors. Witnesses then saw him climbing to the roof of a nearby building with a ladder and holding a rifle. They pointed and shouted at the armed man on a nearby roof.
- A local police officer climbs to the roof after witness reports.
- According to Butler County Sheriff Michael Slupe, the man identified by the FBI as Thomas Matthew Crooks, a twenty-year-old white male, turned his rifle toward the officer, who dropped down to safety.

6:10 p.m.

- Tom Knights, Butler Township manager, stated the police officer lost his grip and was not retreating when he fell eight feet to the ground.
- The roof where Crooks was spotted was an estimated 147 yards from the podium where Trump was speaking.
- While speaking, Trump turns to his right, pointing toward the screen on his right showing border-crossing numbers. Three shots are heard.

6:11 p.m.

- The first shot is heard, and Trump says "Oh," raises his hand to his right ear, looks at it, then quickly drops behind the armored podium.
- Secret Service inner ring agents rush the stage, pile on top of Trump, shielding him, as five more shots are heard.
- Tragically, fifty-year-old former fire chief, Corey Comperatore, rushes to cover his wife and daughter and is shot and killed.
- Two other attendees are critically wounded.
- Forty-two seconds after identifying Crooks, a Secret Service counter sniper fires, hitting Crooks in the head and killing him.

6:12 p.m.

- Approximately one minute after the final shot, Trump gets up on his feet, reaching with his right hand toward his face, which is smeared with blood from his ear. As he stands up, Trump pumps his fist to the crowd, shouting, "Fight, fight!"

6:13 p.m.

- Two minutes after the shots were fired, Trump turns back towards the crowd, again raising his fist, just before the Secret Service agents put him into a vehicle, taking him to the local hospital emergency room.

6:50 p.m.

- The Secret Service releases a statement, "The former President is safe."

***

I said that if there are villains or fools to be found in this story, we might need to look to the leadership of the Secret Service. That would start with Secret Service Director Kimberly Cheatle.

On Tuesday, July 14, 2024, Cheatle appeared on ABC's *Good Morning America* to discuss the Trump assassination attempt. This is from an article in *The Hill*, about her appearance:

> Secret Service Director Kimberly Cheatle said in an interview that aired Tuesday morning that a sloped roof used by the gunman who attempted an assassination of former president Trump last weekend at a rally had "safety factor" considerations.
>
> "That building in particular had a sloped roof, at its highest point," Cheatle said in an interview that aired on ABC's *Good Morning America* Tuesday morning to the outlet's Pierre Thomas. "And so, there's a safety factor that would be considered there that we wouldn't want to put somebody up on a sloped roof. And so, the decision was made to secure the building, from the inside."[318]

Sometimes it all comes down to a single bad decision that results in catastrophe. In my years of training, I have reviewed several such incidents, and have often been shocked at the propensity of certain individuals to make bad decisions. That sets an entire chain of events in motion, and when one looks at all of the other mistakes which might otherwise be unreported, it makes one question the entire enterprise.

As somebody who has served in a protective detail, as well as trained such groups, this is an inexcusable failing. At this point, I am unable to determine whether this was based on a desire to bring about the death of Trump, or simply criminal negligence.

Whatever the truth, Cheatle showed an unparalleled skill at making herself look bad, as demonstrated when Cheatle showed up at the Republican National Convention on Wednesday, July 17, 2024, just days after the unsuccessful assassination attempt. At the event, Cheatle was confronted by some Republican senators, angry over the Secret Service director's previous meeting with the Senate about the assassination attempt, in which she cut off questions. As reported by *Forbes*:

> Two prominent Republican senators angrily confronted Secret
> Service Director Kimberly Cheatle at the Republican National
> Convention in Milwaukee Wednesday, demanding answers about
> security lapses that may have led to Saturday's assassination attempt
> at Trump's rally in Pennsylvania.
>
> Senators Marsha Blackburn of Tennessee and John Barrasso of
> Wyoming were seen closely trailing Cheatle as she walked through
> the arena in video footage of the confrontation in which Blackburn
> yelled, "this was an assassination attempt, you owe the people
> answers!"[319]

Yes, the people of America, and indeed the world wanted answers. A
political candidate targeted by the "justice" system, but popular among
the people, who then nearly loses his life to a crazed gunman who
sneaks past security, would be viewed with great suspicion by a for-
eigner watching these events. If this happened in a foreign country, we
would probably immediately sanction them. The *Washington Examiner*
gave detailed coverage to the specific complaints of the Republican
senators.

> Secret Service and FBI officials briefed House and Senate lawmak-
> ers in separate private briefings Wednesday afternoon.
>
> Barrasso said the suspect, identified as Thomas Matthew Crooks,
> was flagged as suspicious more than an hour before he ultimately
> fired on Trump from a nearby rooftop.
>
> "He was identified as a character of suspicion because [he had] a
> rangefinder as well as a backpack. And this was over an hour before
> the shooting actually occurred," Barrasso told Fox News. A source
> familiar with the call told the *Washington Examiner* the precise lead
> time mention was 62 minutes.[320]

There were a number of failures prior to the Trump assassination attempt,
as well as suspicious activity. This suggests to me that this was more than
a simple lapse of security, and potentially something much more sinister.

***

What else has been reported about this incident that makes it highly suspicious?

The alleged gunman also appeared to possess little or no skill with guns, as reported by ABC News:

> Two former high school classmates of Crooks told ABC News that the suspect was rejected from the high school rifle club and asked not to return.
>
> "He didn't just not make the team, he was asked not to come back because of how bad of a shot he was. It was considered like, dangerous," said Jameson Myers. One of the former classmates said, "On the first day of pre-season he basically couldn't even hit the target."[321]

I know the skeptics will say, "Maybe he improved his marksmanship since being rejected by his high school rifle club." And that's certainly a valid possibility.

Early reports claimed Crooks was a registered Republican, but also that he'd made a fifteen-dollar donation to the group Act Blue and the Progressive Turnout Project on January 20, 2021, the day of President Biden's inauguration, complicating the question of his political affiliations.[322] One of the challenging aspects of figuring out Crooks is the claim he didn't have much of a social media profile. This seems unusual to me for a twenty-year-old. The lack of information on this question renders me unable to come to a strong conclusion, although I do have significant suspicions. It seems to me that *something* about Crooks is being hidden, but I don't have enough information to render a well-informed opinion as to what that might be.

One of the narratives which quickly began appearing in the media is that Thomas Crooks was the victim of bullying. But that picture was dismissed by Vincent Taormina, a classmate of the gunman from middle through high school, as detailed in this article from the *New York Times*:

> He recalled one instance when the two were in seventh grade. During a classroom political debate, Mr. Taormina voiced his support for Mr. Trump. Mr. Crooks seemed incredulous.

"He says, 'Aren't you Hispanic? And you like Trump?'" Mr. Taormina said. "He said, 'That's a little stupid.'"

Mr. Taormina brushed off the encounter and had few other interactions with Mr. Crooks. But he disputed other classmates' accounts that the gunman had been bullied or was a loner, saying that he was intelligent and had his own small group of friends.[323]

The account painted by Taormina does not suggest a loner or misfit, but a highly intelligent individual. What could have motivated him? The *New York Times* article continued with details of the anomalies of this case:

> Over the last several months, the gunman received multiple packages, including several that were marked "hazardous material," according to a federal law enforcement memo obtained by the The *New York Times*. Federal officials reviewed his shipping history after they discovered three explosive devices connected to him, the memo said. One device was found in his home, and two others were found in his car parked near the rally.
>
> Investigators discovered two improvised explosive devices in the would-be-assassin's car that used a radio-controlled initiation system intended for commercial fireworks demonstrations.
>
> While the briefing on Wednesday filled in some blanks, it left many questions unanswered. Federal law enforcement officials are puzzled and exasperated by the lack of evidence on the gunman's two phones, one found by his body on the roof of a warehouse outside the security perimeter of the rally, the other discovered during a search of his house.[324]

When I reviewed this information, I definitely got a Lee Harvey Oswald vibe from the guy. Crooks was getting "packages" delivered to his home? Oswald supposedly obtained his rifle from a mail-order company.[325] I can understand how this might have gone undetected, as there appeared to be no reason for federal law enforcement to be suspicious of this character.

But if it's true that there is little to no information on his phones, all I can say is that's consistent with somebody trained in spy craft. If you're an officer in charge of an asset, you teach them how to avoid detection.

That's what I did with officers assigned to my details.

The options are that Crooks figured all this out on his own or was trained by somebody who knew what they were doing.

Personally, I think it possible there are crooks operating behind Crooks.

Who else might be involved in this assassination attempt? A detective interviewing a suspect is trained to look for claims which don't make any logical sense. Consider this section from the *Times* article:

> Kimberly A. Cheatle, the director of the Secret Service, admitted that her agency made serious "mistakes" during one of the calls, and provided new information about Mr. Crooks's movements during the shooting . . .
>
> During the briefing with senators, officials ran through a time-line of events, noting that law enforcement officers had identified the gunman as suspicious about an hour before the shooting but then lost track of him, according to two people familiar with the contents of the briefing.
>
> About 20 minutes before the shooting, a sniper spotted him again, the people said.
>
> Some senators left the call angry with the Secret Service after learning that officers did not intervene before he opened fire.[326]

In the light of a review, a series of mistakes can easily appear to be part of a well-orchestrated plan. The incompetence of one group can make it appear as if the other side must have been working with a criminal mastermind.

I'm aware of those considerations.

It's also possible that those attempting to cover-up the remarkable stupidity of their organization or decisions they made, can appear to have been guilty of planning the event.

I'm cognizant of wanting to find support for what you want in conflicting evidence.

And yet, there are things which even gross incompetence doesn't seem to explain. Consider this curious fact reported by the *New York Post*:

> BlackRock Inc, the world's largest money manager, has pulled an ad that briefly featured Thomas Crooks, the 20-year-old who shot

and wounded former President Donald Trump at a campaign rally in Pennsylvania.

The company said Crooks was a student at Bethel Park High School and appeared in the 2022 ad with other unpaid teens . . .

The 30-second BlackRock TV ad features an AP and honors economics class that Crooks attended at the time, with the world-be Trump assassin speaking with his teacher.

Crooks graduated the same year the commercial aired from Bethel Park High, where he was one of a dozen students who received National Math & Science Initiative Star Awards, according to the Pittsburgh Tribune-Review.[327]

BlackRock Inc. has been in the news a great deal during the 2024 presidential campaign as a target of independent presidential candidate Robert F. Kennedy Jr. As reported by the *Washington Post* in November of 2023:

In a campaign video titled "I'll help you buy a home," Kennedy especially targets a company called BlackRock, saying that when houses come on the market, it "swoops in" and outbids prospective home buyers with "all-cash offers" and turns the homes into rentals. He also often includes two other investment firms, Vanguard and State Street in his critique.[328] [Author's note – The company Kennedy meant to criticize was not BlackRock, Inc., but another company, Blackstone, Inc., but formed by the same umbrella corporation.]

And the critique of BlackRock, Inc. and its multiple tentacles was not limited to the Kennedy campaign, but also included some of the most powerful voices in the Republican party. From an article in the *Financial Times*, in December of 2023:

BlackRock chief executive Larry Fink has hit out at the candidates for the Republican presidential nomination over their attacks on the $9.1 trillion dollar asset manager during Wednesday's debate, calling the references "a sad commentary on the state of American politics."

Both Vivek Ramaswamy and Ron DeSantis specifically referred to BlackRock in multiple attacks on Nikki Haley, who has risen in the polls and gained backing from some wealthy donors. The men sought to portray her as a pawn of secret financial interests, tying her to their critique of investing based on environmental, social, and governance factors.[329]

When I was at the CIA, one of my jobs was to analyze information. In many instances I wasn't able to determine what was true, just what was suspicious, and worthy of further investigation.

At this point in the analysis, we've identified two curious pieces of information. First, Thomas Matthew Crooks was in a BlackRock TV ad, and second, BlackRock was the target of criticism by top republicans, specifically questioning why presidential contender, Nikki Haley, was being supported by BlackRock.

I'd also be remiss if I didn't note that had President Trump been assassinated on July 13, 2024, prior to having named his vice president, US Senator J. D. Vance, the entire nominating process would have been thrown into confusion. Nikki Haley, as the last candidate to drop out of the race, would have had a valid claim to be the Republican nominee.

Let's leave BlackRock for a moment, and return to the scene of the shooting, with an opinion from an actual sniper. As reported in the *New York Post*:

A veteran of the sniper team with the world's longest confirmed kill refuses to believe untrained gunman Thomas Matthew Crooks was so easily able to shoot former President Donald Trump – saying even "a seventh grader" would know the rooftop he climbed onto was "the most f—king obvious" place to check.

"I'm very familiar with the layout of these types of things and what the job should be," retired sniper Dallas Alexander said in an Instagram post Sunday of the previous day's attempted assassination at Trump's rally in Butler, Pa.

"And yesterday what happened, I have no doubts in my mind that the shooter had help from somewhere within an agency, an organization, or the government," Alexander stated firmly.[330]

I have to add a couple of warnings to his certainty, although I agree with the general thrust of his comments. When a security detail is working on a political campaign, often with multiple events per day, and a rotating group of agents, things can get missed.

I have my strong suspicions, but I am not certain. As one read further in the article, it was clear that even Alexander was softening his comments:

> Alexander continued: "Something happened. I'm not pointing fingers at anyone, it's just too obvious that this guy had help getting there. Whether someone turned a blind eye or it was strategically planned. Events like that, security like that . . . it's not a small thing and that is the most obvious place to be."
>
> Matthew Murphy, a retired Green Beret and a sniper trained to the most elite level, also dismissed the suggestion that "some 20-year-old kid that looks like he played Dungeons and Dragons in his mom's basement" was able to put Trump in his sights.
>
> "You're gonna tell me that the kid went through all these levels of security, somehow got into the closest building to the president and accessed the rooftop, then had the time to go unpack his rifle, lay down and then take five to eight well-aimed shots at the president before he was decisively engaged?" he asked.[331]

Eventually, we will have to point fingers at those who, either through intention, or negligence, allowed this terrifying event to take place. One always has to ask whether an event happened because of evil intentions or simple incompetence.

But here's a final piece of information I'd plug into my analysis.

> The $1 billion asset manager Austin Private Wealth, LLC, a financial planning firm in Texas purchased put options worth 12 million shares of Trump Media & Technological Group Corp (NASDAQ: DJT) a day before his assassination attempt. The short position was taken on July 12, 2024, and was the largest among those listed.[332]

The company later said it was a "clerical error."[333]

To say I'm suspicious would be an understatement. There are claims that Austin Private Wealth has connections to BlackRock, as well as George Soros.

It is common among many of these large organizations that clever accountants and lawyers will conceal who is actually in control of them.

But the allegations of a connection to BlackRock or George Soros are unproven at this time and I have not seen any convincing evidence at this point to convince me the claims are true.

Perhaps it was a "clerical error."

But with the example of Buzzy Krongard's former employer, the Bank of Alex Brown, shorting United and American stock prior to the terrorist attacks of September 11, 2001, I think we need an independent investigation, rather than simply trusting a company's press release.

We must not be fooled again.

We deserve the truth.

***

Let's look at a few other aspects of this case which deserve comment.

From *Forbes* magazine comes this account:

> Local law enforcement had reportedly stationed three snipers inside the building whose roof was used by the gunman who attempted to assassinate former President Donald Trump during a campaign rally in Pennsylvania on Saturday, highlighting the potential security lapses that led to the former president getting injured and one person being killed.[334]

I know you think that must be a mistake. The snipers were "inside" the building, while the shooter was on the roof? Apparently, that's true. Was it just because it was a hot day in July in Pennsylvania?

Sometimes it's important to consider the simplest, non-conspiratorial explanation.

I know in retrospect it seems unbelievable, but when you've looked at enough of these situations, you'll be surprised at how lazy and irresponsible people can be.

Their building was designated as a command center, and "One of the law enforcement officers stationed in the building saw the gunman 'scoping out' the roof and carrying a range finder, before briefly disappearing from the site and returning with a backpack."[335]

The Keystone Kops element of this near tragedy continued.

> The officer managed to take a photograph of the shooter and even radioed the sightings to his command center, but the suspected shooter – 20-year-old Thomas Matthew Crooks – was reportedly able to scale the roof through an air conditioning unit.[336]

It was a hot day in Pennsylvania, but one would think that police in a building might be able to keep somebody from crawling onto the roof, whether with a ladder (in some accounts) or more likely, by climbing up an air conditioning unit. However, having served on protective details, often in combination with other police or security departments, I've seen enough lapses to convince me that these sort of boneheaded actions, are all too common.

We know that Crooks was smart, and there is some evidence that he planned this event, as detailed in a *New York Times* article:

> A cellphone linked to the gunman, Thomas Matthew Crooks, of Bethel Park, Pa., included geolocation data that indicated he could have been in the area of the site, the Butler Farm Show grounds, on July 7, according to federal officials and information provided by the F.B.I. on Wednesday during a congressional briefing. Mr. Crooks opened fire from a warehouse roof at the site on Saturday, grazing the former president's right ear, killing a rally attendee and seriously injuring two others.[337]

As the evidence has shown, Crooks was smart. By several accounts, he was a loner (or at least had a limited group of friends) and also seemed to consider himself better than other people.

It's speculation, but from these sparse facts, I would say he fits the profile of somebody an intelligence agency would try to recruit. If you gave me that profile of an individual and I was operating in a foreign country, that's exactly who I would try to recruit.

And yet there's also other evidence to suggest Crooks was operating completely on his own, as evidenced by the purchase of items he ended up not using.

> He told his employer at the nursing home where he worked, he needed to take Saturday off because he had something important to do.
>
> Then, on the afternoon before the shooting, Mr. Crooks visited a gun range, officials said. The next morning, he bought a ladder at a Home Depot—though officials do not believe he ended up using any ladder to ascend to the warehouse roof—and then purchased ammunition at a nearby gun store, Allegheny Arms and Gun works.
>
> After Secret Service snipers killed Mr. Crooks, the authorities recovered a bulletproof vest and several magazines for the rifle from his car, along with rudimentary explosive devices.[338]

When I look at these facts, it doesn't seem to me that he was being controlled by anybody familiar with offensive operations. The ladder and the bulletproof vest don't make much sense, which is what he probably concluded when he got to the site on the day of the rally. The fact that he was at the site six days before the rally took place, suggests to me he could have stored the rifle at the location.

However, this raises the question of why a security search of the area prior to the rally didn't uncover it.

But as we've seen, the incompetence of fools might explain a great deal. The Judiciary Committee revealed another possible explanation for the failure at the Trump rally, not enough resources to do a proper job. From a *New York Post* article:

> The Secret Service had "little resources" to cover the July 13 campaign rally where former President Donald Trump was nearly

assassinated in Pennsylvania after the conclusion of a NATO summit in Washington, D.C., according to congressional whistleblowers.

The whistleblowers told the House Judiciary Committee that Secret Service Special Agent in Charge Tim Burke revealed the oversight at a July 8 meeting with the FBI, Western Pennsylvania Fusion Center and other law enforcement partners.

The meeting was held to talk over security needs for Trump's fateful event in Butler, Pa., on top of First Lady Jill Biden's separate event on behalf of her husband's campaign in Pittsburgh the same day.[339]

I've seen a lot of bureaucratic ineptitude in my years with the CIA, and so this strikes me as a possible explanation for the screw-ups involved in the event. If you don't have properly trained people in charge of this high-level of security, you're going to have lapses. Even when you have properly trained people, there can be mistakes.

But when we discovered those mistakes, there were certainly consequences.

And to complete the picture of Thomas Matthew Crooks, we also had the *New York Post* telling us how he'd threatened violence against his high school classmates.

Would-be Donald Trump assassin Thomas Matthew Crooks threatened to "shoot up" his high school five years before he put the ex-president in his crosshairs, a detail that criminologists say may offer a clue into the motive behind the assassination attempt.

The future killer's warning was enough to keep dozens of Bethel Park High School students home for the day, but the incident was dismissed by school officials at the time, his former classmates recalled.

"We had this anonymous place you could post things or tell on someone on our computers at school and he posted something like 'Don't come to school tomorrow,' and something that made it sound like he'd put bombs in the cafeteria bathrooms," Vincent Taormina, 20, told the *Daily Mail*.[340]

And if these lapses are not enough to horrify you, it was reported by the *Wall Street Journal* that Crooks was able to fly a drone over the site earlier in the day before his attempt.

> The gunman who tried to kill Donald Trump was able to fly a drone and get aerial footage of the western Pennsylvania fairgrounds shortly before the former president was set to speak there, law enforcement officials briefed on the matter said, further underscoring the stunning security lapses ahead of Trump's near assassination.
>
> Thomas Matthew Crooks flew the drone on a programmed flight path earlier in the day on July 13 to scour the Butler Farm Show grounds ahead of Trump's ill-fated rally, the officials said.[341]

As happens so many times in an intelligence investigation, just as you think a clear picture is coming into view, a detail pops up which makes you question whether you have the complete picture. This from *CBS News*:

> The briefers told lawmakers they are still attempting to access three foreign encrypted platforms that Crooks used on his cellphone, multiple sources told CBS News. Sources said officials told lawmakers that the encrypted sites are presenting challenges to investigators and could take time to decrypt.[342]

The use of encrypted platforms is a common way for intelligence operators to communicate, as well as a way to move funds between groups. The information provided in the press to date is not clear enough to come to a conclusion but is worthy of further investigation.

And in a final complication, there is audio evidence of a possible second shooter. This is from an article in the *International Business Times*:

> Audio forensic experts from the National Center for Media Forensics at the University of Colorado suggest to possibility of a second shooter. Catalin Grigoras and Cole Whitecotton noted differences in the sound of the shots, indicating multiple weapons. While one shooter has been identified, and another was a Secret Service sniper, the third potential shooter remains unknown.

Former deputy undersecretary of defense Stephen Bryen highlighted this controversial analysis, urging further investigation. Initial gunfire came from the identified shooter Thomas Matthew Crook's location, but a second burst came from a different spot. Acoustic evidence suggests at least two shooters, excluding the Secret Service.[343]

Will this initial analysis hold up? I can't tell you. However, similar evidence in a reexamination of the assassination of President John F. Kennedy, caused a House Select Committee in 1979 to conclude there was a second shooter in that incident.[344]

We should not be surprised if additional facts continue to dribble out, providing fodder for both the sinister explanation for the Trump assassination attempt, and the one in which the Secret Service (perhaps hobbled by their DEI obsession) show the incompetence often displayed by most large organizations. A week after the assassination attempt, the Secret Service was admitting that some of the claims made against them were true. This is from *NBC News* on Sunday, July 21, 2024:

> Former President Donald Trump's security detail complained they were not being given enough resources and personnel by the Secret Service over the past two years, and the agency acknowledged Saturday it denied some requests.
>
> A spokesperson for the Secret Service said in a statement Saturday that the agency has not provided certain resources in the past but has instead provided other security measures including from local partners. A Secret Service official told CNN that examples of these alternatives included having local sniper teams in place when the Secret Service could not provide their own, or having hand-held magnetometers and other measures established at certain events where larger, walk-through magnetometers weren't available.[345]

From my experience working on a security detail, this reads as nothing less than a confession. There is no substitute for highly qualified agents, and depending on local police sniper teams, as demonstrated by what happened in Butler, Pennsylvania, is a recipe for disaster. Expect more "confessions" and "inconvenient truths" to be revealed in this story.

I believe we are still a long way from having all the facts about the attempted assassination of former President Donald Trump.

***

Sadly, it is abundantly clear that our government lies to us as a matter of procedure. Government agencies are known for concealing or falsifying information that questions their actions, especially when negligence is involved.

The FBI took total control over the investigation, which is its legal jurisdiction. We must ask ourselves, can Merrick Garland's Department of Justice be trusted to objectively investigate the assassination attempt on Donald Trump? Here are just a few dubious activities of the FBI, many of which we have detailed in this book:

1. The Russian Collusion hoax.
2. Crossfire hurricane and falsified FISA surveillance requests on Trump's campaign staff.
3. Frivolous and politically driven criminal investigations, e.g., The New York Attorney General fishing expedition, charging Trump with falsifying business records.
4. The January 6 (false flag) pipe bomb investigation.
5. Charging and jailing multiple American citizens after the January 6 debacle, with no due process, several who committed no crime (including an innocent grandmother).
6. The FBI is in control of Crooks' laptop. Remember the FBI's suppression of Hunter Biden's laptop information?

And they expect the American people to trust them?

For years there's been a media and democratic narrative that "Trump is Hitler," or the more commonly expressed sentiment that he's a "threat to democracy." (I'd be remiss if I didn't remind readers that historically, when the CIA wants to topple a foreign government or prevent a certain political figure from coming to power, they often employ the use of media propaganda to whip up public sentiment against their perceived enemies. Perhaps this narrative in the American media has been completely organic. Or perhaps it has not.) Regardless of the origin, in a nation of more than three hundred million people, it's only common sense to conclude a few mentally unbalanced people are likely to take it upon themselves to rid the country of a perceived rising fascist tide in response to such rhetoric.

It is abundantly clear to me that the Biden administration and its Department of Justice have disdain for former President Donald Trump and have targeted him for censorship, defamation, and criminal indictments of questionable validity.

Did the Biden administration (and the head of the Secret Service) lead them to place protection of Donald Trump as a lower priority, unworthy of additional resources?

We desperately need answers to these questions if we are to remain a constitutional republic.

***

As a CIA officer, one of my assignments was team leader of a high-risk defector protection detail. All agents on the detail were required to meet several stringent qualification requirements. However, even while I was at the CIA, I could see that what would later morph into DEI (Diversity, Equity, and Inclusion) was already gaining traction at the agency.

In the Trump assassination attempt I can see no evidence that the women on the protective detail were responsible for any of the mistakes that led to the shooting. As far as I can tell at this point, all the mistakes at the event which mattered were made by male law enforcement members, or at the top by Secret Service Director Kimberly Cheatle.

But in watching video of the event over and over again, I believe the women on the detail did not serve the president or the country well. This is from a *New York Times* article on the DEI controversy regarding the Trump assassination attempt.

From an overwhelmingly male phalanx of agents guarding Mr. Trump that day, these critics pointed out a trio—visibly shorter than their peers and with their hair pulled back in a bun, ponytail and with hairpins, respectively, as they put themselves in harm's way to protect the former president—for criticism. Video of their movements, including a moment in which one visibly struggled to holster a weapon, has fueled an outcry among conservatives who have pinned the agency's failings on its women, suggesting they were only hired to diversify the predominantly male organization.[346]

This is the point the *New York Times* reporter missed. Just because the presence of much shorter women around President Trump on that day did not cause any of the actual problems, the fact that Trump was much taller than them, and exposed to possible gunfire by another shooter as he moved off the stage, is an actual problem. The *New York Times* article continued:

> Conservatives have long argued that codified diversity efforts promote left-wing ideas about gender and race and distract from the organizations' core missions. The G.O.P.-led House has repeatedly passed legislation that would eliminate such initiatives at the Pentagon and other government agencies.
>
> "A woke military is a weak military," is a common refrain among right wing lawmakers.
>
> Ms. Cheatle has spoken openly about her efforts to recruit more women into the service, in part to help recruitment and retention issues.[347]

In the pages of this book, I have not hesitated in the least to criticize the male members of the intelligence agencies, when I believe they have deserved it.

I have also not hesitated to criticize bad ideas, when I have seen them.

From my experience working in a protective detail, the most important consideration is whether you can do the job. This is understood by all good men and women of conscience. Let me give you a little background and depth to this issue, which never seems to make its way into the angry coverage of our mainstream media.

I was ordered to accept the first female protective agent on my detail. I would have gladly accepted any woman who could meet the standards of such a dangerous assignment. There are times where a woman can go where a man cannot go and do what a man cannot do, such as close protection of a female official.

However, the female candidate for my detail was selected merely for being female. During firearms qualification she could barely hit the target and could not qualify. While we all went to lunch, the firearms instructor had to stay behind with her and help her hold the gun to qualify. She was a good officer and became a friend.

She confided in me that she was forced to take the assignment and did not want it, because she did not like firearms and did not want a dangerous assignment. She eventually left the detail and the Office of Security because of this and became a top performing analyst in the Directorate of Intelligence.

I also sat on promotion panels where the highest performer happened to be a white male, but was secretly denied promotion, which was given to the favored gender.

Finally, I was the senior CIA security briefer for counterintelligence cases. I was called in by my supervisor and asked to remove one historical case because the perpetrator's race cast a bad light on that minority. The order came from the chief of the new diversity office.

Of course, I refused and told them I did not place the individual in the lecture for that reason and was not going to remove the case brief for that reason.

Following all of this, I wrote an article for the internal CIA employee's unclassified internal discussion database. The title was, "Will the Real Multicultural Diversity Please Stand Up." In the article I documented both the hypocrisy and risks involved in demoting qualified officers and placing less qualified officers in their place to force DEI on the workforce.

The response set a record of responses in the database with employees of all races and genders agreeing and writing they were tired of being told how to think.

In American today, DEI represents not only a threat to corporate and government efficiency, but also is a risk to our national security, as we just saw in the Trump assassination attempt.

***

This brings us to ask some critical questions regarding this horrible and historic event. We the American people must demand these questions be answered:

- Why did it take 26 minutes for police to respond to the shooter?
- Who was in charge of the Secret Service advance?
- What was the Secret Service advance plan?
- What was the communication protocol between police and the Secret Service command center?
- Did the Secret Service receive the police alerts?
- How did Crooks get *a rifle* past security?
- Why did the Secret Service counter sniper wait 42 seconds to fire when you could see Crooks had a rifle? Was he restricted by management politics?
- Why do before and after photographs show Crooks laying on the roof slope, down 10–15 feet from the peak?
- Donald Trump is 6' 3." Why was the female inner ring agent only 5' 6"? Why did she not handle her firearm correctly (it took four minutes for her to pull out her firearm)?
- Why were the other female agents, looking confused as Trump entered the vehicle, with one unable to holster her firearm, also much shorter than Trump?
- Why was the stage evacuation so chaotic? Had the agents never trained together?
- Who waived physical and training requirements for female Secret Service agents?
- Why were multiple requests for additional security denied?
- What are the "explosive materials" the FBI recovered from Crook's care and home?
- What is the status of Crook's laptop?
- What was ever done about the congressional investigation into Secret Service DEI hiring?
- What was Thomas Crooks's motive?

- Was Crooks on any psychiatric medication? News reports claim he had done internet searches for "major depressive disorder."[348]
- How did Crooks know which building to take position on?
- The police were looking for Crooks; why wasn't the Secret Service?

We need answers to these questions. We must not allow the Deep State, the Shadow Government, to stonewall for weeks, months, and years, under the claim of a "continuing investigation." We must be shown the facts as they are revealed.

Any other response is not what we deserve as a free people.

***

What Must Be Done?

There are several actions we must demand following this tragic and deadly incident.

1. Fire or demote the Secret Service advance agent.
2. Fire the director of the Secret Service.
3. Find out which Secret Service personnel were responsible for the breakdown in communication and fire or demote them.
4. Scrutinize the Secret Service shoot/no shoot policy.
5. Reexamine and make communication protocols mandatory.
6. Return qualification standards back to those of the original merit-based qualifications.
7. Eliminate DEI hiring and enforce current EEO standards based on qualification and experience.
8. Conduct an independent investigation of this incident—outside of the FBI.

***

My provisional opinion at this time is that the assassination attempt on former President Donald Trump was not the result of a conspiracy or an inside job.

However, I need a lot more information before I render a final judgment.

I encourage you to do the same.

I think a complete review will likely lead most people to conclude there was intentional negligence on the part of those involved in protecting former President Trump, based partly on their antipathy toward him, and an indifference as to whether he lived or died.

But we are at the beginning of trying to make sense of this event, not the end.

What does appear to be confirmed is Secret Service senior command arrogance, incompetence, and gross negligence, especially Secret Service Director Kimberly Cheatle's decision not to have agents on the sloped roof of that building because of concerns for their safety nearly cost the life of a presidential candidate.

Secret Service agents put their life on the line to protect government officials, political leaders, and other high-value individuals.

They can handle a sloped roof.

And they should be tall enough to protect a candidate as he makes his way to a secure vehicle.

I have warned the CIA, since 1994, that false diversity standards are counterproductive, dangerous, and harm other employees (and their families). It's often said that excellence is the result of a lot of small things being done well.

The reverse is usually true when there are tragedies, such as when there's an airplane crash. The investigations often reveal a number of small mistakes leading to a catastrophic outcome.

The Shadow Government makes too many decisions without our oversight.

We see the consequences of their actions all around us.

But the responsibility is on us, to pull them out into the light, to speak honestly about what we believe, to engage with others about our concerns, and when presented with information which might challenge our beliefs, to change those opinions when in accord with reason.

In the end, no single person can tell us what is true.

But two things are obvious.

Donald Trump narrowly escaped a bloody disaster.

And so did America.

***

My coauthor and I were racing to finish this chapter about the Trump assassination attempt on Saturday, July 13, 2024, when on Sunday, July 21, 2024, came the news that President Joe Biden was dropping out of the presidential race, although remaining in the Oval Office for the next five months. This is how it was covered in *NBC News*:

> President Joe Biden announced Sunday that he will end his presidential re-election campaign, bringing an abrupt and humbling conclusion to his half-century-long political career and scrambling the race for the White House just four months before Election Day.
>
> Biden, 81, could not reverse growing sentiment within his party that he was too frail to serve and destined to lose to Donald Trump in November. He backed Vice President Kamala Harris to replace him as the Democratic nominee.[349]

Many were not surprised by Biden's withdrawal from the 2024 race, but it certainly threw the race into chaos.

At this moment, it appears former President Donald Trump is likely to win the 2024 race.

The theme of this book is that the intelligence agencies have been manipulating our political discourse, probably since the Kennedy administration. The tactics used by the CIA overseas, as detailed in books written by former agency officials, Allen Dulles and Ted Shackley, have likely been deployed in our own country.

With that understanding, it's reasonable to ask whether the intelligence agencies are continuing to manipulate our political system, throwing into doubt what we think we know.

If we've been living in a manipulated reality for decades, how are we to discern what is true?

In the wake of the Trump assassination attempt and the Biden resignation, some commentators anticipate further chaos, perhaps the poisoning of Trump, truck-bombs outside of political rallies, or the all-too common plane crash which kills a leading political figure.

I acknowledge these as possibilities, but do not anticipate them happening.

The Shadow Government may have more tricks up their sleeve, but an ever-increasing number of eyes are watching them.

That matters.

Whatever disruptions the Shadow Government may have planned for the upcoming months and years, they are in their twilight.

In recent days some commentators have claimed the American Republic died years ago. It died with the merger of corporate and government power, the censoring of alternative voices on social media, and in the weaponization of our justice system. But I believe the courageous example of many citizens is resurrecting our American dream. They are picking up the shattered pieces of our most sacred rights and reforging them into a mighty country.

The Shadow Government can only hold power when it remains in the darkness. When brave citizens stand to fight, shining the light of truth upon them, the villains, the cowards, and the fools take flight.

The power to make a better future is in your hands.

It's up to you.

AFTERWORD

My battle with the CIA led directly to the breakup of my marriage with Lorena.

However, God had another plan for me, as I later met and married my best friend, Sue. It was a divine appointment. We are soul mates, something you rarely find and is so precious. To counter the CIA's attempts to silence me and destroy me financially, I planned a completely off-the-grid farm on an old piece of farmland left to Sue by her parents, which had not been touched for decades.

The piece of land was overgrown and the area where I would build our house was a vine forest. For six months, I cleared the vines and trees making the property ready for our house. Living in Jacksonville Beach, Florida at the time, we traveled on weekends, staying in the empty shell of a metal building (I had purchased from the royalties of my book, *From the Company of Shadows*), cooking on an outdoor propane burner, and taking showers outside with a camping shower.

These were weekends of hard work, but they were exciting because we had a vision; being totally independent from "the system."

Instead of a medium-size traditional house, I purchased several small metal buildings, each with its own function. It is like a tiny village, which was my vision. The first was our main house, the second was the utility building with washer, dryer, and freezer, and the third was my office and studio, where I film my commentaries on the CIA. The fourth building is a larger metal building that functions as a barn for farm equipment.

Over the next five years, we worked on the houses and the land. We put in a deep well (critical to survival) and installed a solar power system that powers the entire farm, not connected to the grid or the internet, where bad actors could shut it down.

After five years of carpentry, plumbing, electrical wiring, and installing small house appliances, the farm was complete. I learned everything I built from YouTube videos! I finished the inside of the live-in building with tongue and groove local pine, and the door handles and window frames made from cutting in half the large vines I removed when clearing the site for the house. We moved in full time and began planting fruit trees that would provide food: blueberries, apples, pears, plums, figs, persimmons, and strawberry patches.

We built four above ground gardens (the soil in the area is terrible), making our own soil and using compost—each garden having four raised bed gardens, where we plant a variety of healthy vegetables, broccoli, mustard greens, crowder peas, onions, garlic, romaine lettuce, etc.

I built a self-sustaining chicken coop, with a DIY automatic feeder and water dish and hatch in the back where we can collect eggs without having to go into the coop. The ladies run free on the farm during the day and give us about eight eggs every morning. Chickens are hilarious to watch, and they have become our egg-laying pets. They are rascals.

For a former biologist, this was my dream come true, a totally off-the-grid set of cabins, completely solar powered and independent of the electrical grid, all plants and trees providing a natural staple of healthy food. Sue, a master gardener, landscaped the areas around the house, making the farm a beautiful and colorful garden. We planted several plants that would help the bee pollinator and butterfly population (including milkweed for Monarchs), with colorful flowering plants of several kinds everywhere. Sue and I call it our little Calloway Gardens.

After all the trauma and suffering the CIA caused, by the grace of God we live in a paradise on earth, peaceful, serene, and beautiful. We are made for each other and are blissfully happy. We attend a wonderful little home church and help people in need whenever we can.

All through the process, as we look back, we can see the hand of the Lord protecting us, miraculously providing for us, and giving us true happiness. I am convinced Psalm 23 is true, "He prepares a table before me in the presence of my enemies."

May God's grace find you all as well.

APPENDIX A:
MERITORIOUS UNIT
CITATION

C05605878

(b)(3)
(j)(1)

The United States of America

Central Intelligence Agency

Citation

OFFICE OF SECURITY

is hereby awarded the

MERITORIOUS UNIT CITATION

in recognition of their accomplishments in providing a safe environment for _____ personnel from January 1990 to May 1991. These officers performed their duties in a highly professional manner while working in a stressful and dangerous environment. It is a credit to the officers dedication to duty that during their tours of duty not one Agency official was harmed _____ All of the officers deployed _____ met the highest standards of the Central Intelligence Agency and for this reason are worthy of this commendation.

APPENDIX B:

PERFORMANCE APPRAISAL

REPORT – AUGUST 28, 1987

CONFIDENTIAL
(When Filled In)

CAUTION: BLANK FORM REQUIRES
SECURE STORAGE IN FIELD

PERFORMANCE APPRAISAL REPORT

*(NOT to be completed without
using Form 45i directions)*

SECTION A	GENERAL INFORMATION					
1. SOC SEC NUMBER	2. NAME (Last, First, Middle) SHIPP, Kevin M.	3. DATE OF BIRTH ..	4. SD	5. SCHED GS	6. GRADE 07	
7. AFFILIATION STAFF EMPLOYEE-CAREER		8. OCCUPATIONAL TITLE SECURITY PROTECTIVE OFF				
9. OFFICE/DIVISION/BRANCH OF ASSIGNMENT SEC		10. CURRENT STATION WASHINGTON, D.C.				11. HQS.
12. REPORTING PERIOD 861101 - 870617		13. DATE REPORT DUE IN OP ASAP		14. TYPE OF REPORT 2/R		

SECTION B	QUALIFICATIONS UPDATE

Qualifications Update (Form 444n) is _____ is not _____ attached. (Submit only if there are changes.)

SECTION C	PERFORMANCE RATINGS

Rating Number

1. Individual consistently fails to meet the work standard for the key job element performed. Performance is unsatisfactory.
2. Individual frequently fails to meet the work standard for the key job element performed. Performance is marginal.
3. Individual occasionally fails to meet the work standard for the key job element performed. Performance is acceptable.
4. Individual fully meets the work standard for the key job element performed.
5. Individual occasionally exceeds the work standard for the key job element performed. Performance is good.
6. Individual frequently exceeds the work standard for the key job element performed. Performance is excellent.
7. Individual invariably exceeds the work standard for the key job element performed. Performance is superior.

(b)(3)
(b)(6)
(j)(1)

APPROVED FOR
RELEASE⊓ DATE:
06-May-2011

KEY JOB ELEMENTS

KEY JOB ELEMENT NO. 1 AND RATING

Provides protection for the office suite of the Director and Deputy Director of Central Intelligence. Responsible for the processing and monitoring of all visitors to the suite.

6

KEY JOB ELEMENT NO. 2 AND RATING

Provides protection for [____] the Director of Central Intelligence and has direct responsibility for [____] Command Post.

6

KEY JOB ELEMENT NO. 3 AND RATING

Provides daily administrative and communications support for the DCI Security Staff.

6

KEY JOB ELEMENT NO. 4 AND RATING

During DCI/DDCI travel assists the DCI Security Staff in providing personal protection for the DCI and DDCI and is responsible for the protection of the classified material(s) that is in their possession. As such, is responsible for, among other matters, security with liaison, transportation, and communications.

6

KEY JOB ELEMENT NO. 5 AND RATING

SECTION D	OVERALL PERFORMANCE RATING LEVEL

Taking everything into account about the employee which influences his/her effectiveness on the job, I rate the employee's overall performance at this level.

6

FORM 45 USE PREVIOUS
10-82 EDITIONS

CONFIDENTIAL

(4)

CONFIDENTIAL

C05605786

SECTION E	NARRATIVE COMMENTS

1. By Supervisor

Mr. Shipp is recommended for continued employment.
Mr. Shipp was selected for a rotational assignment as a Protective Security Officer (PSO) with the DCI Security Staff and he served in that capacity from 16 June 1986 until his entry into the [   ] Program in June 1987.

The undersigned supervised Mr. Shipp from December 1986 and he consistently demonstrated maturity and a genuine dedication to the mission of the DCI Security Staff. One of his most impressive attributes was his willingness to address issues that required considerable thought and research. For example, Mr. Shipp realized the need for Standard Operating Procedures for the PSO's in both the office and [   ] Command Post environments. With a minimum of supervision, he pursued the development and implementation of this critical initiative. The final product has provided the DCI Security Staff with an important benchmark from which staff operations are conducted.

During Mr. Shipp's tenure, the DCI Security Staff maintained a 24-hour Command Post at the residence of the former Director of Central Intelligence, William J. Casey. His maturity and sound judgement attracted the Casey family and they relied heavily on him for guidance and support. During a time of personal crisis, the Casey's knew they could count on Mr. Shipp.

With regard to his office responsibilities, he developed a solid, professional rapport with the occupants of the DCI suite. He was always tactful, polite and eager to assist as required. He accepted his security responsibilities in a serious manner and his attention to detail reflected favorably on the entire DCI Security Staff.

In conclusion, Mr. Shipp's assignment to the DCI Security Staff was an unqualified success. He enhanced the stature of the rotational assignment to the DCI Security Staff by an outstanding performance of his assigned duties. He also will, in the opinion of the undersigned, be a success in the future for the Office of Security.

Months employee has been in this position 14	Months employee has been under my supervision 14	Interim discussion was X was not ___ held.	Reason for NOT showing employee the report is attached. Yes___ No ___
DATE 8/1/87	TITLE DC/DCI/SS		

Employee Certification

I have reviewed my supervisor's comments and discussed my job performance ratings with him/her. My signature does not necessarily imply my agreement with either.	DATE	TYPED OR PRINTED NAME AND SIGNATURE Kevin M. Shipp unavailable

2. By Reviewing Official

I agree wholeheartedly with the above assessment of Mr. Shipp. He was an excellent addition to the staff and should do well as a staff agent. He will be invited back to the staff in the future.

DATE 8-20-87	TITLE C/DCI/SS	

3. By Employee

I have read my reviewing official's comments. My signature does not necessarily imply my agreement with them.	I have ___ have not ___ attached a statement containing my comments about this Performance Appraisal Report.	
DATE	POSITION TITLE	TYPED OR PRINTED NAME AND SIGNATURE Kevin M. Shipp unavailable

APPENDIX C:
PERFORMANCE APPRAISAL
REPORT – JULY 30, 1999

SECRET
SECRET
Classify for Appropriate

APPROVED FOR
RELEASEn DATE:
06-May-2011

PERFORMANCE APPRAISAL REPORT

Complete in Accordance with HR 20-30. See: Performance Appraisal Handbook for Supervisors

SECTION A — GENERAL INFORMATION

1. SOCIAL SECURITY NUMBER	2. NAME (Last-First-Middle)	3. SD
	SHIPP, Kevin M.	

4. SCHEDULE	5. GRADE	6. AFFILIATION	7. OCCUPATIONAL TITLE
GS	13	Staff Employee - Career	

8. OFFICE / DIVISION / BRANCH OF ASSIGNMENT	9. CURRENT STATION	10. HQS
DDO/CTC/	Washington	1

11. REPORTING PERIOD	12. DATE REPORT DUE IN HRM	13. TYPE OF REPORT
01 Jul 1998 - 22 May 1999	30 July 1999	

SECTION B — QUALIFICATIONS UPDATE

QUALIFICATIONS UPDATE (FORM 444N) IS   IS NOT [X] ATTACHED (Submit Only If There Are Changes) ☐

SECTION C — PERFORMANCE RATINGS

RATING NUMBER
1. Individual consistently fails to meet the work standard for the key job element performed. Performance is unsatisfactory.
2. Individual frequently fails to meet the work standard for the key job element performed. Performance is marginal.
3. Individual occasionally fails to meet the work standard for the key job element performed. Performance is acceptable.
4. Individual fully meets the work standard for the key job element performed.
5. Individual occasionally exceeds the work standard for the key job element performed. Performance is good.
6. Individual frequently exceeds the work standard for the key job element performed. Performance is excellent.
7. Individual invariably exceeds the work standard for the key job element performed. Performance is superior.

(b)(1)
(b)(3)
(b)(6)
(j)(1)
(k)(1)

KEY JOB ELEMENTS

Key Job Element No. 1 and Rating
Perform as a team member and leader in the planning, administration, and presentation of

| | 7 |

Key Job Element No. 2 and Rating

| | 7 |

| | 6 |

Key Job Element No. 4 and Rating

Key Job Element No. 5 and Rating

SECTION D — OVERALL PERFORMANCE RATING

Taking everything into account about the employee which influences his/her effectiveness on the job, I rate the employee's overall performance at this level   ➡   7

Form 45 (EF)
9-98
PREVIOUS EDITIONS OBSOLETE

Classify as Appropriate
SECRET
SECRET

C05605759   SECRET
                                 SECRET

SECTION E (Continued)	NARRATIVE COMMENTS
SOCIAL SECURITY NUMBER	NAME
	SHIPP, Kevin M.

COMMENTS - *continued from page 2*

On every ☐ that Kevin went on he acted as the team leader supervising staff officers and independent contractors. Mr. Shipp was universally viewed a ☐ expert instructor, and as such, he was charged with indoctrinating new officers in how to provide ☐ course materials ☐ In the ☐ be coordinated, supervised and taught a ☐ Kevin mentored a new CTC officer through the course, ☐ Nothing would please ☐ management more than for each new officer to perform at Kevin's level.

The same new officer was treated to a second ☐ Kevin's mentoring of this officer proved to be outstanding, however, the new officer proved to be immature and a discipline problem. Mr. Shipp dealt with his less professional ward with maturity, tact, and discipline. During a difficult month, Mr. Shipp proved himself to be an effective manager and true leader. Comments from a former Deputy Director of the United States Secret Service praised Kevin for his handling of a sensitive and difficult situation ☐

☐ within ☐ are the backbone of any tour, but in between ☐ officers show their mettle. ☐ He manned the Agency's counterterrorist nerve center ☐ Additionally, Mr. Shipp doggedly worked on improving course materials. He crafted ☐ ☐ In true team spirit, he shared the fruit of his labors with all of his coworkers. His slides became the office standard, and he unselfishly put all of the graphics on floppy disks to share. Kevin created course schedules that became the office standard, and his coworkers accepted the schedules faster than fraternity brothers grab an "A+" term paper from a historical resource file.

As testament to Mr. Shipp's outstanding performance in CTC ☐ he was awarded a $1500 Exceptional Performance Award. He was also offered the opportunity to Gateway to the Directorate of Operations, which carried the promise of attending the coveted ☐ Even without ☐ Kevin was the highest intelligence producing SOPO in ☐ His production helped boost ☐ in the last year, and infinitely since he arrived in the branch. Mr. Shipp was universally viewed as the best officer in ☐ and his departure was a devastating blow. Mr. Shipp's performance in CTC proved that he is destined for future career ascension, and those of us who benefited from his expertise and hard work can only wish him the success he has earned.

Form 45 (EF)
9-98

Classify as Appropriate

SECRET
SECRET

PAGE 3

APPENDIX D: GAG ORDER

SECRET//███

UNITED STATES DISTRICT COURT

████████████████████

JOHN DOE and ANN DOE,   )
Individually and as next friend for)
Mark Doe and Barbi Doe, minors   )
And JOHNNIE DOE   )
)
            Plaintiffs,   )
)
        v.   )   No. SA-02-CA-573-OG
)
UNITED STATES OF AMERICA   )   ████████████████
)
            Defendant.   )

STIPULATION AND PROTECTIVE ORDER

The undersigned counsel for the parties in this case, subject to the approval of the Court, hereby stipulate to the following terms and conditions.

1.

SECRET//███

JUN-24-2004 THU 02:48 PM U S ATTY   FAX NO. 2103847312   P. 04/07

SECRET//█

subject to █████████████████████████████

5. ████████ has granted to Plaintiffs' attorneys
limited security approvals to have access to information
classified up to the SECRET level. By doing so, ███████
██████ has not, and does not forego the authority of ████████
████████████████████████████ assert the state secrets
privilege over any specific information, even if that
information is classified no higher than SECRET.
Plaintiffs' counsel, in connection with this case, have
signed secrecy agreements obligating them not to disclose
classified information.

3

SECRET/█████

NOTES

Introduction

1   Adam Westbrook and Lindsey Crouse, "It Turns Out the 'Deep State' Is Actually Kind of Awesome," *New York Times*, March 19, 2024, https://www.nytimes.com/2024/03/19/opinion/trump-deep-state.html.

2   Ibid.

3   Ibid.

4   Ibid.

5   Ibid.

6   David Moschella, "It's Not Just Facebook – "Old Media" Spreads Misinformation, Too," Information Technology and Innovation Foundation, January 10, 2022, www.itif.org/publications/2022/01/10/its-not-just-facebook-old-media-spreads-misinformation-too/.

7   Ibid.

8   Ibid.

9   Ibid.

10 Ibid.

11 Adam Westbrook and Lindsey Crouse, "It Turns Out the 'Deep State' Is Actually Kind of Awesome," *New York Times*, March 19, 2024, https://www.nytimes.com/2024/03/19/opinion/trump-deep-state.html.

Chapter One

12 Bob Woodward personal website, "Biography," (Accessed March 24, 2024), www.bobwoodward.com/biography.

13 Ray Locker, *Haig's Coup: How Richard Nixon's Closest Aide Forced Him from Office*, (Lincoln, Nebraska, Potomac Press, an Imprint of the University of Nebraska Press, 2019), p. 357.

14 Ibid. at 358.

15 Bob Woodward Personal Website "Biography," (Accessed March 24, 2024), www.bobwoodward.com/biography.

16   Rick Perlstein, "Watergate Scandal," *Encyclopedia Brittanica*, (Last updated February 4, 2024), www.brittanica.com/event/Watergate-scandal.

17   Annette McDermott, "How 'Deep Throat' Took Down Nixon from Inside the FBI," History Channel, April 29, 2022, www.history.com/news/watergate-deep-throat-fbi-informant-nixon.

18   Ibid.

19   Ibid.

20   Bob Woodward Personal Website, "Biography," (Accessed March 24, 2024), www.bobwoodward.com.biography.

21   Kevin Shipp, *From the Company of Shadows* (Tampa, Florida, Ascent Publishing, 2012), p. 22–23.

22   Bob Woodward, *Veil: The Secret Wars of the CIA, 1981–1987* (New York, New York, Simon & Schuster, 1987), p. 19.

23   Ibid. at 516.

24   Ibid. at 517.

25   Ibid.

26   "Calls Interview in Book 'Fabrication': Widow Denies Casey, Woodward Talked," *Los Angeles Times*, September 28, 1987, www.latimes.com/archives/la-xpm-1987-09-28-mn-6991-story-html.

27   Charles Colson, "The Meeting Could Not Have Taken Place," *Washington Post*, October 1, 1987, www.washingtonpost.com/archive/opinions/1987/10/02/the-meeting-could-not-have-taken-place/0b4409ca-1538-48d0-9dac-542a09dee147/.

28   Kevin Shipp, *From the Company of Shadows* (Tampa, Florida, Ascent Publishing, 2012), p. 47.

29   Tim Mack, "Bob Woodward Controversies," *Politico*, April 30, 2012, www.politico.com/story/2012/04/6-bob-woodward-controversies-075738.

30   Ibid.

31   Ibid.

32   Ibid.

33   Ibid.

34   John Cassidy, "Bob Woodward Throws an Interception," *The New Yorker*, February 28, 2013, www.newyorker.com/news/john-cassidy/bob-woodward-throws-an-interception.

35   Carl Bernstein, "The CIA and the Media," *Rolling Stone*, October 20, 1977, www.carlbernstein.com/the-cia-and-the-media-rolling-stone-10-20-1977.

36   Ibid.

37   Ibid.

38   Ibid.

39   President Barack Obama, "Executive Order 13721: Developing an Integrated Global Engagement Center to Support Government-Wide

Counterterrorism Communications and revoking Executive Order 13584," Federal Register, March 14, 2016, www.federalregister.gov /documents/2016/03/17/2016-06250/developing-an-integrated-global -engagement-center-to-support-government-wide-counterterrorism.

40 Ibid.

41 US Senator Chris Murphy (D-CT), "Senate Passes Major Murphy-Portman Counter-Propaganda Bill as Part of NDAA," Press Release, December 8, 2016, https://www.murphy.senate.gov/newsroom/press -releases/senate-passes-major-murphy-portman-counter-propaganda-bill -as-part-of-ndaa.

42 Len Colodny and Robert Gettlin, *Silent Coup: The Removal of a President* (New York, New York, Saint Martin's Press, 1991), p. 7–8.

43 Richard Reeves, "Missile Gaps and Other Broken Promises," *New York Times*, February 10, 2009, https://archive.nytimes.com/100days.blog .nytimes.com/2009/02/10/missile-gaps-and-other-broken-promises/.

44 Ibid.

45 Peter Kornbluth, "End C.I.A. Covert Operations," *New York Times*, December 21, 2014, www.nytimes.com/roomfordebate/2014/12/21 /do-we-need-the-cia/end-cia-covert-operations/.

46 "Nixon's Side of '60 Story," *U.S. News & World Report*, April 2, 1962, www.cia.gov/readingroom/docs/CIA-RDP75-00149R000500440047-1. pdf/.

47 Len Colodny and Robert Gettlin, *Silent Coup: The Removal of a President* (New York, New York, Saint Martin's Press, 1991), p. 8.

48 Ibid. at 9–10.

49 Ibid. at 70.

50 Ibid. at 71.

Chapter Two

51 "The State-Secrets Privilege, Tamed," *New York Times*, April 29, 2009, www.nytimes.com/2009/04/30/opinion/30thu1.html.

52 Steven Lee Myers, "Former C.I.A. Director Left Secrets Open to Theft, Agency Investigator Says," *New York Times*, February 23, 2000, www .nytimes.com/2000/02/23/us/former-cia-director-left-secrets-open-to -theft-agency-investigator-says.html

53 Lorraine Adams and David A. Vise, "Reno Defends Decision to Stop Prosecution," *Washington Post.* February 3, 2000, https://www .washingtonpost.com/wp-srv/pmextra/feb00/03/A5923-2000Feb3.html.

54 "The Russia House – A Virtuoso Comb. Player – 1990), MovieClips, *YouTube*, 2014, https://youtube.com/watch?v=ulMNuwN1C-8.

Chapter Three

55 "High Finance Gives Way to Espionage Change: In What He Calls His Final Interview, 'Buzzy' Krongard Explains Why Moving from Alex Brown to the CIA isn't Such a Long Step," *Baltimore Sun*, February 1, 1998, www.baltimoresun.com/1998/02/01/high-finance-gives-way-to-espionage-change-in-what-he-rtc-calls-his-final-interviewbuzzy-krongard-explains-why-moving-from-alex-brown-to-the-cia-isnt-such-a-long-step/.

56 Ibid.

57 Ibid.

58 Ibid.

59 Ibid.

60 Ibid.

61 Ibid.

62 Ibid.

63 Ibid.

64 George Tenet with Bill Harlow, *At the Center of the Storm: The CIA During America's Time of Crisis* (New York, New York, Harper, 2008), p. 19.

65 Vernon Lee and Greg Schneider, "Colorful Outsider is Named No. 3 at the CIA," *Washington Post*, March 16, 2001, www.washingtonpost.com /archive/politics/2001/03/17/colorful-outsider-is-named-no-3-at-the-cia /a90d6354-4600-425d-9727-27d5cda77078/.

66 Ibid.

67 Ibid.

68 Ibid.

69 George Tenet with Bill Harlow, *At the Center of the Storm: The CIA During America's Time of Crisis* (New York, New York, Harper, 2008), p. 27.

70 Charlie Savage, "Ex-C.I.A. Agent Goes Public with Story of Mistreatment on the Job," *New York Times*, February 10, 2011, www .nytimes.com/2011/02/11/us/politics/11secrets.html.

71 Ibid.

72 Ibid.

73 Clinical Report from Dr. Ronald Schmal on Shipp Family, Licensed Clinical Psychologist, September 8, 2003.

74 Charlie Savage, "Ex-C.I.A. Agent Goes Public with Story of Mistreatment on the Job," *New York Times,* February 10, 2011, www .nytimes.com/2011/02/11/us/politics/11secrets.html.

75 Ibid.

76 Christian Berthelsen and Scott Winokur, "Suspicious Profits Sit Uncollected/Airline Investors Seem to be Lying Low," *San Francisco Chronicle*, September 29, www.sfgate.com/news/article/suspicious-profits -sit-uncollected-airline-2874054.php.

77 Chris Blackhurst, "Mystery of Terror 'Insider Dealers,'" *The Independent*, October 14, 2001, www.independent.co.uk/news/business/news/mystery-of-terror-insider-dealers-9237061.html.
78 Mark H. Green, *Black 9/11: Money, Motive, and Technology* (Chicago, Illinois, Independent Publisher's Group, Chicago, 2012), p. 33.
79 "Freud in Quotes," Freud Museum in London, (Accessed July 1, 2024), www.freud.org/2019/04/30/freud-in-quotes/.
80 Mark H. Green, *Black 9/11: Money, Motive, and Technology* (Chicago, Illinois, Independent Publisher's Group, Chicago, 2012), p. 33.
81 Ibid.
82 Ibid. at 34.
83 Ibid. at 34–35.
84 Ibid. at 35.
85 "9-11 Commission Report", endnote 130, p. 499, www.9-11commission.gov/report/911Report.pdf.
86 Amy Mulvhill, "Cameo: Ed Hale," *Baltimore Magazine*, November 2014, www.baltimoremagazine.com/section/community/q-a-with-ed-hale/.
87 Ibid.
88 Kevin Cowherd, *Hale Storm: The Incredible Saga of Baltimore's Ed Hale, Including a Secret Life with the CIA* (Loyola University, Maryland, Apprentice House Press, 2014), p. 125.
89 Ibid. at 126–127.
90 Ibid. at 128–129.
91 Ibid. at 129.
92 "How the CIA Underwrote Big Tech," *Kickback News*, May 19, 2022, https://kickback.news/2022/05/19/a-buzzy-interview-a-b-krongard-and-the-cia-ipos/.
93 Ibid.

Chapter Four

94 "Settlement Agreement in Principle," In the Matter of Mediation of John Doe, Et Al v. United States of America, W.D. Tex, No. SA-02-CA-573-OG, Mediator Harold Himmelman, December 12, 2003.
95 "January 29, 2004 Letter from the U.S. Department of Justice to Shipp Family Attorney."
96 "Plaintiff's Preliminary Response to Defendant's Consolidated Notice by the United States of Assertion of State Secrets and Motion to Dismiss," United States District Court for the Western District of Texas, C.A. No. SA-02-CA-0573-OG, March 19, 2004.
97 "The State Secrets Privilege: National Security Information in Civil Litigation," Congressional Research Service, April 28, 2022, p. 23,

(Accessed July 1, 2024), https://crsreports.congress/product/pdf/R
/R47081.

98 Letter from Assistant U.S. Attorney Glenn W. McTaggart to G.P. Hardy,
III," March 26, 2004.

99 Isaiah 40, verses 10-13, King James Bible Online, (Accessed July 1,
2024), www.kingjamesbibleonline.org/Isiah-Chapter-40/#10.

100 "George Tenet Resigns as CIA Director," *NBC News*, June 3, 2004, www
.nbcnews.com/id/wbna5129314.

101 Ibid.

102 Carl Bernstein, "The CIA and the Media," *Rolling Stone*, October 20,
1977, www.carlbernstein.com/the-cia-and-the-media-rolling-stone
-10-20-1977.

103 Ibid.

104 Ibid.

105 Ibid.

106 Ibid.

107 Ibid.

108 Ibid.

109 "Review of Four FISA Applications and Other Aspects of the FBI's
Crossfire Hurricane Investigation," Office of the Inspector General,
U.S. Department of Justice, December 2019, ii, www.justice.gov
/storage/120919-examination.pdf.

110 Ibid. at v.

111 Kimbery Strassel, "Brennan and the 2016 Spying Scandal," *Wall Street
Journal*, July 19, 2018, www.wsj.com/articles/brennan-and-the-2016
-spy-scandal-1532039346.

112 Review of Four FISA Applications and Other Aspects of the FBI's
Crossfire Hurricane Investigation," Office of the Inspector General,
U.S. Department of Justice, December 2019, vi, www.justice.gov
/storage/120919-examination.pdf.

113 Ibid.

114 Ibid. at x.

115 Ibid. at viii.

116 Ibid. at xiii.

117 Ryan Lucas, "Justice Department IG Finds Widespread Problems
with FBI's FISA Application," NPR, March 31, 2020, www.npr.
org/2020/03/31/824510255/justice-department-ig-finds-widespread
-problems-with-fbis-fisa-applications.

118 "Jordan and Johnson Press Wray on Broken FISA Process" Website of
Congressman Mike Johnson, January 27, 2022, https://mikejohnson.
house.gov/news/documentsingle.aspx?DocumentID=1031.

119 Nick Mrodowanec, "US House Speaker Mike Johnson Will Feel the
Wrath of His Party if he Pushes Warrantless Surveillance," *Newsweek*,

December 13, 2023, www.newsweek.com/edward-snowden
-warns-mike-johnson-against-crossing-red-line-1852238.

120 Ibid.

121 Ibid.

122 Rebecca Beitsch and Mike Illis, "Johnson Shifts from FISA Critic to
     Champion as Speaker," *The Hill,* April 11, 2024, www.thehill.com
     /homenews/house/4589152-speakership-turns-johnson
     -from-fisa-critic-to-champion/.

123 Ibid.

124 Ibid.

125 Nick Robertson, "Rand Paul Blasts Johnson for Going Against FISA
     Amendment: He Hasn't Held His Ground," *The Hill,* April 14, 2024,
     www.thehill.com/homenews/house/4593903-rand-paul-blasts-johnson
     -for-going-against-fisa-amendment-he-hasnt-held-his-ground/.

126 Sean Moran, "Thomas Massie: Speaker Johnson Lit Constitution on
     Fire By Casting Deciding Vote for Deep State Spies," *Brietbart,* April 12,
     2024, www.breitbart.com/politics/2024/04/12/thomas-massie-mike
     -johnson-lit-constitution-on-fire-by-moving-for-deep-state/.

Chapter Five

127 Ted Shackley with Richard A. Finney, *Spymaster: My Life in the CIA*
     (Sterling, Virginia, Potomac Books, 2005).

128 Ibid. at ix.

129 Ibid. at 39.

130 Ibid. at 39–40.

131 Ibid. at 43.

132 Norman Solomon, "Why the *Washington Post*'s New Ties to the CIA
     are So Ominous," *Huffington Post,* January 13, 2014, www.huffpost.com
     /entry/why-the-washington-posts_b_4587927.

133 Ibid.

134 Ted Shackley with Richard A. Finney, *Spymaster: My Life in the CIA*
     (Sterling, Virginia, Potomac Books, 2005), 43–44.

135 Bess Levin, "An Exasperated Pentagon Responds to the Taylor Swift
     Conspiracy Theories," *Vanity Fair,* February 2, 2024, www.vanityfair
     .com/news/an-exasperated-pentagon-responds-to-the-taylor
     -swift-conspiracy-theories.

136 Ted Shackley with Richard A. Finney, *Spymaster: My Life in the CIA*
     (Sterling, Virginia, Potomac Books, 2005), xv–xvii.

137 David Corn, *Blond Ghost: Ted Shackley and the CIA's Crusades*
     (New York, New York, Simon & Schuster, 1994), 134.

138 Ibid. at 12.

139 Ibid. at 13.

140 Tim Weiner, *Legacy of Ashes: The History of the CIA* (New York, New York, Random House, 2007), 71–72.

141 Ibid. at 72–73.

142 Ibid. at 73–74.

143 Ibid. at 76.

144 Ibid. at 76–77.

145 Ibid. at 67.

146 Ibid. at 67–68.

147 Seth Ferranti, "This Guy Infiltrated Hollywood for the Mob and Pulled Off a Major Scam," *VICE*, November 11, 2018, www.vice.com/en /article/j5zq44/this-guy-infiltrated-hollywood-for-the-mob-and -pulled-off-a-major-scam.

148 Ibid.

149 Ibid.

150 Nicholas Gage, "Mafia Said to Have Slain Roselli Because of His Senate Testimony," *New York Times*, February 25, 1977, www.nytimes. com/1977/02/25/archives/mafia-said-to-have-slain-rosselli-because-of-his -senate-testimony.html.

151 Ibid.

152 Ibid.

153 Ibid.

154 Ibid.

155 Phillip Shenon, "Yes, the CIA Director Was Part of the JFK Assassination Cover-up," *Politico*, October 7, 2015, www.politico.com/magazine /story/2015/10/jfk-assassination-john-mccone-warren-commission -cia-213197/.

156 Ibid.

157 Ibid.

158 Ibid.

159 Ibid.

160 Jefferson Morley, "Nixon's Plan to Threaten the CIA on JFK's Assassination," *Politico,* June 5, 2022, www.politico.com/news /magazine/2022/06/05/nixon-helms-cia-jfk-assassination-00037232.

161 Ibid.

162 Ibid.

163 Ibid.

164 Jack Anderson and Dale Van Atta, "Death in Dallas: a Plot that Backfired," *Washington Post*, November 1, 1988, https://www.washingtonpost.com /archive/lifestyle/food/1988/11/02/death-in-dallas-a-plot-that-backfired /fe09d891-ebb4-450f-9d1f-33a8a964d831/.

165 Ibid.

166 Tom Leonard, "The Most Convincing Account Yet of How – and Why – the Mob Killed JFK: New Film by Relative of Mafia Boss Sheds Fresh

Light on the President's Assassination Nearly 60 Years On," *Daily Mail*, July 15, 2022, www.dailymail.co.uk/news/article-11019271/New-film -relative-Mafia-boss-sheds-fresh-light-Presidents-assassination-60 -years-on.html.

167   Ibid.

168   Ibid.

169   Ibid.

170   Ibid.

171   Ibid.

172   Ibid.

173   Fred P. Graham, "Nixon Commutes Hoffa Sentence, Curbs Union Role," *New York Times*, December 24, 1971, www.nytimes.com/1971/12/24 /archives/nixon-commutes-hoffa-sentence-curbs-union-role-teamster -served.html.

174   Tom Leonard, "The Most Convincing Account Yet of How – and Why – the Mob Killed JFK: New Film by Relative of Mafia Boss Sheds Fresh Light on the President's Assassination Nearly 60 Years On," *Daily Mail*, July 15, 2022, www.dailymail.co.uk/news/article-11019271/New-film -relative-Mafia-boss-sheds-fresh-light-Presidents-assassination-60-years -on.html.

175   Ibid.

176   Ibid.

177   David Corn, *Blond Ghost: Ted Shackley and the CIA's Crusades* (New York, New York, Simon & Schuster, 1994), p. 105.

178   Ibid. at 105–106.

179   Ibid. at 106.

Chapter Six

180   Ibid. at 172.

181   Ibid. at 172–173.

182   Ibid. at 175.

183   Ibid. at 175–176.

184   Ibid. at 179.

185   Ibid.

186   Ibid. at 181.

187   James P. Sterba, "The Controversial Operation Phoenix: How It Roots out Vietcong Suspects," *New York Times*, February 18, 1970, www.nytimes. com/1970/02/18/archives/the-controversial-operation-phoenix-how-it -roots-out-vietcong.html.

188   Ibid.

189   Ibid.

190 Tom Buckley, "Phoenix: To Get Their Man Dead or Alive," *New York Times*, February 22, 1970, www.nytimes.com/1970/02/22/archives /phoenix-to-get-their-man-dead-or-alive.html.
191 Ibid.
192 Felix Belair Jr., "U.S. Aide Defends Pacification Program in Vietnam Despite Killings of Civilians," *New York Times*, July 20, 1971, www .nytimes.com/1971/07/20/archives/us-aide-defends-pacification-program -in-vietnam-despite-killings-of.html.
193 Morley Safer, "Body Count was Their Most Important Product," *New York Times*, October 21, 1990, www.nytimes.com/1990/10/21/books /body-count-was-their-most-important-product.html.
194 Jeremy Kuzmarov, "The Phoenix Program Was a Disaster in Vietnam and Would be in Afghanistan – And the NYT Should Know That," History News Network, www.hnn.us/article/the-phoenix-program-was -a-disaster-in-vietnam-and-.
195 Tim Weiner, *Legacy of Ashes: The History of the CIA* (New York, New York, Random House, 2007), 556.
196 David Corn, *Blond Ghost: Ted Shackley and the CIA's Crusades* (New York, New York, Simon & Schuster,1994), 229.
197 Ibid.
198 Ibid. at 314.
199 Ibid. at 315.
200 Ibid.
201 "The Parrott Memo," November 22, 1963, Accessed May 5, 2024), www.wikispooks.com/wiki/The_Parrott_Memo.
202 "'63 F.B.I. Memo Ties Bush to Intelligence Agency," *New York Times*, July 11, 1988, www.nytimes.com/1988/07/11/us/63-fbi-memo-ties-bush-to -intelligence-agency.html.
203 Ibid.
204 Steven Hager, "The George Bush Connection to JFK's Assassination," The Tin Whistle, November 22, 2013, www.stevenhager.net/2013/11/22 /the-george-bush-connections-to-jfks-assassination/.
205 Gregg Grandin, "George H.W. Bush, Icon of the WASP Establishment – and of Brutal US Repression in the Third World," *The Nation*, December 4, 2018, www.thenation.com/article/archive/george-h-w-bush-icon-of -the-wasp-establishment-and-of-brutal-us-repression-in-the-third-world/.
206 Ibid.
207 Joseph McBride, "The Man Who Wasn't There: George Bush, CIA Operative," *The Nation*, July 16, 1988, www.aarclibrary.org/notices /George_Bush_CIA_Operative_by_Joseph_McBride.pdf.
208 Ibid.
209 Ibid.

210 David Corn, *Blond Ghost: Ted Shackley and the CIA's Crusades* (New York, New York, Simon & Schuster, 1994), 315.
211 Ibid. at 349.
212 Ibid. at 353.
213 Ibid.
214 Ibid. at 360.
215 Ibid. at 361.
216 Ibid. at 376.
217 Ibid. at 376–377.
218 Ibid. at 378–379.
219 Ibid. at 380.
220 Ibid. at 382.
221 Ibid. at 383.
222 Ibid. at 387.
223 Telephone Interview with Danny Sheehan by Kent Heckenlively, May 26, 2024.
224 Ibid.
225 David Corn, *Blond Ghost: Ted Shackley and the CIA's Crusades* (New York, New York, Simon & Schuster, 1994, 402.
226 David Stout, "Ted Shackley, Enigmatic C.I.A. Official, Dies at 75," *New York Times,* December 14, 2002, www.nytimes.com/2002/12/14/us/theodore-shackley-enigmatic-cia-official-dies-at-75.html.
227 Ibid.
228 From the *Washington Post*, "Theodore Shackley, 75; CIA Leader Was Legendary Operative," *Los Angeles Times*, December 14, 2002, https://www.latimes.com/archives/la-xpm-2002-dec-14-me-shackley14-story.html.
229 "Episode 102 – Tucker Carlson Interviews Felix Rodriguez, X Platform, May 6, 2024, www.x.com/TuckerCarlson/status/1787603250822193463.
230 Ibid.
231 Ibid.

Chapter Seven

232 Paul L. Williams, *Operation Gladio: The Unholy Alliance Between the Vatican, the CIA, and the Mafia* (Amherst, New York, Prometheus Books, 2015), 34.
233 Ibid. at 35.
234 Ibid at 36–36.
235 "The *S.S. Normandie* Catches Fire," This Day in History, February 9, The History Channel, www.history.com/this-day-in-history/the-normandie-catches-fire.

236 Paul L. Williams, *Operation Gladio: The Unholy Alliance Between the Vatican, the CIA, and the Mafia* (Amherst, New York, Prometheus Books, 2015), 36.

237 Ibid. at 37.

238 Ibid.

239 Ibid. at 38.

240 Ibid. at 39.

241 Ibid. at 31.

242 Ibid.

243 Ibid. at 39–40.

244 David Talbott, *The Devil's Chessboard: Allen Dulles, the CIA, and the Rise of America's Secret Government* (New York, New York, Harper Perennial, 2015), p, 15.

245 Ibid. at 18–19.

246 Ibid. at 19.

247 Ibid. at 32–33.

248 Ibid. at 33–34.

249 Ibid. at 35.

250 Ibid. at 35–36.

251 Paul L. Williams, *Operation Gladio: The Unholy Alliance Between the Vatican, the CIA, and the Mafia* (Amherst, New York, Prometheus Books, 2015), 40.

252 Ibid.

253 Ibid. at 41.

254 William F. Buckley, Jr., "My Friend, E. Howard Hunt," *Los Angeles Times*, March 4, 2007, www.latimes.com/archives/la-xpm-2007-mar-04-op-buckley4-story.html.

255 Ibid.

256 James D. Robenalt, "A Plane Crash 50 Years Ago Changed the Course of U.S. History," *Washington Post*, December 8, 2022, www.washingtonpost.com/history/2022/12/08/dorothy-hunt-united-crash-watergate/.

257 Ibid.

258 William F. Buckley, Jr., "My Friend, E. Howard Hunt," *Los Angeles Times*, March 4, 2007, www.latimes.com/archives/la-xpm-2007-mar-04-op-buckley4-story.html.

259 Paul L. Williams, *Operation Gladio: The Unholy Alliance Between the Vatican, the CIA, and the Mafia* (Amherst, New York, Prometheus Books, 2015), 40.

260 Ibid. at 42.

261 Daniele Ganser, *NATO's Secret Armies: Operation Gladio and Terrorism in Western Europe* (New York, New York, Frank Cass, 2005), xi.

262 Ibid. at 28.

263 Ibid. at 29.

264 Ibid. at 33.
265 Ibid.
266 Ibid.
267 Allen Dulles, *The Craft of Intelligence: America's Legendary Spymaster on the Fundamentals of Intelligence Gathering for a Free World* (Guilford, Connecticut, Lyons Press, 1963), 4–5.
268 Ibid. at 37.
269 Ibid. at 142.
270 Ibid. at 171.
271 Ibid. at 235–236.
272 Ibid. at 245–246.

Chapter Eight

273 "Senate Select Committee to Study Governmental Operations with Respect to Intelligence, (The Church Committee)," Landing Page, (Accessed May 13, 2024),www.senate.gov/about/powers-procedures/investigations/church-committee/.
274 Ibid.
275 Ibid.
276 Ibid.
277 Ibid.
278 James Risen, *The Last Honest Man: The CIA, the FBI, and the Kennedys – One Senator's Fight to Save Democracy* (New York, New York, Back Bay Books, Little Brown & Company, 2023), 3–4.
279 Ibid. at 4–5.
280 Ibid. at 5–6.
281 Ibid. at 7.
282 Ibid. at 346.
283 Steven V. Roberts, "One Year Later; the Murder of the C.I.A.'s Chief Officer in Athens Remains a Mystery Without Solid Clues," *New York Times*, December 26, 1976, www.nytimes.com/1976/12/26/archives/one-year-later-the-murder-of-the-cias-chief-officer-in-athens.html.
284 James Risen, *The Last Honest Man: The CIA, the FBI, and the Kennedys – One Senator's Fight to Save Democracy* (New York, New York, Back Bay Books, Little Brown & Company, 2023), p. 358.
285 David Shortell, "What Barr's Work Under Bush 41 Tells Us About How He'll Handle His New Job," *CNN*, March 7, 2019, www.cnn.com/2019/03/02/politics/william-barr-george-hw-bush/index.html.
286 Marie Brenner, "I Had No Problem Being Politically Different,' Young William Barr Among the Liberals," *Vanity Fair*, October 7, 2019, www.vanityfair.com/news/2019/10/the-untold-tale-of-young-william-barr.

287   James Risen, *The Last Honest Man: The CIA, the FBI, and the Kennedys –
      One Senator's Fight to Save Democracy* (New York, New York, Back Bay
      Books, Little Brown & Company, 2023), 362.
288   Ibid. at 363.
289   Ibid. at 369.
290   Ibid. at 397.
291   Ibid. at 397–398.
292   David Barstow, "Behind TV Analysts, Pentagon's Hidden Hand," *New
      York Times,* April 20, 2008, www.nytimes.com/2008/04/20/us/20generals
      .html.
293   Ibid.
294   Ibid.
295   Ibid.
296   Alex Thompson, "The CIA's Least Covert Mission," *Politico,* September 8,
      2021, www.politico.com/news/2021/09/08/cia-least-covert-mission-510043/.
297   Ibid.
298   Tyler Durden, "Exposing the CIA's Secret Effort to Seize Control of Social
      Media," *ZeroHedge,* May 26, 2024, www.zerohedge.com/political/twitter
      -files-cia-exposing-secret-effort-us-intelligence-seize-control-social-media/.
299   Ibid.
300   Ibid.
301   Editorial Board, "Edward Snowden, Whistle-Blower," *New York Times,*
      January 1, 2014, www.nytimes.com/2014/01/02/opinion/edward
      -snowden-whistle-blower.html.
302   Ibid.
303   Ibid.
304   Stuart Taylor Jr., "The Big Snoop: Life, Liberty, and the Pursuit of
      Terrorists," The Brookings Essay, April 29, 2014, www.brookings.edu
      /articles/the-big-snoop-steps-for-american-business-to-protect-privacy/.
305   Ibid.
306   Ibid.
307   Ibid.
308   Ibid.

Chapter Nine

309   Lee Ferran, "ODNI, Pentagon Reveal FY23 Intelligence Budget at
      Nearly $100 Billion," Defense Budget 2024, October 30, 2023,
      www.breakingdefense.com/2023/10/odni-pentagon-reveal-fy23
      -intelligence-budget-at-nearly-100-billion/.
310   "Intelligence Community Spending Trends," Congressional Research
      Services, January 9, 2023, Appendix A), https://crsreports.congress.gov
      /product/details?prodcode=R44381.

311 "US Intelligence Agencies 'Black Budget' Detailed," August 30, 2013, BBC, www.bbc.com/news/world-us-canada-23903310#:~:text=A%20 breakdown%20of%20US%20intelligence's,agencies%2C%20 according%20to%20the%20files.

312 Harry S. Truman, "Limit CIA Role to Intelligence," *Washington Post*, December 22, 1963, www.cia.gov/readingroom/docs/CIA-RDP75 -00149R000700550045-9.pdf.

313 Zachary B. Wolf, "The Number of People with Top Secret Clearance Will Shock You," CNN, August 16, 2022, www.cnn.com/2022/08/15/politics /classified-information-what-matters/index.html.

314 Dana Priest and William M. Arkin, *Top Secret America: The Rise of the New American Security State* (New York, Little Brown, 2011).

315 Dana Priest and William M. Arkin, "A Hidden World, Growing Beyond Control," *Washington Post*, July 19, 2010, www.washingtonpost.com /investigations/top-secret-america/2010/07/19 /hidden-world-growing-beyond-control-2/.

316 Ibid.

317 Brent Durbin, *The CIA and the Politics of US Intelligence Reform* (New York, New York, Cambridge University Press), 2017, 11.

Epilogue

318 Tara Sutter, "Sloped Roof Used by Trump Rally Gunman Had 'Safety Factor' Considerations; Secret Service Director," *The Hill*, July 16, 2024, www.thehill.com/policy/national-security/4776617-secret-service -director-assassination-attempot-roof/.

319 Sara Dorn, "GOP Senators Angrily Confront Secret Service Director at RNC," *Forbes*, July 17, 2024, www.forbes.com/sites/saradorn /2024/07/17/gop-senators-angrily-confront-secret-service-director -at-rnc-you-owe-the-people-answers/.

320 Anna Giaritelli, "Furious GOP Senators Confront Secret Service Director at RNC Convention," *Washington Examiner*, July 18, 2024, www .washingtonexaminer.com/news/campaigns/congressional/3088474 /furious-gop-enators-confront-secret-service-director-rnc/.

321 Bill Hutchinson, "After Trump Assassination Attempt, Questions Swirl About What Happened," ABC News, July 14, 2024, www .abcnews.go.com/us/trump-attempted-assassination-investigation /story?id=11926565.

322 Julia Ingram, "Did the Trump Gunman Make a Donation to Democrats? Here's What the Records Show," CBS News, July 18, 2024, www.cbsnews .com/trump-shooter-thomas-crooks-donation-to-democrats-registered -republican/.

323 Glenn Thrush, Jack Healy, and Luke Broadwater, "Gunman's Phone Had Details about Both Trump and Biden, F.B.I. Officials Say," *New York Times*, July 17, 2024, www.nytimes.com/2024/07/17/us/trump-shooting -crooks.html.

324 Ibid.

325 "JFK Assassination Records – Purchase of Rifle by Oswald," National Archives (Accessed July 20, 2024), www.archives.gov/research/jfk/warren -commission-report/chapter-4.html.

326 Glenn Thrush, Jack Healy, and Luke Broadwater, "Gunman's Phone Had Details about Both Trump and Biden, F.B.I. Officials Say," *New York Times*, July 17, 2024, www.nytimes.com/2024/07/17/us/trump-shooting -crooks.html.

327 Ronny Reyes, "BlackRock Yanks 2022 Ad Featuring Trump Shooter Thomas Matthew Crooks," *New York Post*, July 15, 2022, www.nypost .com/2024/07/15/us-news/blackrock-pulls-ad-that-featured -trump-shooter-thomas-matthew-crooks/.

328 Glenn Kessler, "The 'Black Hole' in Robert F. Kennedy Jr.'s Housing Conspiracy Theory," *Washington Post*, November 30, 2023, www .washingtonpost.com/politics/2023/11/30/black-hole-robert-f-kennedy -jrs-housing-conspiracy-theory/.

329 Brooke Masters, "Larry Fink Dismisses 'Sad' Criticism of BlackRock in Republican Debate," *Financial Times*, December 7, 2023, www.ft.com /content/b985a3ad-f0fa-4463-bcfl-7ff3435e0f23.

330 Isabel Keane, "Veteran Sniper from Team with the Longest-Confirmed Kill says Roof used by Would-Be Assassin Thomas Crooks was "the Most F—king Obvious' Risk," *New York Post*, July 15, 2024, www.nypost .com/2024/07/15/us-news/veteran-sniper-weighs-in-on -trump-assassination-attempt/.

331 Ibid.

332 Vinod Dsouza, "US Asset Manager Shorts Trump Stock a Day Before Assassination Attempt," *Watcher Guru*, July 19, 2024, www.watcher.guru /news/us-asset-manager-shorts-trump-stock-a-day-before-assassination -attempt.

333 Frank Chung, "Investment Firm Says Massive Short of Truth Social Stock Before Shooting was 'Filed in Error,'" *AU News*, July 19, 2024, www .news.com.au/finance/money/investing/investment-firm-says-massive -short-of-truth-social-stock-before-trump-shooting-was-filed-in-error /news-story/8f9886b3ecf6flc53d7ad3737387d2a.

334 Siladita Ray, "Three Snipers Were Inside Building Trump Rally Shooter Fired From, Reports Say," *Forbes*, July 16, 2024, www.forbes.com/sites /siladityaray/2024/07/16/trump-assassination-attempt-three-police -snipers-were-reportedly-inside-building-where-gunman-fired-from/.

335 Ibid.

336 Ibid.

337 Adam Goldman, Glenn Thrush, and William K. Rashbaum, "Gunman Might Have Scoped Out Site Six Days Before Trump Rally," *New York Times*, July 18, 2024, www.nytimes.com/2024/07/18/us/politics/guman -site-trump-rally.html.

338 Ibid.

339 Josh Christenson, "Secret Service had 'Little Resources' to Cover Trump Rally After NATO Summit: Whistleblowers," *New York Post*, July 18, 2024, www.nypost.com/2024/07/18/us-news/secret-service-had-little -resources-to-cover-trump-rally-after-nato-summit-whistleblower/.

340 Katherine Donlevy, "Thomas Matthew Crooks Threatened to 'Shoot Up' High School Classmates Years Before Trump Assassination Attempt," *New York Post*, July 18, 2024, www.nypost.com/2024/07/18/us-news /thomas-matthew-crooks-threatened-to-shoot-up-high-school/.

341 Sadie Gurman and Aruna Viswanatha, "Trump Gunman Flew Drone Over Rally Site Hours Before Attempted Assassination," *Wall Street Journal*, July 19, 2024, www.wsj.com/politics/national-security/trump -gunman-flew-drone-over-rally-site-hours-before-attempted-assassination -2d0e21a.

342 Ellis Kim, Robert Legare, Andres Triay, and Chris Liable, "Trump Shooter's Online Activity Shows Searches of Rally Site, Use of Encrypted Platforms, Officials Say," CBS News, July 18, 2024, www.cbsnews.com /news/trump-shooting-online-evidence-lawmaker-briefings/.

343 Anshul Panda, "More than One Shooter? Second Shooter's Role in Trump Attack Sparks Mystery and Investigation," *International Business Times*, July 17, 2024, www.ibtimes.sg/more-one-shooter-second-shooters-role -trump-attack-sparks-mystery-invesitgation.75310.

344 "JFK Assassination Records – Summary of Findings of Select Committee on Assassinations in the Assassination of President John F. Kennedy in Dallas, Tex., November 23, 1963," National Archives, (Accessed July 20, 2024), www.archives.gov/research/jfk/select-committee-report/summary .html.

345 Kristen Holmes and Homes Lybrand, "Secret Service Says It Denied Trump Additional Resources in Recent Years, Even as His Team Complained," CNN, July 21, 2024, www.cnn.com/2024/07/21/politics/secret-service -trump-security-requests/index.html.

346 Catie Edmonton, "After Trump Assassination Attempt, Right Points Finger at Female Agents," *New York Times*, July 16, 2024, www.nytimes .com/2024/07/16/us/politics/secret-service-female-agents.html.

347 Ibid.

348 Joe Marino, Larry Celona, & Chris Nesi, "Trump Shooter Thomas Crooks Might Have Been Battling Undiagnosed Mental Illness: Sources,"

New York Post, July 18, 2024, www.nypost.com/2024/07/18/us-news /trump-shooter-thomas-crooks-may-have-suffered-from-mental-illness/.

349 Peter Nicholas, "President Joe Biden Drops Out of 2024 Presidential Race," NBC News, July 21, 2024, www.nbcnews.com/politics/2024 -election/president-joe-biden-drops-2024-presidential-race -rcna159867.

ACKNOWLEDGMENTS

I would like to thank my dear friend Robert Kennedy Jr. for your support and encouragement in writing this book. You are a modern-day hero, courageous and brilliant in your stand against government tyranny. Next, I want to thank Skyhorse president, Tony Lyons, for your encouragement in making this book a reality and leading one of America's truly free publishing companies. Hector Carosso, thank you for your hard work, grace, and skill in editing this manuscript.

Special thanks to my coauthor, Kent Heckenlively, for your courage in taking on this project, your dedication and hard work, and for being the best literary teammate I have ever had. My deep respect and love to my wife Sue, who has supported me through this entire project, knowing the risks involved. Finally, I want to thank Milly and Roger Kennedy, as well as Rhonda Dasher and the small group that meets in their house for their prayer and encouragement as I decided to accept the risk and write this book.

—Kevin Shipp

I'd first like to thank my wonderful partner in life, Linda, and our two children, Jacqueline and Ben, for their constant love and support. You make every part of this journey an adventure. I'd also like to thank my mother, Josephine, and my father, Jack, for teaching me to have both courage and grace. I have the best brother in the world, Jay, and am appreciative to his wife, Andrea, and their three children, Anna, John, and Laura.

I've been fortunate enough to have some of the greatest teachers in the world, Paul Rago, Elizabeth White, Ed Balsdon, Brother Richard Orona, Clinton Bond, Robert Haas, Carol Lashoff, David Alvarez, Giancarlo Trevisan, Bernie Segal, James Frey, Donna Levin, James Dalessandro, and Eddie Abasolo.

Thanks to the fantastic friends of my life, John Wible, John Henry, Pete Klenow, Chris Sweeney, Suzanne Golibart, Gina Cioffi Loud, Eric Holm, Susanne Brown, Rick Friedling, Max Swafford, Sherilyn Todd, Rick and Robin Kreutzer, Christie and Joaquim Perreira, Rick and Heidi Bindi, Trina and Conrad Walker, and Tricia Mangiapane.

My life has been immensely enriched by the brave whistleblowers I've come across in my writing, such as Judy Mikovits, Frank Ruscetti, Robert F. Kennedy Jr., Nobel Prize winner Luc Montagnier, Zach Vorhies, Ryan Hartwig, Mikki Willis, Michael Mazzola, Henry Marx, Tyson Yee, Cary Poarch, David Johnson, and of course, James O'Keefe, who provides a platform for many of these brave individuals.

I also wish to acknowledge the wonderful staff at Skyhorse: the fabulous Caroline Russomano, the amazing Hector Carosso, and my wonderful publisher, Tony Lyons. I am honored to serve with all of you in the fight for freedom.

—Kent Heckenlively

INDEX